This is a war story through the eye  invent such a tale. But then who of war itself?

—*Pollyanna Pool*

Much has been written concerning the infamous camps in Poland and other places under the Nazis, but nothing about the women and children in Japanese prison camps. This is a first-hand account of this time period, when civilians had to go through an ordeal of slavery at the hands of absolutely merciless barbarians. Alice is the most courageous person I know, surviving the indignities, cruelties, and humiliations heaped upon her as an innocent child. These acts are unforgivable. I hope everyone will be able to read this moving true story.

—*Joanne Schartow, classical violinist*

It's about time someone gives credence to a little girl's fears and faith. This book describes a friendship that was horribly interrupted by a pantheon of fiends. I have cried with Alice over the loss of our little friend from school days. I was there at Lily's memorial service in our boarding school chapel and sang those same hymns she used to love so much. We must take care this never happens again.

—*Harriet Hammond, old school friend*

I have had the opportunity of reading *CHILD POW, A Memoir of Survival*. It is a child's memoir of suffering that ends with a message of hope.

—*Rose Ruze, social worker*

Alice's story points vividly to the terrible things the Japanese did to civilian prisoners, whose only crime was being tourists in the Philippines at the wrong time. The senseless brutality unleashed upon this little girl should not be forgotten as we buy our Sony, Nissan, and Mitsubishi products. It is to Alice's great credit that she grew into a lovely woman, who has been a valuable member of society, all the time harboring these terrible memories, which until now she has been prevented from revealing.

—*John Schartow, teacher*

Not enough is known about what civilians went through under the Japanese. The outrageous behavior of our government at suppressing the POW's stories in the interest of endorsing the re-building of our defeated enemy appalls me. The indifference to common courtesies and despicable malingering by our own country to keep these POWs from their families is atrocious. This child's story pulls the plug on all the covering-up for all these years.

—*Peter Nick, attorney*

I knew some of the atrocities of war. I was not, however, prepared for what Alice told me. I was in the Navy on an aircraft carrier and we went to the Philippines.

I remember seeing wrecked ships on some of the beaches, and the jungle coming right down to the waters' edge. I thought at the time, *What a hell of a time the Marines and soldiers must have gone through to retake those islands.*

We had a neighbor by the name of Beauregard, descendant of the general of the same name in the Civil War. He showed me his Bronze and Silver Stars for saving the lives of fellow marines. He received a battlefield commission for this and became a colonel before retiring. He is still on medication.

I asked him, "How bad was it over there?"

His answer was, "You don't know fear until bullets are flying around you like bees."

What kind of fear runs through the mind of an eight-year-old as she watches a 14-year-old boy drowned? What runs through the minds of a young girl and her mother as they witness a beheading?

Is it fear or is it courage or a resolve to do anything to see one more day? You know one day war will end, but you don't know the outcome or when. Nonie somehow turned this fear into a resolve to endure. A resolve to find the courage to live one day at a time, until they found a way out.

In war there are only losers, and it's important to know that it not only affects the soldiers doing the fighting, but it affects the innocent men, women and children caught behind enemy lines. Of all the books I have read, none have been written from a young person's perspective, and that's what makes this book unique.

Not only is this about atrocities or the horrors of war, but a love story. The love of a mother to do anything to make sure her daughter made it home. I think they fed off each other, so they could survive this ordeal.

Would Nonie have made it by herself? I don't know. Would Alice? No. Alice is Alice, and she would have made someone mad enough to shoot her on the spot. It didn't make any difference to the Japanese how old a person was.

—*Ted Schmidt, former U.S. Navy*

I've known these two ladies but never knew the background until I read this story of love written by a daughter about her mother. It made me wonder if, as a lad of ten years old, I could have kept my mum and me alive in the desperate circumstances these two were forced into. Would I have thought to forage for bird's nests or thought to sell my own hair for fishhooks to keep us alive? We never know what we'll be called on to do in this life after we decide no one is going to vanquish us. Bravo to this wonderful survival story of devotion between Nonie and Alice. I salute the ladies.

—*Joe Amundsen,Sr.,*
Princess Patricia Canadian Light Infantry, Retired

CHILD P.O.W.

CHILD P.O.W.

A MEMOIR OF SURVIVAL

A . L . FINCH

A Division of WinePress Publishing Group

ISBN 13: 978-1-59977-008-6
ISBN 10: 1-59977-008-3
Library of Congress Catalog Card Number: 2007920793

DEDICATION

This memoir is for my mother, who kept us alive against
terrifying odds and who gave me life, not just at birth,
but once again in war. If she had not succeeded,
I would not now be able to recount the tragedies of
the terrible World War II.

Also this is for my daughter Jeannie, the star in my universe,
the lady who makes my sun come up in the morning.

This book is also a memorial to all the dear, brave people,
military and civilian, whose lives were taken
from them so cruelly, for no reason, by those who could
not value decency and goodness and who chose instead
to wear the face of terror.

TABLE OF CONTENTS

THE PASSAGE OF YEARS WITH CLOSELY APPROXIMATED DATES

Commence	Leave	Destination	Purpose
August-1941	January 1942	Manila	captured
January 1942	May 1942	Cabanatuan	prisoners and starving
May 1942	October 1942	Baguio	the officers' camp
October 1942	January 1943	China	Foochow/Guanxi/Foochow
January 1943	February 1943	Fukuoka	detention camp
February 1943		The Hell Ship	final trip to Japan
February 1943	March 1945	Kobe	working the docks
March 1945	April 1945	Australia	return to the world
late April 1945	May 1945	Brisbane to Norfolk	transit to USA
late May 1945		Norfolk to California	transit for rehabilitation
very late June		Lakewood	released from military custody
June 26 To June 29, 1945		We finally come home to our family.	

INTRODUCTION

A
t the end of the Japanese-Russian war in 1905, the newly modernized Japanese navy, under Admiral Togo, successfully mauled the Russians into an agreed upon cessation of conflict. The United States voted for Japan to be given the whole Korean Peninsula for their colonial territory, providing the Japanese made no fuss over America's recent acquisition of the Philippine Islands, at the end of the Spanish-American war. Japan's long-planned march into history began in earnest twenty-five years later.

In 1931 Japan invaded and quickly conquered Manchuria. Japan then invaded China, through the Manchurian corridor, in 1932 and Shanghai in 1935. They used that military action as training for a future conquest of Southeast Asia, later known as the Greater Southeast Asia Co-Prosperity Sphere.

Under this guise, Japan planned to come into feudal owner-ship of immense quantities of rubber, oil, foods, gold, many precious minerals, and an immense, available work force. Japan told the Southeast Asians they would share in the co-prosperity. "Asia for the Asians" ads appeared in several languages, in every newspaper, on every kiosk and wall.

The Southeast Asians, who had reason to distrust Japanese colonialism, didn't believe a word of it. They recognized that the treasures of all the Orient might be Japan's, if Japan held the lands in Southeast Asia, Indo-China, the Philippine Islands, and Malaysia.

Few of the countries of Southeast Asia were self-governing. Most were territories, colonies, or protectorates of European countries, as well as of the United States. Sadly, all these Asian countries and their various colonial masters together couldn't assemble an army strong enough to forestall hostile Japanese occupation or aggressive action.

Japan had a superbly trained Army and Navy, with much field practice in China and Manchuria over the previous ten years. If the Japanese were to attack another country, the only real threat to them would be from the United States Navy's huge Pacific fleet. It was important, therefore, to neutralize this naval threat, if the Japanese wanted to dominate Southeast Asia and the Pacific. The Allied powers soon came to know exactly how well-trained and equipped those Japanese forces were.

The Japanese plan for a complete seizure of Southeast Asia depended on keeping America out of any early direct conflict. If successful inroads were made into Southeast Asia, the Japanese could better dictate future international discussions. They wanted a negotiated peace, with broadened trade and colonial possessions.

General Hideki Tojo, Chief of the Imperial General Staff

Japanese Emperor Hirohito and his War Party, led by General Tojo, was advised in September 1941, by Franklin D. Roosevelt, President of the United States, through the Unites States Ambassador to Japan, Joseph Grew, that if the outward expansion of this so-called Co-Prosperity Sphere wasn't halted, the United States would blockade all oil and goods from Indochina.

3

The American blockade threat propelled the Japanese military into immediate action and set the scene for attacks on Pearl Harbor, the Philippine Islands, the rest of Southeast Asia and the South Pacific, in early December, 1941. Japan had planned for the eventuality of this war for over ten years, even as they had planned ten years ahead for their march into Manchuria—not the exact date or minute—but the plan for battle, and the reason for it.

How secretive and horrendous of men to decide to begin a war against America and all her allies! It was typical of the Japanese military cadre to arrogantly believe they would be the certain victors. The Japanese War Party, under General Tojo, had taken over the government and moved toward the commencement of hostile actions in the Pacific. At this point, no voice of influence outside the War Party was heard. Moderation no longer existed in Japan. General Tojo had superseded the emperor as the predominant man in government.

Admiral Isoroku Yamamoto, who had studied in America and was culturally quite aware of our attitudes, developed the plan, based on three important details: surprise, swiftness of attack, and the crippling of the United States fleet.

Fleet Admiral Isoroku Yamamoto – (1884-1943)

Striking out in this type of warfare would enable Japan to negotiate treaties heavily weighted for their own benefit. They expected to mandate import and trade futures for generations to come. It was all about greed and economics, personal power, and national prestige. All wars are.

Yet the eternal questions remain: why are those who plan the catastrophes of war never the ones to fight? Why do the good die young? Why do we continue to sacrifice our best and our brightest in bloody battlefields? Eventually, retribution comes, but it is slow and not thoroughly applied to those who should be recognized as the most grievous malefactors.

Alice and Nonie – 1940

PROLOGUE

*The history of the great events of this world is scarcely
more than the history of crimes.*

——Voltaire

I began to write this eyewitness account for my children
and my grandchildren, so they would understand not all
history is in books, and not all books are accurate. Years
after these events occurred, the remembrance of those times is
as clear to me as it was during that fateful time.

One advantage for me now is that I finally understand why
some of the things happened. Not that I agree, of course. Concerning certain happenings, I have often wondered whose side
our government was on at that time? Why did they dissemble
so much, regarding incontrovertible facts?

Many historians and economists agree a country is never
quite as prosperous as when it is at war. Munitions industries
flourish, as do producers of hard goods, aircraft manufactur-
ers, transportation, and all ancillary industries, such as mines,
smelters, energy sources, and even agriculture.

With a sustained increase of all this production comes ac-
celerated employment, which is touted as the cure-all for a
financial depression, such as that which existed pre-WWII.

Suddenly, war becomes politically correct as a resolution for a badly depressed economy.

This book, then, is the story of two ordinary American civilians from Puget Sound, who were caught in the middle of a war, with only two ways out. Our choices were simple in one way, yet complicated in another: We could work hard and survive, yet perhaps die anyway in captivity, or we could give up at the outset and die helplessly.

In this life we might be called on to do strange, incomprehensible things. At that instant, we make a choice to be either survivors or the poor souls who give up and whine, "My life is really worthless." The latter is wrong. We must never, never give up. We must focus on the excellence and superiority of our individual personhood. It is important to embrace life, including all its interesting, tragic details. We must seize life with both hands. That is how we become survivors.

I'll recount just a few of many stories. I'll also give the benefit of my personal observations and opinions, however outrageous you may think they are. Regardless of how outrageous, the opinions are mine, and I'll defend them.

During this time of war there was a plethora of villainy, but also an abundance of heroism. Perhaps one of the greatest unrecorded heroes in my eyes was my dear mother. What I'm about to share is more My Nonie's story than my own, but I am her only child, so I will tell it.

My Nonie – 1940
Eleanor Gilderoy Ponko 1910–1999

As a small child, because she was so tiny, quick, and elfin, Nonie was called "Brownie" by her family of five brothers and sisters. "Nonie" was simply the childhood name I gave my mother, when I couldn't properly say her name and elided Brownie into Nownie and finally into Nonie. In our family, among her closest friends and those she loved the most, she preferred to be known as Nonie. We pronounced it "know-knee."

She gave me life at birth, then she gave me life a second time by teaching me to survive through vigilance, courage, hard work, persistence, and faith. These are the lessons I want to pass on to my children and their children.

Many names have been changed. In some cases, survivors or their family members could not be reached for their consent; in some cases, memories were too traumatic to be reopened, and a name was changed to avoid asking the person to relive the issue after so many years; in some cases, my own continuing fear of retribution from exposing the surviving Jap demons demanded that I use a pseudonym for that person. People who knew me then and know me now will believe they can identify this or that person. Perhaps. Don't be too sure, though.

Don't ever tell me that you liked my book. I'll be so disappointed in you. This is not a book to "like." I want you to hate it but remember it and try to change your little corner of the world so nothing like this ever happens again. And please... feed the hungry.

Questions will arise as you read about our experiences, but be patient—I believe all will be answered by the end of the story. Try especially to learn two lessons My Nonie taught. First: We must never be so afraid to die, that we can't fully live. Second: Be a survivor!

ACKNOWLEDGMENTS

S pecial thanks to my daughter, Jeannie. I could not, and would not, have written this book without her encouragement and enthusiasm. Her driving intelligence kept me at it when I felt defeated by the immensity of the task. She has supported me by proof-reading, asking for more elaboration, and by encouraging me to stand fast and not soften my narrative. She has brought me great joy throughout her life, and for this reason, foremost among many, I am glad to be a survivor. She has replaced tears with joy in my life. I love her immensely and am so proud to be the mother of this wonderful and unique woman.

I am grateful to other people for their important support: my grandson, Jon, serving with the United States Army overseas, who has urged me to get this personal history on paper; my cousins Jim Gilderoy and John Westine, who held me in their hearts when I cried the tears of memory; Major General Don Brown and dear Joan, his wife, who through the gifts of love and friendship were My Nonie's closest and best friends in the

11

whole world; my mother's sweet friend, Margaret Moore, who gave My Nonie the kind of devoted friendship only very special people can share between each other; my closest friends and supporters, Joanne and John Schartow, who share my anger and disgust and continue to offer counseling at each step along my way; and especially for Ted Schmidt and his Jeanne, for Ted's tears and his unflagging belief the story should be told.

Heartfelt thanks go to John Schartow, editor pluperfect, who because of his own military service could intelligently edit this compilation of autobiography, travelogue, horror tale, and, as one person has called it, the love story of a daughter for her mother. This book will now be the volume I always wanted it to be and I am forever grateful that John agreed to take it on.

In the previous edition there were mistakes. Charitably, I accept responsibility for the editing errors and deletions. At the time I did the final review I had a serious vision problem and simply didn't "get it right", hence the necessity for this re-issued volume.

Through John's magic fingers and acute sensitivity to task, and the fact that John knew My Nonie, Papa and me for many years, he has helped me make the book the way it always was meant to be. Kudos, John.

Many thanks to my publisher, Athena Dean, and her staff at WinePress Publishing. These good people have helped me leave a remembrance of a time that will never be seen again, and a time that should never have happened at all. Perhaps not all new authors are impatient and abrasive, but I have been. The publishers have been exceedingly gracious not to have returned this attitude in kind. Thanks, Athena.

The book was originally titled "Nonie's Story." Athena, my publisher, said, "But, Alice, it's your story, too." The name was changed but the book largely remains the story of my mother's heroism as seen through my eyes. She was a unique lady who saw the world the way she wanted it to be, rather than how it really was. She had the magic.

My Nonie survived one of our country's deadliest times and kept me, a young girl at that time, alive against terrifying odds. I am left to tell the story. During our ordeal she harmed no one, but she defeated the entire Japanese Empire's attempt to extinguish her, armed only with intellect, determination, imagination, and faith. I loved her greatly and continue to mourn her passing.

As a memoir, this book would not exist without remembering all those dear, brave people whose lives were taken so cruelly. The book must remind us not to make the same mistakes again.

In any recitation of events, errors may creep into the narrative—ask any police officer. Different witnesses see an event from varying perspectives. This book is as free of errors as I can make it. Any errors that exist are certainly my own, perhaps colored as remembered through the eyes of a young child, but no one else should be held at fault.

The opinions are mine. If, as a reader, you agree, thank you for your support. If you should disagree or even become quite vexed with my opinions, so be it. Write your own book. I'll be glad to read it. This one's mine.

A.L.Finch
Lakewood, Washington
February 2007

CHAPTER 1

THE BEGINNING

*Parents we can have but once. The longer we live, the
higher the value we learn to put on the friendship
and tenderness of parents.*

——*Samuel Johnson*

While the Japanese planned their conquest of the Pacific, on the other side of the world, Del, my natural father, was graduating from veterinarian school. Aunt Lucy and My Nonie had accompanied their husbands to college, financially supporting the men.

Each of the ladies worked at good jobs on the university campus. They also rented a very large house, which they opened with board-and-room for other vet students. It was quite successful, since both ladies were excellent cooks and good housekeepers. The university years passed by and life was good.

Each of the men talked about opening their private practices and appeared to be happy. On the day of graduation, after the honorees had headed to the stadium to robe for their graduation, my mother busily set the table for the buffet she and Aunt Lucy had prepared. A knock sounded at the door; a process server handed Nonie divorce papers. This was akin to saying, "Thanks for putting me through school, but I've found someone else. Bye now."

15

Del was gone from our lives forever, from that moment on. He didn't even come back to get his clothes at the boarding house. He simply walked away. My Nonie's surprised hurt was beyond explanation. We rarely discussed him after that. If we did, I instigated the discussion.

I did learn my father went first to China, then to Mexico, for hoof-and-mouth disease eradication. Consequently, since he was out of the country, the meager child support award was never enforceable nor obtainable, and he didn't volunteer it. But through several local vets with whom I kept in touch over the years, I learned quite a bit about him.

I was told my father amassed a fortune in China. It is said that he dealt in stolen Chinese artifacts, which were shipped out of the country, for sale to dealers who transshipped them mainly to Europe and South America. On his proceeds, he lived rather "high on the hog" in Mexico, as the vets say, where his search for personal indulgence and opulence could be satisfied more cheaply.

Later, as the children he fathered grew, he moved to the United States to educate them. My father later became state veterinarian of what was then our largest American state. He eventually retired in Florida.

I attempted to contact him once as I was interested to learn about my siblings and about familial health traits, but I received no response and my mail was not returned to me. I'd heard he had five children with his second wife. Should any of them find me, my door is open to them. And so is my heart. The past is gone.

As a child and an adult I never felt the need for him in my life. His abrupt departure was the first abandonment my mother and I would survive. Our lives became quite symbiotic after that.

We were a unit of two, each who lived for the other's welfare and happiness. Life was good.

In my mother's ultra-conservative family in 1938, divorce was such an unnatural idea that, in their eyes, it became My Nonie's fault. Relationships in her family were strained because of the divorce, and any social life was considered ended. It was customary in similar instances, among families like ours, to retire gracefully from the active world and become a caretaker of remaining family members. While this may sound bizarre by our 21st century moral standards, it was quite customary at that time. It was presumed that Nonie could live quietly in her family's home and work to support her child in boarding school.

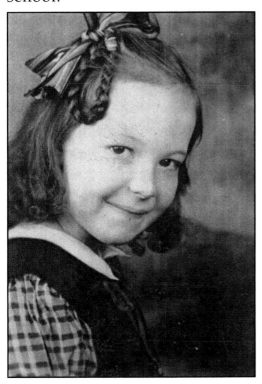

Boarding school – 1938

To put this attitude into context, understand that she was only 28 years old. It seems literally an application of the old phrase "Get thee to a nunnery." I remember one of her sisters asked, "What did you do to cause this?" Others assumed it had been her choice or her fault, rather than the opposite. I think my natural father was intimidated by her perfection.

Nonie worked for a large insurance company; I went to boarding school. I loved it. Life became regular, quiet—and very, very boring—so periodically I felt a need to stir things up a bit in my own sector of the world. My Nonie was, unfortunately and frequently, asked to find me another school. The issues always were quite trivial, so I didn't listen to the criticism of what I had done.

There was one cross, crabby teacher who never should have been around young children. We little girls delighted in annoying her. Once we hung her nightgown on the flagpole. It was such fun. She was red in the face and wouldn't come out for dinner that night. The way we tormented her was a singular lesson in why an adult should never set out to antagonize a group of little children. We became tyrants.

We girls hatched a plan to turn the newly installed speaker system volume very high at morning chapel service because this teacher was due to lead Morning Prayer. I had been deputized to do the deed at the proper time.

Unknown to me, the Presiding Bishop of the Diocese of Olympia (housed in Seattle—go figure!) came that particular day to lead Morning Prayer while our disliked teacher merely remained part of the staff attendees. From my vantage point, I couldn't see the pulpit or who had approached it. At the proper time, following the Prayer Book's order of service, I stealthily crept to our audio equipment, pegged the volume high and scooted back to my seat. Suddenly our Bishop's voice, ordinarily loud enough to call crows, boomed out as though he was God Almighty Himself addressing the multitudes.

"God be with you," he thundered in his resonant and very deep voice. "Who did that?" he boomed again. Admittedly, it was pretty loud, alright. Set your teeth right on edge.

The smaller students were terrified; a first grader began to cry. Older students, kneeling, thrust their faces into their piously folded hands and rocked with laughter, heads bent "en chapelle," as though they were praying. Their shoulders shook with accompanying snorts of poorly stifled laughter. Our dear Headmistress walked quickly to the equipment, modulated the dial, then noticed me sitting on the end of the pew, with "Guilty" pulsating across my innocent face. She and other faculty members then grabbed up the culprit, who was given a good hard shake, and I was sent to my room for the day. What a treat! since I could read without interruption. I loved this particular school. It was quiet and orderly, but it may have needed an ounce of excitement.

Off to a new school.

I regret that the Headmistress was so humorless, but I could read my future in her face—once again—another school. I felt sorry about that. My Nonie was always patient when I was expelled, though it meant relocation, a job search, new living conditions, new friends. She said they simply hadn't understood me, and she never criticized me for my sudden expulsions. Nonie always accompanied me to the new location. I never knew why she just didn't send me off to school. She never did. My grandmother was quite vexed about another of our moves one day and told me, "You'd better thank your lucky stars she always goes with you. If it were up to me, I'd give you to the next gypsy who came along."

Several years passed before Nonie met a man who stole both our hearts. She wanted to marry again, but her family considered remarriage an absurd, questionable idea. Our rigid, straight-laced, controlling family wondered what *decent* man would marry a woman with a child?

After an abbreviated courtship, My Nonie and her gentleman friend went to Vancouver, British Columbia. They completed necessary forms, a waiting period, and were married on June 14, 1941, in the Bishop's Rectory of a beautiful Church of Canada. For as long as they lived, they celebrated this day as their anniversary.

Papa leaving for 1940 summer cruise

Unfortunately, they were informed a few weeks later that their marriage was invalid, since an attorney hired by my natural father, the plaintiff in Nonie's first marriage, had never filed adjudicated, endorsed divorce papers. Because of that, her first marriage was still valid, and Nonie was now legally a *bigamist*. Good grief!

Kind and sensible, as Canadians usually are, they recognized this as a clerical error, rather than as a nefarious scheme to amass husbands, and they set aside the marriage that was accomplished in Canada. After she later contacted a U.S. court with the proper jurisdiction, Nonie was finally free of Del, her first husband, but her status remained that of an unmarried woman.

Our family members went into a tirade about this situation. The greatest problem? They had not been consulted before the marriage. Nonie had "eloped," and no relative had agreed on her choice of husband. Later, after we were missing in Asia, my new Papa was extremely attentive to my grandparents and so brave in war—with medals to prove it! Finally, all the family's attitudes toward him changed completely, and they not only accepted, but honestly loved him as one of their own.

At the moment, in the early summer of 1941, after being advised he was not a married man, he was on a sea-cruise. He'd joined the U.S. Naval Reserve several years earlier. He was a teacher who loved the sea, and with school summers off, reservists' cruises appealed to him. Neither he nor Nonie anticipated the problems their elopement produced. Now, he suggested if he wasn't around as an irritant to anyone, it might clear the air a bit, making it easier for Nonie to deal with her family situation. It seemed the answer to their dilemma was the naval summer cruise. They didn't know it then, but it would be four long years before they would see each other again.

Things did calm down with our family during this time, and the mutual decision of a naval deployment appeared wise. Subsequent developments led both My Nonie and her darling to rue the day they allowed themselves to be swayed and separated by outside opinions. Over the years, I heard them talk about how they should have stayed together, avoiding the tragic war events which later occurred. They demonstrated the true love of a couple who were only complete together.

Nonie's confidante in affairs of the heart was her oldest sister, my Aunt Alice, an Army nurse stationed in the Philippines. Aunt Alice was good to me all of her life. When it seemed I was regularly in one self-designed difficulty or another, more often than not Alice took my side. One terrible transgression was when I painted my cousin, five years younger, bright green so we could play "Jack and the Beanstalk." It took years for me to live it down, and almost as long for the paint to wear off! Aunt Alice thought it was hilarious, as did I. I think I inherited my "banana-peel humor" from Aunt Alice and my grandmother. I have always been grateful to her because when she intervened, it gave me a moment to assemble my thoughts and my defense, despite the barrage of criticism or anger from others.

Mail took two to three weeks by sea, when the sisters wrote each other. It was not satisfactory nor practical to discuss such a personal and emotional issue as remarriage via long distance sea mail. Strangely, though I was a chatterbox, at an early age I was also a reliable and inveterate secret-keeper. I remember overhearing conversation that there was no use trying to learn anything from me. "She won't say a word unless her mother tells her it's OK," my grandmother once told Aunt Lucy.

In late June, 1941, Aunt Alice sent my mother and me two round-trip plane tickets to Manila, via the Pan American China

Clipper. We were thrilled, but our relatives were less than joyful. Sourly, my aunties sicced the uncles onto Nonie, like a dog after a gopher, saying, "Why go to such a part of the world?" Uncle Jack even flew in from Cheyenne to give his two cents worth. He offered Nonie, his younger sister, a job with United Airlines in Cheyenne and said we could live with his family until she could afford our own place.

Boeing B314 – The China Clipper Flying Boat
San Francisco to Manila via Honolulu, Midway, Wake and
Guam in August 1941

The Philippine Islands? In the South Pacific? Why not go to Eastern Canada? Or the Caribbean Islands? Yet if we didn't go soon, although the fighting remained only in Britain, France, and Belgium, we might never be able to go at all.

We went to seek Aunt Alice's assurance and support that this marriage was truly the best for us. With her endorsement, however, the way would be cleared in Nonie's mind to quickly proceed. I believe she wanted one relative on her side, perhaps to avoid total disenfranchisement from our family. Therefore, she simply refused to listen to the others, in spite of their badgering.

Many times my aunties, uncles, or my grandparents cajoled me to learn why we were determined to fly to the South Pacific, and why we refused to go elsewhere. Finally though their consensus was at least Nonie was unavailable to her gentleman while she traveled.

A few relatives still thought us quite odd, yet after we went to the Philippines and in spite of what later ensued, no one ever said, "It served you right." It was an act of loving kindness that overcame their usual sarcastic criticism and was totally unexpected.

CHAPTER 2

THE CHINA CLIPPER

The winds of war have blown away these flights
of beauty—now but a far distant memory
of gentler times past.

—*Juan Trippe*

I haunted the county library van on our street each week. If what I was after wasn't available, it was ordered from the state library. I was obsessed to discover every detail about China Clippers and the Philippines.

At boarding school I'd had a sweet friend from Manila, whose family was highly placed in business and government, so I knew about the Philippines in vague terms. Although she was two years older, we were quite close. Since I thought she was much smarter, I deferred to her a lot. She had the tiniest hands and most beautiful eyes I'd ever seen. I didn't envy her, but I did stare at her often, to memorize her face and voice.

My Sweet Friend and her family invited me to spend a summer with them, several times. Each time before she flew home, a relative came to America to accompany her, usually an uncle. My family was assured, if I visited, I would be safe and cared for until we two girls returned to America for school at summer's end. I'm sure My Nonie might have allowed me to go, but I think her refusal hinged on the cost of plane fare. Now, joy of joys, I could get to see her again, while I visited Aunt Alice. I was totally overjoyed! I could hardly sleep at night, thinking about the trip.

We left for the South Pacific in August, 1941. I missed My Sweet Friend, in many loving ways. She was often the buffer between the school administration and me for antics of which I was frequently—and most often fairly—accused.

Even My Sweet Friend wasn't able to keep me from punishment one time, when it was discovered, after a frantic all afternoon school search, that I wasn't missing, nor had I been kidnapped.

I had climbed the heavy ivy outside my third floor bedroom window and was ensconced in a big copper rain-diverter on our roof, reading Nancy Drew detective stories. My punishment that day was mild, considering how frightened our staff had been. I felt quite put upon, since I hadn't disobeyed anyone. No one had ever told me *not* to climb the ivy onto the roof of the huge school.

Kidnapping was in the minds of all adults in those days. The little Weyerhaeuser boy and Doctor Mattson's baby had each been kidnapped, barely a few blocks from our school and it was also only a few years since the Lindbergh baby's tragic death.

Members playing at the nearby Lawn Tennis Club had sighted me in my aerie close to dinner time and had thought it strange that a child was allowed there. They called our school to inquire about "the little girl on the roof." I was retrieved and sent to bed with a glass of milk and a piece of bread for supper. My Sweet Friend brought me a small bottle of orange juice, a huge chocolate bar from the commissary, and her own jar of macadamia nuts. We shared this feast under my blankets after lights out.

About five o'clock in the morning we both began vomiting. Our moans and honks in the bathroom brought ever-vigilant staff who discovered we had simply eaten too much chocolate and too many macadamia nuts. They considered our stomach upsets punishment enough, so the case of the missing child was closed, but this may have been an additional reason I was asked to attend school elsewhere the next year. I'm sure that this, coupled with the previous chapel episode, was the straw that broke the camel's back.

"We have made more than adequate attempts to teach her self-control," the headmistress wrote to My Nonie. I still have the letter from her. The headmistress is so gentle and her language so soft. Her vexation with the unruly brat never comes through. You can see why I loved this place.

"She is a dear little girl, but she is the focus of attention and leads disruption among our younger students. She is a born leader but her inventive exploits are sometimes beyond the grasp of the younger children, who see these activities as exciting ways to circumvent our rules. We hope that she will be able to attain an understanding of self-control, and in achieving this, will be able to return to us for the following year." Isn't that endearing?

My Sweet Friend had gone to a Catholic boarding school in Switzerland on the border with France for 1940-41 while my new school was in California. She would be home in Manila from Europe by the time we would arrive in early August 1941, and I realized I had missed her more than I recognized. She was a sister figure in my life, and I loved her dearly.

I tried hard to remember details about the Philippines. I kicked myself for not paying more attention to descriptions of her homeland and family relationships. All I remembered well was her reply when I asked if she got homesick. She nodded her head. Her eyes filled with tears. Then she softly said, "Mostly for my amah."

Her amah was her baby nurse, her teacher, her confidante, and her well-loved friend. My Sweet Friend loved her large family with total devotion and told me long, happy stories about her three uncles, five aunties, and cousins. They all lived on the same large acreage in Manila. Each family had its own house. At random, different relatives joined others for meals, activities, and companionship. In spite of how dearly she spoke of each one, it was her amah to whom My Sweet Friend was closest; whose whole lovely purpose in this world had been to cherish my friend. I imagined what a good feeling it must be to have an amah, though I didn't need one. I had My Nonie. She was my sun, moon, and stars.

The big event was at hand. Surely no seven-year-old had ever been as excited as I was to be on such a wonderful journey. The first week of August we flew by Western Air Service to San Francisco. I thought we'd leave from Los Angeles, since it was closer to Hawaii, but before dawn the next day we went in a hired car from our hotel to Treasure Island on San Francisco Bay.

Arriving at the Pan American terminal area, we were met immediately by uniformed personnel who took our bags from the car and ushered us into the terminal. Nonie produced her passport identification, although technically she didn't need a passport as the Philippine Territories were U.S. possessions. We were greeted warmly as though we were expected guests and asked to proceed out to the airplane. I was quite fascinated with the décor of the terminal itself. The big room was all done up in shades of greens and blues and seemed to be an introduction to the tropical paradise where we were heading. The furniture was very blonde wood, not like anything I had seen before this time. It had very straight legs and the tables were curved into free-form shapes. Quite exotic to the eye of a kid who had grown up with Sheraton and Chippendale and heavy dark fabrics and color. I was entranced by all of it.

Western Air Service –
Seattle to San Francisco –
The first leg of our trip to the Orient

Although the giant passenger flying boats each had individual names, a Pacific crossing was generically called "the China Clipper" or "the Boeing Clipper." Our beautiful airplane was *Pacific Clipper,* and a true princess of the Pacific she was. I was thrilled; I could barely swallow! I was a kid accustomed to four door sedans and railroad compartments, but this air travel idea superseded anything heretofore in my imagination.

We walked across a large landscaped patio to the huge plane and across a ramp with cables attached to stanchions for a guard rail. Nonie held my hand as we approached. Stepping into the aircraft, we were welcomed as though we were very important passengers and we were shown directly to our seats. The uniformed gentleman assisting us said we'd be given a tour later after we were in flight. It was very exciting. Soon everyone was boarded and the cabin door was shut, not to be opened until Honolulu. What fun!

We taxied to our take-off point in San Francisco Bay, and to provide a clear flight path, escort boats kept away other watercraft in our vicinity. Even the Oakland ferry was required to yield the right-of-way to us. How important I felt. The pilots gradually revved the engines, checked magnetos, and our plane roared forward and bumped repeatedly as we hit small waves in the bay. As we left the sea plane base at Treasure Island behind, we were jostled and jerked, like riding a bronco in a rodeo! The booms were thunderous, like banging trash cans, then suddenly we lifted into the silent air.

Alcatraz Federal Penitentiary

With the Golden Gate Bridge on our left and Alcatraz Penitentiary on our right, we climbed smoothly and steeply over the early, quiet California coast. I wondered aloud why we didn't fly directly *under* the bridge, finished in 1937, but to my surprise, someone explained it wasn't legal. I had never thought about airplanes, so free in the air, abiding by rules or laws, but

I learned. My analogy, which I kept inside my seven-year-old head, was that while one law made you curb your dog, no law should control a free-flying canary. Some canary!

This plane was a giant compared to the little DC- 3 we had flown in from Seattle's Boeing Field. Here, we were surprised with the rich decor of our main cabin. It resembled travel in the Pullman train car we took to visit relatives in Iowa. There was ample room to walk around, unlike the cramped aisles on the DC-3. These windows were larger and the seats much wider and more comfortable, more like in our living room at home. Beds folded down from the ceiling in our area, with side curtains to provide privacy. One climbed a ladder, crawled onto the bed, buttoned the curtains, and undressed or dressed, as needed.

I wrote the tail number, 18602, on a postcard which we mailed to my grandmother from Honolulu. She saved it in a scrapbook and I have it now. It seemed important to me to let our family know our conveyance had a proper number. I wonder why I thought so?

Our aircraft had a double-deck, with flight officers and other crew members seated on the top level. A large area there was devoted to the flight controls, with a great bank of radio equipment and a table for the navigation officer. Many dials, levers, and meters needed attention to keep us on course and in touch with various air stations along our route. We flew at about 175 miles per hour, although we were told the airplane could fly over 200 miles per hour. How marvelous it seemed to go that fast!

P.A.A. (B314) Flight Deck Showing Crew   *La Guardia Field*

Clipper Flight Deck

Uniforms and manner of speech followed formal naval patterns, with a captain, first officer, and other ranks. Our plane held 68 day passengers, 36 sleeping passengers, and a crew of 11, including two stewards. Day passengers might go as far as Hawaii or Midway Island, or might be picked up at Guam, bound for Manila. Long-distance passengers, such as we were, had sleeper bunks. Others, with tickets for a shorter flight, used the chair seats which reclined into sleeping cots with a pillow and blanket.

A circular staircase connected the two decks, which I thought was especially grand, like in the movies. There were six separate passenger compartments in addition to a large lounge seating 12, and a separate deluxe VIP compartment near the tail, offering complete isolation.

I watched carefully to see who used that area, thinking it might be a beautiful movie star or an admiral or a president of a country. To my chagrin, it was only inhabited by an unassuming small, silent Caucasian man in a business suit, who stayed to himself and mixed with no one. This unremarkable man's presence whetted my appetite for adventure.

I was sure he was a spy or even a "spy master," since these were the days my imagination thrived on Charlie Chan, the famous oriental detective in the movies and on "thriller" radio stations. My imagination sought adventure wherever I was.

A galley crew prepared our meals. There were restrooms and lavatories separate for men and women. We had impressive sound-proofing, heating, and air conditioning. I hadn't thought heating was necessary. After all, wouldn't we fly in the sun all the way? I learned the air is very cold at high altitudes, and we'd have been in dire straits without these comforts.

To pass the time there were earphones to enjoy music or spoken books. In addition, someone had recorded many quarter-hour and half-hour radio programs. I enjoyed episodes of "The Green Hornet," "The Shadow," "Gangbusters: Your FBI in Peace and War," and "Captain Midnight." Children's programs were limited to "The Lone Ranger," "I Love a Mystery," and "The Chase and Sanborn Hour," with Edgar Bergen and Charlie McCarthy.

I spent many hours listening as I looked out the window, and with the drone of our mighty engines, I often fell asleep hugging my favorite doll. Unknown to me, My Nonie had brought two wonderful new dolls to give to My Sweet Friend and me when we were together in Manila. All in all, this was a marvelous flying machine—our home for the next five days.

In later years I have thought how wonderful it would have been if every child of that era could have had the same travel experience. A blessing on Pan Am for giving a little girl a memory to recall when times were tough and bleak with despair. Pan Am gave that little girl—who grew to be an adult—sweet memories of a time that's gone forever and can never happen again.

We two rubber-neckers wanted to see everything and everyone; we had a variety of military personnel, government officials, business men, and families on rotation with U.S. corporations. My Nonie never put up a facade and was quite amused at those who did, because there were more than a few passengers who acted like snobs. Nonie lived by the standard that if a person was courteous and kind, they were as rich and grand as King Midas himself.

Quite a few appeared to seek our admiration, acting like high society. We could easily tell by the way they talked, and what they talked about, they were impostors of the socially elite. Nonie recalled reading about the extraordinarily rich Astor family of New York, their wealthy friends and parties. She said all pseudo-sophisticated and suave mannerisms should have been thrown overboard from our Clipper, but we observed several who seemed well acquainted with "Madame Astor's horse," by trying to be someone they were not.

This phrase was derived from an episode at an Astor mansion dinner party, when a silly guest tried too hard to impress Mrs. Astor. The unfortunate woman attempted to display a level of social greatness, which she didn't possess. She slipped on an icy step as she entered the mansion. Newspapers of the day recounted how, rather than grandly approaching her hostess: "Mrs. Dalrymple shot through the door in reverse, like the rump of Madame Astor's horse."

Nonie said we were there to enjoy ourselves, and we ignored behaviors of those who tried to act overly grand, yet used improper language, which gave us giggles later. One woman—definitely not a *lady*—had black roots showing on bleached hair, dirty fingernails, and acted in a most superior manner. She needed to brush her teeth.

"I dropped my handbag, and all the powder flew out of my 'convict'," she complained at one point. She meant her "compact," of course. Another time, a gentleman described a lovely concert he attended in a most "exotic" location. The blonde woman huffed and proclaimed,

"I, for one, don't want anything to do with all that sex stuff." We were perplexed until one of the teachers with us asked her if she referred to "erotic" rather than "exotic"?

Her frowning rejoinder was, "Isn't that what I already said?"

We stifled our giggles, although two ladies sitting with us pretended to cough into their handkerchiefs until they could control their snorts of laughter. We eventually embarrassed ourselves by laughing at her, which was not good, and not how true ladies act.

I remember one large man who drank almost continually. In his own eyes he was the epitome of social and financial greatness.

He told us often how he was on the way to look over "some big deals" in the islands. To his misfortune, however, he had a continual battle to keep his trousers buttoned. In those days men's garments didn't have zippers. With use, the buttonholes enlarged. Of necessity, women of the family, or the gentleman's dry-cleaning establishment, often restored security to the plackets by the addition of a few stitches to lessen the size of the buttonholes. Apparently this man had no one to sew for him. Also apparent, the man had gained a bit too much weight, thus putting a strain on the already stretched buttonholes. All of a sudden, as he moved or turned, the placket would burst open leaving his rotundity in an "exposed" position. Ever watchful male crew members kept a close eye on his couture and on our level of embarrassment, and assisted as necessary. Eventually they convinced him to go to the men's "smoking room." (There actually wasn't one.)

Most passengers were delightful. Several families were returning to Manila from summer vacation in America. Three of our group were contract school teachers who laughed and anticipated a grand time instructing in China. Nonie and I enjoyed them and wished them well. We wondered to ourselves how they could afford the cost of the clipper tickets.

We aimed to have fun for these few days on our Clipper, so we used our best manners and avoided any attempt to impress our fellow passengers. When we took off for the Pacific Ocean vistas and the start of our adventure, little did we know what harrowing experiences we'd have before we ever saw the precious coast of America again.

We flew only by day, since passengers on all airliners of those days were far too fearful to fly at night; our trip took nearly six days. In those early years of air travel, hilariously, a rumor said one could "help" the plane fly if they hunched their bum and pressed their feet tightly against the floor, while they pulled up on the arm rests. This was to ensure we stayed in the air by not putting down too much of our weight. At first I was a proper "armrest-clutcher," but I soon saw the folly of it and relaxed the rest of the flight to Manila.

My Nonie had flown in small airplanes quite often with her brother Jack, an official with United Airlines, and one who also loved private aviation. In the 1930s, Uncle Jack frequently had a WWI barnstormer buddy come through Cheyenne, Wyoming, who gave the family all the airplane rides they could handle in return for a good bed, a bath, and a few free meals.

Jack hired on, back in the late '20s, as a dirty hand mechanic's supervisor in Pat Patterson's Ford garage in Cheyenne. A short time later, Pat brought several smaller airlines together and formed United Airlines. They flew mail bags and freight for a number of years, before offering passenger service.

United Airlines 220hp Waco
"flying the mail" – 1935
Cheyenne to Denver to Omaha to
Kansas City

These were the days when there was no such thing as radar or even radios in planes. Instruments consisted of a compass, RPM indicator, and an altimeter. The pilot knew only what direction he was going, how high he was and about how much fuel he had, based on an exposed length of wand. The wand was attached to a cork, which floated in the wing gas tank, within the pilot's field of vision—that was it! Everything else was conjecture, even the height of mountains and weather forecasts.

Pat took Jack along with him to United, where Jack eventually became director of maintenance until he retired in the 1970s in San Francisco. Nonie liked to fly, and I followed her lead. My adventuresome grandmother flew unaccompanied well into her nineties to her adored World Series baseball games every year. In her youth she had traveled through what became Yellowstone Park in a covered wagon. What a contrast of transportation methods. It's clear—flying has been in our family a long time.

My husband with the first airplane I bought him.

Charles and Anne Lindbergh surveyed an air route over the Pacific Ocean for Pan American World Airways in 1931.

Overseas air travel was incredibly complicated. Facilities had to be constructed and in operation to refuel, repair, and to serve passengers. With a rapidity historically unequaled by other forms of transportation, intercontinental flight became a reality.

Intercontinental flight was a totally new mode of transportation across distances that continued to take weeks by ship. One of the biggest hoops to jump through was convincing civilians air travel was readily available and safe, and that domestic flights were affordable. It was such a very new form of transportation. Although Clippers already flew the short European route, it was 1935 before the first China Clipper landed in Manila. That in itself shows the need for air travel and perhaps the search for adventure exhibited by the American populace in the 1930s.

Imagine, only four years after the Lindberghs devised a route over water, Clippers landed in Manila. Outstanding progress! The Clippers to Europe and South America had been flying longer, although passenger airplanes were still an exotic novelty to most people. Certainly only the most adventuresome considered going long distances over great bodies of water. According to our fellow passengers, it was reassuring that after all, we might land on the ocean and remain afloat in an emergency. Many years later I learned ocean landings and take-offs were probably a bit of the fantastic.

The ocean, by nature, has swells, is seldom calm except in certain latitudes, and emergency repairs on such a large aircraft could hardly be handled on the open sea, without a hangar. Minor repairs could be done in flight by crawling through a tunnel in the huge wing to the engines. On base, there was a greater risk of damage to an airplane by attempting an ocean landing, than limping along to the next land available or making an emergency landing near a friendly ship.

The ocean's expanse made us feel small, defenseless. For most people, when one traveled and wanted a bit of luxury, railroads remained the answer. Railroads had dining cars and Pullman cars, where seats folded into beds at night. Roomettes had Pullman beds and a sitting area, a private bathroom, and porters who took care of every need.

Curiously, I have never understood why people travel for the sake of travel alone, but many do. I know a few who get on airplanes, arrive at a destination, then take the next flight home again, purely for the thrill of travel—which I find quite peculiar. Why would anyone leave their comfortable home to be subjected to the whims of strange people and settings?

Today we have those who travel for months at a time in their motor-homes, simply for the sake of going somewhere. How sad that they can't be satisfied with their homes. These same travelers might have idly taken lengthy train trips and ocean voyages, with no particular destination in mind. Ocean liners remained the choice of less stalwart souls who fancied crossing the Pacific.

We, however, had a true destination and were very excited about arriving there as soon as possible—by air. One should have a destination, travel, do what needs doing, and return with alacrity. It would have been good had we been able to do that.

While our airplane's range of almost 3,000 miles was more than adequate for long flights, passengers required shorter hops. Most people did not like to fly at night, making overnight land stops a necessity, in spite of our plane being fully equipped to sleep. Our entire Clipper flight was about 57 to 60 airtime hours, depending on winds aloft. We landed at predetermined islands, with fully staffed accommodations, much the same as a modern bed and breakfast facility today. All this was part of the airline's service. Each stopover offered a variety of recreational activities like beach combing, ocean swimming, and hotel pools, which filled with each incoming tide. There were motorboat forays, small sailboats, and snorkeling along inner reefs of landing lagoons.

There was always an open bar on shore, regularly enjoyed by several passengers. Pan Am also maintained a plane-to-shore-station library. One could check out a book on Midway Island, leave it on the Clipper when deplaning, and the book made its way back to Midway with a future passenger. Absolutely everything was designed for passenger comforts.

Three Clipper-type airlines served world travelers: Pan American World Airways, British Overseas Aviation Corporation, and Deutschland Luft, each loosely called Pan Am, BOAC (Bow-ack) and "the Heinies." The latter two flew comparable routes with similar non-Boeing aircraft, but both had fewer passenger comforts than Pan Am. Supposedly, they were all quite supportive of each other, but I doubt it was true.

Pan American and other airlines also flew Martin aircraft, now Lockheed Martin. Foreign lines favored planes built by their own nationals, however. Britain bought Boeing planes but also had Sunderland Aviation Corporation, and Germany had Heinkel Deutschland Luft Corporation, yet no other planes were as large as our Boeing 314 China Clipper—nor as grand.

All were serviceable, but Juan Trippe, the founder of Pan Am, had done his homework and knew that adventurers who flew long distances over water would want the ultimate in available luxuries. His customers certainly hit the jackpot; between Juan Trippe's dream and Bill Boeing's construction, the luxury air travel market was cornered by Pan American.

We stopped one early afternoon. After dropping a flare to check wind direction, our pilots made a 90-degree landing to the beach in the lagoon of what appeared to be an uninhabited atoll. While circling, I was unable to tell if the land was composed of a group of volcano tops which had erupted above sea level in a circle, or if it was an entire atoll. It seemed we were viewing a water-filled partial caldera of a single extinct volcano, therefore an atoll.

Being raised on "The Ring of Fire," as the Pacific Ocean volcanos are called, makes many school children of the Pacific coast more informed than others about related geology. Our background in Puget Sound with our resident volcanos made it especially exciting and stimulating to circle that day.

Later, while the Clipper anchored in the beautiful blue-green lagoon, most of the passengers loaded into small rubber boats and motored to the beach. The crew explained that controlling factors concerning extemporaneous stops had to do with weather, storms, and even passengers' votes. These choices gave our trip added interest. If a Pan Am official was on board, we were told the schedule often became even more flexible. They were generally pilots themselves, and like pilots everywhere, including the one I later married, they liked a grand adventure. On this day we were ahead of schedule, so we spent several hours beach-combing for beautiful shells on the seaward side of the atoll. We also had a picnic on the beach. I don't think I ever knew this island's name.

In those days, smaller, uninhabited islands were designated with numbers by which ships and planes would navigate. Many Pan Am pilots flew in Europe for Lafayette Escadrille in World War I and continued to be extremely patriotic. Since the United States Navy was aware of Japanese intentions in the Pacific, I have always wondered if a bit of surreptitious spying was perhaps coincidental to our landing in the lagoon that day.

I remember years later talking to a long-time Pan Am top-echelon official who was the relative of a college friend. He told me our landing in the lagoon could never have happened; the liability to passengers and the aircraft was far too great. To show respect for my friend's parent, I didn't argue the point, but it was true, because I was there; we had done it.

"You know what the answer is; it was because of national security," Nonie said in jest and laughed when I told her later about the conversation. Then we both laughed ruefully. We knew her comment was not hilarious, nor untrue.

After one in-flight dinner, we climbed into our bunks early and slept. In the morning we found ourselves moored near an island, having slept though the landing during the late evening. In another memorable incident we deplaned on an island shortly before sunset. At the airline's tropical inn we dined and had a social evening, while local people played music and sang; it was quite festive. Then we enjoyed baths and beds for a few hours.

In the early morning darkness we were hustled into our robes and slippers and driven down to the sea to board the plane. It took off as dawn peeked into the far eastern sky. Then we slept again, as our mighty Clipper droned peacefully through the morning, above the liquid silver Pacific. Hours later we were roused for breakfast, served on china and white linen tablecloths, with crystal-like glassware—no modern sacks of peanuts or plastic cups on *our* Clipper.

Stewards prepared the most wonderful food for every meal. Every breakfast had beautiful, fresh pineapples sliced before our eyes, then doused with coconut milk and powdered sugar and served with warm, soft croissants, ham and hot chocolate. Oatmeal—a passenger favorite—was presented with cream so thick and heavy we could eat the cereal and topping with our forks.

Incredible luncheon offerings included a smörgåsbord of small sandwiches, cheeses, sliced fresh fruit, and tarts. Everything was as beautiful to our eyes as it was delicious to our taste buds, as though all had been prepared by magic elfen fingers. Lovely little ham roulades, touched with our first savoring of Asian salsa, were wrapped around the thinnest stalks of celery, cucumber, melon, and shaved green beans.

Dinners were extravaganzas of seafood and roasts. One evening was Prime Rib night; the next was Lobster. One evening featured a "Deep South" country dinner, American style. Naturally, they served fried chicken, mashed potatoes, and gravy. From one meal to another, everyone was pleased. Pan Am had planned well, and they surpassed themselves with each day's menu.

In later months, when we dreamed, talked, obsessed, and cried over food—or the absence of it—we cherished our many memories. We even remembered precisely how many slices of peaches we ate at a specific meal. For many years in the camps, food was all we talked about, because our hunger was so excruciating.

My Nonie and I laughed together, imagining my rigid grandmother and her childless daughters attempting to stay overnight in an island guest house. The tropical climate doesn't need standard glass windows; movable shutters sufficed. My grandmother would have stationed each of her daughters as sentinels, with pistols on the edge of the bed, to listen for "a man." It would mean sleepless nights for those women, and we laughed at their self-imposed terror.

My mother had been witness to some of our relatives' previous, silly escapades. It's a wonder no one was ever harmed, since all these older women carried and used pistols, with varying degrees of proficiency and judgment. My grandmother, for target practice, would prop a broom upright with rocks, then pace off 50 feet, aim, and shorten the broomstick, an inch at a time, without a single miss. Her favorite pistol was a floppy-action old .45 caliber Bisley, which my grandfather used to shoot coal mine mules if one fell and broke a leg. I was always sure that Bisley might blow up in her hand, but it never did.

My grandmother was terrible about gun safety, but I tried to emulate her in other ways, and I adored her all of my life. Her sons and my mother used to chasten her about reckless shooting. Uncle David finally filed off the firing pin and the New Year's Eve gunfire stopped forever. We were all so relieved.

My grandmother would stick her aquiline nose in the air and say, "Oh, don't be so silly. The only people I've ever hit were ones I aimed at!" Probably true. She was born in 1878 and lived her life fully until age 102, still of right mind, eccentric, funny, lovable, domineering, and controlling.

I believe the tickets on our Clipper were outrageously expensive in proportion to today and more than the SST Concorde in later generations. Our two tickets must have cost Aunt Alice close to $7,000 each in 2007 dollars. In 1936 when Clippers first began flying to Great Britain the fare was $1600 and $1438 to Manila on a Martin M-30. This was before the day of the Boeing B314 which we were flying in. We had a much longer flight and one lasting many more days, also.

Of course, in the 1940's, respectable, well-made ladies' shoes cost $1.50, and a nicely furnished three bedroom house rented for $25 a month; a ranch mink coat was all of $500; a deluxe Ford car cost $900; a doctor charged $25 to delivery a baby; and tickets from Seattle to Alameda, California, where we flew to board the Clipper, cost $18.75. On the other hand, My Nonie, regarded as being very well paid for a woman of her time, earned $35.00 per week as the secretary to the insurance company president.

I often wondered how Aunt Alice came by our tickets, but she never revealed it. Her priorities were first being an Army Major, then a senior surgical nurse. More relevant to my mind was the fact—not coincidentally—that she was a professional-grade poker shark. In any community to which she moved, Aunt Alice quickly become notoriously successful. Therefore, I've always guessed she paid for the tickets with her card winnings. She *was* a case.

In later years she told me that in 1946, after the war was over, she received a courteous refund from Pan American for the unused portion of the two tickets which Nonie and I never used for a return trip from the Philippines. Then demonstrating her adventurous spirit, rather than saving that windfall, she bought a shiny, new 1947 Ford convertible. I imagine her speeding along with her adorable little Boston terrier called Nuisance wedged in behind her head, laughing and barking out the window at other cars. People would point and laugh at the little dog who seemed to be driving the car. Alice loved to drive with her windblown short hair and a grin wide as the sky. Her new toy was baby blue with a white top—the proper color for a convertible in the 1940s. All of her cars for years were baby blue.

After WWII, Pan Am told her their Clippers had almost all been sold or destroyed by one means or another. With the advent of new types of aircraft, Clipper service was no longer available to the public. Newer DC-6s, able to cross the Pacific in fewer leaps, were now either built or on the drawing boards. This was right before jets blanketed air travel. It's too bad Clippers went the way of the winds. They provided a calm, slow, sophisticated adventure. In today's travel, people use autos, sailboats, hang gliders, and slower conveyances. There surely might still be a market for the China Clippers and their leisurely luxury.

As an adult I have flown first-class with major airlines, stayed in the grandest hotels, been in limousines, traveled in compartments on exclusive trains, and have sailed on the very finest cruise lines. Yet I tell you the luxury and pampering given to Clipper passengers has never been surpassed—nor equaled. There are not enough superlatives to describe a long flight on a China Clipper.

It always makes me smile to remember the pleasure Aunt Alice showed, to provide us with this dream trip, a type which no longer exists. It has passed into memory and into history, yet for those involved as passengers, the experience will be treasured to the end of life.

Our flight route was from Los Angeles to Honolulu, Midway, Wake Island, Guam, and finally Manila. We heard the flight occasionally diverted for an additional day in beautiful Yokohama to refuel, shop, sightsee, and provide an overnight for tourists. Unfortunately, we were told their facilities had recently been "out of service," so our flight plan was directly from Guam to Manila.

Of course their facilities were out of service! The Japanese were training and assembling invasion fleets there, near Yokohama harbor, and in August they didn't want sharp eyes recognizing what they were doing. Three invasion fleets were assembled. One was to approach the Hawaiian Islands. A second was to overrun and capture the American possessions: Wake, Guam, Midway, and French Frigate Shoals.

The third fleet steamed into history in The Thousand Mile War, in the Aleutian Islands. American forces endured a terrible winter in 1942 as they battled to dislodge the Japanese from Attu, Agattu, Kiska, and other remote Alaskan islands. The Thousand Mile War, referencing the Alaska-Aleutian campaign, stretched far across the North Pacific Ocean and Bering Sea, from Alaska almost to the Japanese Kurile Islands, which are part of the Ring of Fire in the Pacific.

Nonie and Papa –1941.
Before he left on his "summer cruise"

My new Papa made his first assault landing at Massacre Bay on Attu, where our American casualties were heavy. It had long before been named Massacre Bay, since early Russian sailors sheltered there while they slaughtered seals on the beach. My Papa was a Landing Boat Group Commander on an attack transport, responsible to guide assault landing crafts to the beaches.

As a distinct target with his revolving orange light, he was injured for the first time on Attu, the second time at Tarawa, and the third time at Saipan. Finally he was sent to the United States Naval Hospital at San Diego to recover, and his active duty overseas was over.

All in good time and on time, we arrived in Manila late one August afternoon. We planned to stay two weeks then return for my school matriculation; uniforms awaited me at home. I had been readmitted—on parole, so to speak—to my favorite boarding school. My Sweet Friend planned to accompany us, and all was ready for our return to Puget Sound.

CHAPTER 3

MANILA

Match me such a marvel, in any Far East clime,
to find a white-walled city half as old time.
——*After M. Arnold*

At first glimpse, the islands overwhelmed us with the green velvet carpet of mountainous jungles. It was a huge contrast to our days and days of flying over the silver Pacific. As we approached Manila Bay, harbors and inlets were filled with ships of every description and size. We planned to deplane, navigate Port of Entry, get our luggage, then contact Aunt Alice by telephone at her Army Hospital to receive directions on how and when to meet. Nearby we saw several ranks of pedicabs and taxis, as well as street cars—which I love. Of course we had no idea which one to take or in what direction we should go.

"Be patient. People will pick you up, and they will recognize you," Aunt Alice said on the telephone.

We were mystified. How could anyone recognize us? We were foreign tourists. After an interval of half an hour, loud honking drew our attention. Four limousines whipped into the curb. Out of the second car popped My Sweet Friend from school, who ran and hugged us both. We were so surprised to be warmly welcomed by a delegation of ladies from her family; her mother, her aunties, and her cousins had come to greet and take us to their homes. The ladies were dressed in beautiful, colorful floral frocks with sleeves like butterfly wings. We were absolutely astounded. They chattered as though we had known them all our lives. Questions came at us in exhilarating rapid fire.

"How are Uncle David and Aunt Dorothy? Did their little boy ever get chicken pox?"

"How is grandfather's brother's hotel sale coming along? My husband deals with people in the Bay area all the time and said to tell you he'd help if you all needed him to."

"Did grandmother discover who robbed her mailbox? The paper boy?"

"What happened with Aunt Betty and Uncle Carl's house-hunt? Did they have their baby?"

"Is old Freckles still alive? Bull dogs do live a long time, don't they?"

My Nonie was pleased by this reception, but she asked repeatedly how they knew all about us. We figured it out quickly enough; My Sweet Friend had kept them informed. Aunt Alice was also in touch with them about our arrival; she had notified them when we would arrive. Together, they developed a welcome plan, all in advance.

This lovely family lived much like ours, on a single, large piece of property with four or five houses quite separated from others, though our American homes were very much smaller and far less grand in décor. The relatives of both families could be splendidly isolated or have much interaction, so we felt nurtured, and as included as though we were at home.

We were treated with love, not exclusion by this Brahmin-like upper-class bastion of Manila society, rather than like American "hoi-polloi." They were as kind and inclusive as if we were related. Apparently, the favored little daughter, My Sweet Friend, had also fully advised them of our inseparable friendship at boarding school, since she spent many weekends and all holidays at our home in America.

She was included in everything, from trips to Mount Rainier and Pacific Ocean beaches to vacations on Vancouver Island, Victoria, B.C. In Cheyenne at Frontier Days, we spent one August with Uncle Jack. The spring vacation one year had her sequestered at Uncle David's house with chicken-pox; she exposed and might have infected his entire household. There was no immunization available in those times for chicken-pox. Two weeks later she emerged healthy again, with only one small scar underneath her chin; no one got the disease from her. Aunt Dorothy had taken *such* good care of her.

Much more than a house guest, My Sweet Friend was treated as another adored granddaughter among our close family. When she departed from America for Manila the final time, she took along a piece of everyone's heart. I was never jealous of her. It was fun for me to see how my family members each loved her so intensely. Aunties and even an uncle or two had tearful eyes and hearts when she left in July of 1940. She was barely nine years old.

She was such a happy, bright light in all our lives during these vacations. Pretty, impeccably dressed, socially well-mannered, she was also well-traveled for her age and could speak responsibly on many matters to any in our family. She was trained, even as a nine-year-old girl, eventually to step into the business world of her relatives' many commercial interests. Her

55

grandfather, mama, and daddy were effusive in their support for the new generation of women getting involved. It took another four decades before the United States stepped forward with similar, though very reluctant, support for women.

This family certainly showed appreciation for all the happy times when Aunt Alice first arrived in the Philippines, early in 1940. Alice contacted the family to deliver letters from their little one in America; they immediately expressed joy and gratefulness. They welcomed Alice into their homes, much as My Sweet Friend had been treated in Washington State. I think they were secretly delighted to find another card player in their midst.

Aunt Alice was so funny. She had a happy disposition, a wicked sense of humor, and a laugh that should have been given by the Lord to a tall man, not a petite woman, as she and her sisters were. When Aunt Alice laughed, everyone laughed—some with her, others at her. Aunt Lucy was the tallest, My Nonie was the most beautiful, Aunt Betty was the gentlest, but Alice was the fastest driver and most reckless. She always had a fender dent. "It was kissed by another car, because my little car is so gorgeous," she'd explain. Then everyone would laugh, but only a wise few refused to ride with her.

In the early evening after our arrival, Aunt Alice arrived in a taxi, with several nurses and doctor friends, after duty hours. They were all welcomed and included. This was a time of high hilarity, indescribable quantities of food—some of which we didn't recognize but loved at first taste—music, songs, dancing, and lots and lots of hugs until late that night.

My Nonie gave the new dolls to us and we little girls were positively joyful. It seemed our worlds were complete. We had our families together and we were together.

We were introduced to local dignitaries and more relatives, prominent members of Manila society, and others influential in government, banking, and corporations. It was a gala like none I had ever seen. It was hard to imagine they hosted this for us. Finally, we met My Sweet Friend's amah, Karja, whom she loved greatly, a beautiful lady of about 45 years, with dark skin and fine features, from Bombay.

Her striking bright blue sari was heavily lined in cotton, with a tight, short-sleeved, collarless blouse. Sari skirts are made of straight yards of fabric, folded into pleats, but not stitched in any manner. Long panels of each skirt were left unpleated, to drape over the shoulder. The few ladies who wore a sari looked for all the world like enormous, fluttering, gorgeous blossoms.

Even at age seven I was amazed how similar a sari skirt was to ancient Scottish kilts, in the way they were wrapped and belted. I remember how I stared at grandfather and his brothers, like exotic birds, when they dressed in formal kilts for weddings, funerals, and important events like Bobbie Burn's birthday celebrations. Kilts also were an extremely long piece of fabric; a hand-pleated plaid, then cinched around their waists with a leather belt. They laid the remaining tartan over their left shoulder, toward the front, from the back. It was attached at the leading edge of the skirt with a large pin and at the front of the shoulder with a cairngorm badge, an amber gem quarried in Scotland, and known elsewhere as a topaz. The belt also held their oval leather purse, the sporran, on a chain, in the middle of their colorful raiment. My grandfather always carried a pocketknife and a ten dollar bill in his sporran with his pipe and a small disc of tobacco. His brother, Uncle Billy, carried a Derringer in his.

Karja, the amah, stayed quiet in the background. Yet every time she attempted to leave the area, my friend called her back, or ran and took her hand. Finally, the father invited her to stay and enjoy our party. I think I grew to love her also by the end of the evening.

Although we were well-rested after many lazy days on our wonderful flight from America, it appeared I must have become overly tired, because suddenly I fainted. Adults at the gala, including doctors and nurses, concurred fatigue, travel, and the day's excitement was enough to cause my collapse. They were proved quite wrong.

CHAPTER 4
POLIO

Bright angels, guard the child
whose sickness breaks her mother's heart
—Gordon

During the next two days I grew more gravely ill, until I was hospitalized and diagnosed with Infantile Paralysis, a technical term for Poliomyelitis, or polio. Doctors said it was important to move me from Manila Hospital to the contagion hospital, so I could not expose others. I was deathly sick, and My Nonie was furious about the move. It was not a good time for either of us; she felt helpless; I was out of my head with fever and knew no one. Fortunately, Aunt Alice was there and often brought doctor friends to observe and advise. Nonie was finally convinced she really had no word in the matter. Laws required patients with communicable diseases to be quarantined—and polio was terrible, during its course.

Polio causes great muscular pain, accompanied by a high fever and a semi-comatose state, in which patients can hallucinate for days. I recognized no one and spoke gibberish. Nonie was beside herself with worry. She sat by me, swathing my small body with cool, wet towels. Aunt Alice gave me alcohol rubs.

My Sweet Friend's relatives encouraged Nonie; they called private physicians from the University of Santo Tomas medical school. They made special arrangements to have Nonie telephoned of changes in my condition, day or night. Her father also arranged a Trans-Pacific radio call to my grandparents, who were distraught, but glad to know Nonie was with people who'd care for her.

Grandfather, whom I had called Bum Bum since I was a baby, sent special loves for Nonie to give me. He would kiss and nuzzle my neck saying, "Yum, yum. You're as sweet as candy." As a toddler, I tried to copy his words, and he became Bum Bum.

My Sweet Friend and her kind family were as worried about me as was My Nonie. Left to her own devices, with me to worry over, Nonie may not have taken good care of herself without the support of these good people.

Sadly, I never saw any of Manila as a tourist. We girls never got our chance to study together again as planned. Later, during our first days of incarceration, we only glimpsed their family from a distance; we never spoke with them again.

Although there were fine physicians in Manila, and Aunt Alice's physician friends were also on hand, none had an answer on how to treat polio. The etiology was unknown; world-wide, the treatment was Gothic, at best. It consisted of metal braces and body casts. In a few cases, an iron lung, thumped up and down, to perform a manic-pressured CPR on the patient who was locked into the device, with only head and feet stuck out each end.

Since I didn't like confined places, the iron lung, which kept others alive, was not a good solution for me. I think I was too claustrophobic, perhaps to the point of making myself worse.

Once again I was lucky. I didn't need the device, since my respiration was not that seriously involved.

Time inched by with little done except to treat my fevers. This was maddening for Nonie, who repeatedly demanded action for her child. Fortunately, nothing was done. In this case that was perfect because I had the good luck to fall into the hands of nurses trained by Sister Kenny, the great Australian nurse who developed a radical treatment for polio. She professed a strapped, buckled, and laced patient in rigid steel braces or body casts was detrimental to the desired outcome of the therapy. Her system of gentle exercises was done by para-professionals called physical therapists, and eventually by a patient's family. This kept muscles from terrible body torsion and paralysis, which most often accompanied progressive polio.

Conventional physicians either ignored Sister Kenny or tried to dissuade patients from allowing her treatment. She was far ahead of her time and a true blessing! Physical therapy was not widely known in the United States. At that time it was practiced to any great degree only in Australia, New Zealand, and in military hospitals as treatment for Anzacs and Kiwis, military forces from Australia and New Zealand. American doctors regarded physical therapy with much skepticism. Most conventional doctors appeared to equate physical therapists with shamans and witch doctors.

The Sister Kenny nurses gave me range of motion exercises and kept well-intentioned doctors from trussing me in a body cast to prevent leg contortion. Of course, I had also raised a bit of Cain about wearing a cast in the motionless, humid, hot September in the Philippines, near the equator. Bless those nurses for sparing me that discomfort.

CHILD POW

The height of my disease was several weeks of unremitting fever, constant, severe pain from muscles attempting torsion, spells of limited consciousness, and a great sense of helplessness. I found it extremely difficult to restrain myself from complaints or whining. I tried to be brave, to not worry My Nonie unnecessarily.

In the throes of fever all I wanted was my grandfather! My dear Scottish grandfather was a terrific comfort whenever I was ill. During bouts of chicken pox and other childhood diseases, he read to me in his deep, sweet, Scottish-accented English. While I recuperated from scarlet fever, he read me the entire Hurlburt's *History of the World*, then Hurlburt's second volume *Geography of the World*. I loved both those books and am sorry they ever got away from me.

Since he only completed third grade before descending into the coal mines of Scotland, he always read for information, not for leisure. My grandfather had accumulated a formidable home library of high school and college text books about geography, history, written English, and mathematics. He was a true self-educated man who often read in bed until late at night. I never heard him read any subject that did not edify.

Sometimes when I was sick, I saw him cry with worry. His tears healed us both. I needed him to rub my head and croon the soft Gaelic songs of his own childhood. It's the only language I can say a few phrases of, but never learned to fully speak. Now, in great physical distress, he was thousands of miles away; my comforter was not available.

No one, at that time in 1941, knew how polio was transmitted. Since most epidemics occurred in summer months in the States, or as we said, back in the world, many authorities thought perhaps cold water swimming or bathing when one's body was overheated might be to blame. In the United States we did have many outdoor, unheated pools in summer use, commonly called plunges.

A few physicians thought polio was related to moonlight exposure, when rising night mists might lift harmful soil bacteria and possibly float an illness to anyone the mist touched.

Many other doctors thought this disease resulted from eating chickens infected with coccidiosis, since polio epidemics and dying poultry flocks seemed to occur simultaneously. It is also true hundreds of thousands of chickens were slaughtered in coccidiosis outbreaks.

In those days, many preachers harangued on radio and swore epidemics were a response to the sins of the wicked. This was the least believable cause of polio. Apparently, wickedness could be lessened by generous donations to some preachers' pockets. The Bible thumpers haven't changed much today. I knew I wasn't wicked, and neither was My Nonie. She was an angel.

We had previously planned that I would return to Washington for our boarding school's September matriculation. We were to take My Sweet Friend with us; we were registered at the seminary together. She definitely did not want to return to France, where she had spent the prior year, alone. It was also becoming too dangerous due to the spreading war in Europe. She loved both our American seminary and the nuns who taught at her Swiss-French school. She found French girls snobbish; they excluded her from all activities and called her Bebe Noire, Black Baby, though her skin was not black at all; it was like golden honey.

Today I despise those narrow-eyed, skinny-nosed creatures. She was absolutely gorgeous. I told her they were pea-green jealous of her beauty. That phrase made her laugh each time she told anyone about her year in Europe. I know I was right about those brats, since she did not have a single negative aspect in character, appearance, or manner with others; she was simply an adorable little girl.

After consultation with doctors, friends, and associates of Aunt Alice, we concluded our best plan was to stay in Manila through December, so I could recover well and go back to Washington State for school in January. Nonie remained with My Sweet Friend's relatives and had use of a car and driver to visit me as often as she chose. She passed the evenings teaching the ladies of the family how to tat. Tatting is needlework which uses a shuttle and thread to create beautiful lace edgings and tatted inserts for luxury clothing. Tatting makes lovely doilies and is easy, once mastered, but difficult to learn.

In the meantime, though separated, we girls were pleased to learn we'd be tutored in Manila for now, until the government health department removed me from quarantine. We would return to our seminary together. Although we hadn't resumed our friendship face-to-face, we spoke daily on the telephone. I had an October birthday party planned and was sorry she couldn't attend.

My Sweet Friend often accompanied her relatives when they had business in other island countries. In this way, they believed her generation would meet people they might do business with now and in the future. She loved these trips and planned to return in plenty of time for our tutoring, later in the fall. Since we were both good students, it should be no trouble to stay abreast. We were giddy with anticipation.

As it turned out, I was lucky to have only a mild, permanent affliction from polio. The course of the disease did leave me with a marked limp, left-side weakness, and one lung that doesn't fully inflate in normal respiration. Affected muscles never recovered and were useless. As other muscles strengthened to support my skeleton, they underwent excessive strain. In my older age a few have become useless, so my gait is compromised, irregular, with bouts of muscle collapse. Suddenly, my legs can begin to ache, then refuse to respond, to walk, or even allow me to stand. It happens so quickly I take care to have a cane at the ready, whenever I'm out of my house. It makes me sad. My dancing days are gone. I loved to dance.

CHAPTER 5
HELL COMES TO EDEN

More than an end to war,
we want an end to the beginnings of all wars.
—*Franklin D. Roosevelt*

I was in the contagion hospital Neustra Senora de Socorro de la Santa Spirito for six weeks before being released to my mother's care. During that time, Nonie was befriended by acquaintances of Aunt Alice who went to the United States for six months. They agreed to let us live in their cabana in the hills; to keep it occupied in their absence. The cabana was in a marvelous area of verdant plants and trees, where it stayed cooler in late September, one of the hottest months. Gratefully, we went there for my recovery.

This home was not what one would usually designate as a cabana. More usually it would be called a villa. It had begun in the 1920s as a modest three room retreat used on an occasional weekend away from the Manila heat. Over the years, the original family added second stories and spreading wings, and the current building became a beautiful and quite grand creation. The now vacationing second generation owners loved their home very much as evidenced by their care in choosing furnishings, paintings, and even garden statues.

The outer patio at our cabana with a lovely vine covered gazebo where I spent many hours with the household kitties

This place was on a hillside with broad green lawns and lush gardens decorated with religious statuary around several rock pools filled with koi. I couldn't identify the broad variety of palms, shrubs, and flowering bushes, though I knew a few were bougainvillea, amazing orchids, and ferns. From our hilltop palisade with comfortable stone seats, steps, and tiers of patios, we marveled at intense sunsets and a breath-taking panorama. The entire area was lantern lit at night for parties.

Our cabana was a sprawling two story house with five enormous bedrooms and a collection of heavy, dark rattan furniture with colorful pads and pillows. The bedrooms were each large enough to have two or three big beds for the family's grown sons and their friends who came so often to stay for weeks on end. Tables built of light mahogany matched nearby cushioned, velvet-covered wing chairs, inhabited by several enormous yellow-eyed cats, begging to be handled and loved. Their beauty was exceeded only by their patience, as I dressed them daily in a variety of doll clothes.

A large dining room held only a narrow, double-long table with 20 chairs, nine on each side and one at each end, as I discovered one rainy day. I learned how many guests we could serve at a seated dinner, which we did many times. I stretched blankets across the top of the vast table to make hideaways and royal castles underneath. I populated my fairy tale lands with a few dolls, a vivid imagination, and any available and willing cat. The large library was immediately put to use, and I thought surely this must be like heaven. With kitties, many books, and My Nonie, what else could I ever need?

We happily celebrated my eighth birthday in October, 1941, in our cabana. My Sweet Friend had accompanied her immediate family to Sarawak to visit an uncle and attend to their banking business. I missed her at the party, but looked forward to seeing her soon. Children of U.S. Rubber company families attended, and we had such a wonderful time, with a clown, trained goats who danced upright in costume, and a boy with a happy monkey to entertain us all.

October is the perfect month for a birthday. It breaks the winter stretch before the holidays. Fall colors are striking, and the weather is mild both there and in America. Constantly warm weather in the Philippines gave us flowers all season, and thankfully the monsoons had passed while I was in Our Lady of Help contagion hospital. At home, back in the world, fall weather changed greens oaks, maples, birches, and alders to warm oranges and gold. It seemed that wherever I lived, my birth month was beautiful. I am so lucky.

They had frequently added more space as their social group grew larger, more varied, and as their immediate family expanded with the birth of three sons. Most rooms were large, with dark tile floors. A high wall around the main houses and gardens created private patios, which made me feel completely secure. The eldest son, now grown, also worked for U.S. Rubber. He lived in the cabana with his family of five, but they currently vacationed at Yellowstone Park and the Grand Canyon in America for six months, so the retreat was ours! We were very grateful for their willingness to let me recover there for the autumn months.

Our home stayed cool with 12 foot ceilings in some places, 15 feet high in others. Large ceiling fans, called punkas, had long ropes to pull for increased circulation. The tapestry-like fabric swept air back and forth, creating quite a breeze and cooling the room to a great degree. I was surprised at how efficient the punkas were.

The cabana could sleep many guests if people shared rooms, but the structure was interesting in that intersecting hallways could open unexpectedly onto a bedroom wing, a storeroom, a patio or modern bathrooms, in totally unique places—like a secluded, walled shower in the garden—this due to difficulties in placement of plumbing pipes. A large central stairway climbed to more bedrooms where it was almost always cooler at night.

The inner patio entering directly into the living room

The house was roughly Y shaped. The wings housed live-in staff. The man and woman who lived there took good care of us as gardener/handyman and cook/housekeeper. After the war started, their seven small children were evacuated to relatives in Borneo. Thankfully, the entire family survived WWII.

This hilltop Utopia was a great change from Manila's city heat and busy streets. The verdant canopy was peaceful, totally unlike Manila's noisy, confusing environs. Before many months passed, we would remember and long for that graceful getaway with its many comforts.

One Monday afternoon, several carloads of civilians and nurse and doctor friends of Aunt Alice's arrived for a long planned wonderful vacation week of games, cards, and food. Most of these single military people took vacations early in December, prior to more demanding schedules around the holidays later

71

in the month, when staff with families were given extra time to be with their loved ones at Christmas. They were all medical personnel, and since they had worked the past weekend and planned to work again the next weekend they had earned the five consecutive days off at our hideaway.

My mother was a magnificent hostess with a gracious manner, sharp intellect, and natural sweetness. Nonie had already drawn a coterie of friends to her. It was such fun to watch her maneuver through a crowd of guests. The focus of all eyes, and she left each person smiling as she passed, happy to be noticed by her.

I remember that day she wore a two-piece dress of aqua silk with widely spaced tiny white polka dots. Her dress had a long, slightly full skirt, topped by a short-sleeved jacket with a mandarin collar and small pearl buttons. Her hair was pinned in an "up-sweep." She wore the pearls Papa had given to her for their wedding in Canada. Nonie was absolutely stunning, as usual. Quiet, smiling, dignified, she was never loud, nor made inappropriate comments. My Nonie was as perfect as any lady, and I tried my best to emulate her, but surely fell short as a young girl, even in new holiday clothes.

That memorable day I wore a white lawn blouse with ruffles around the sleeves and collar, new white patent leather shoes, and a black and white checked and gathered taffeta skirt. My long hair was fashioned into a heavy braid, laced with lavender ribbons. Nonie lent me one of her cameos; I was excited and felt perfectly outfitted for the start of our party week.

We had barely welcomed our guests who had caravaned out to the hills, when our cook ran to the front of the house yelling that we needed to turn on the radio. What we heard stunned us all.

"Air raid! Air raid! This is no drill! Attacks now at Manila, Clark Field, Cavite, Subic Bay! Japanese bombing Manila! This is no drill! Air raid Manila! Active military return to duty! This is no drill! Air raid! Air raid! Civilians remain indoors to avoid strafing from airplanes! Remain calm! This is no drill! Air raid Manila! This is no drill!"

All service-connected people with us, mostly single people who were nurses and doctors, listened intently, then scampered for their cars and raced back down the mountainside toward their duty stations. What excitement!

Finally, our radio announced news about the attack on Pearl Harbor in the Hawaiian Islands. It was hard to believe My Nonie and I were there only a few months before, and now that idyllic place was in harm's way. The media repeatedly referred to the Pearl Harbor attack as occurring on Sunday, December 7, yet *for us* it was now Monday, December 8. It was difficult for us to determine if they meant the battle had raged for two days, or did they mean the International dateline, or what?

The few civilian people with us became hysterical and spoke incoherently. Many sobbed; others cried quietly. Some began to pack in a frenzy; a few sat docilely, waiting to be told what to do. No one was sure of the next wise move.

Nonie called Pan Am, requesting an earlier than scheduled flight off the island on any plane that could fly us to a safe location. To our complete shock, they refused us transport because I was recovering from polio, and its contagion potential was unknown.

Clark Field, P.I. 12-9-41   w/ permission W. albertson

Clark Field near Manila was heavily damaged
by air attacks on 12-8-41

Later Pan Am declared we missed our flight. In 1947 they sent Aunt Alice a refund for half the cost of the round-trip tickets. It's a hoot if you think of the reasons behind their tardy refund. They stated our return plane waited for us as long as they could, yet along with the refund, Pan Am was ruefully apologetic, but never admitted they had denied us passage because I had been ill. Since airlines don't generally refund without being threatened,

I've always regarded it as a back-handed apology. It's a long time ago. No harm was intended. The world had turned into a place of chaos then. Let it go.

Incidentally, the last Clipper flight out of Manila went directly to Australia, with no interim stops for any reason, to clear the immediate war zone quickly. Safety was paramount and with that flight the era of the China Clippers had ceased forever.

Eventually, late that night, General Douglas MacArthur, High Commissioner of the Philippine Territory, announced assurances over the radio. He stated that while this was a troublesome event, we were: "...not to worry, since an American fleet is on the way to set things right. However, in the interim, we will continue to be under martial law."

Our gardener came to my mother and explained he and his brothers planned to stand guard during the night. He said not to expose any lights, since we might be strafed by Japanese airplanes. He asked My Nonie to take great care and get as much sleep as possible in the next few days.

This nice man, who took such good care of us, told my mother he and one of his brothers planned to leave early in the morning to sail the children to relatives in Borneo. He felt it was imperative to get them to a safer area. This was a huge undertaking. Borneo was hundreds and hundreds of miles away. There was open sea. He was right, but it was an extremely long trip, even with two sails to help. They needed an ample supply of fuel and fresh water for their fishing boat, yet no trouble was anticipated if they left quickly. He felt they would appear to be a solitary family, fishing as usual. We felt such fear for their safety.

We subsisted on snacks that night. Our cook, the mother of the departing children, was inconsolable in anticipation of their journey, its danger, the distance, and the uncertainty of when they could all be reunited. She finally suppressed her nervousness about the news and worked her kitchen magic. Soon we had a sumptuous supply of tasty baked goods.

Later, after our capture, our cook left the Manila area. She was able to sail to Borneo later in the war with other fleeing refugees in two of the family's fishing boats. It was a trip of great hardship, overcrowding, and insufficient supplies. When one boat broke down, the other towed it. If one boat ran out of potable water, the other shared until they could make landfall where they could re-provision. Sometimes they took short sea passages at night, from island to island. Sometimes they were in open seas for days.

All told, she finally rejoined her children and husband in December 1942, one year after separation. Everyone was safe, so they lived quietly and grew vegetables—which were frequently requisitioned by marauding Japanese troops—but this dear family came to no personal harm.

In the meantime, my mother, of course, felt an enormous responsibility to those who remained at the cabana with us. She did everything possible to assure their safety, until they finally departed. She slept little for many nights. From a child's viewpoint, sleep was difficult for me too, though I also found much excitement in the middle of this history-making activity.

Our radio was constantly tuned to whatever station was most clear. Smoke in the distant southwest left no doubt about the bombing of Manila and her environs. Towering, black oil clouds churned skyward. Fuel designated for the southern fleet burned from some of the many "oil tank farms," as they were called. Later, when our forces eventually pulled out of the area, the Navy torched all the oil, rather than let it fall into Japanese hands.

We heard and saw airplanes for days, but we didn't know whose. Later, we learned all were Japanese bombers. Manila was declared an "open" city to avoid great damage on the infrastructure, buildings, and people. However, the Japanese ignored this. The naval station and submarine base at Cavite Navy Yard and Subic Bay were obliterated by bombs. American planes at Clark Field were either destroyed on the ground or flown elsewhere, available for use. The city itself was heavily bombed.

It appeared the military prepared to abandon us. If so, Nonie said perhaps we should also leave, though a dozen civilian guests still lived with us. We thought if there was no army to fight, the Japanese might bypass us. We later realized that was a foolish hope.

All roads were closed to civilians, to ensure our military could travel as needed. Radio reports told of traffic jams in the city as civilians tried to flee the bombs. Curfews were established. No one was allowed on the roads or out in the open before eight in the morning, or later than five o'clock in the evening. In most areas no one obeyed those new laws; people were far too frightened to listen to a bunch of old men with a lot of gold braid. Officers and bigwigs wrote their own travel passes and had them counter-signed by staff in General MacArthur's offices, the governing military body.

SUBIC BAY- 12-8-41
SUBMARINE PEN AND SURFACE FACILITIES BURNING

Prior to the start of hostilities, we had planned a long vacation week to include all our new acquaintances. My Sweet Friend and a few relatives planned to stay with us also. I was thrilled. I hadn't seen her since the first day we flew into Manila.

She was not allowed to visit me in the hospital because no one was sure about the contagion period for polio. She attended classes for that short period at a nearby young ladies' academy, and lived at home. Between the quarantine period, which the health authorities impressed on us, her family's business affairs,

78

and the fact that we had no car, we had not interacted face to face for many months. We did, however, talk incessantly on the telephone, as girls do. We were thrilled at the idea of seeing each other again.

I had planned many wonderful things to show her at our cabana. I knew she'd love the koi ponds, where we could pet the fish. When we called them, these multi-colored aquatic creatures clamored and splashed on top of each other for food. They were a wonder, called "pond flowers" by our gardener. Like submerged blossoms they swam from sunlight into shadows. I knew My Sweet Friend would love watching them, even as I did. Unfortunately, that very Monday morning as they left their home in Manila to visit us aerial attacks began. We never resumed our close friendship.

I think, perhaps, *if* they had only made it to the hills with us.... She was the sister I was never lucky enough to have. In memory, I see her face, as lovely as the flower for which she was named... Lily.

Since much of our entertaining was food-based, and our friends knew the difficulty we always had shopping without a personal car, they had bought food at their military or corporate commissaries for the planned vacation week. Many had left us abruptly during the air raid for their military or governmental duty stations, so we found our larder and refrigerators stocked with excellent supplies. These could easily have lasted a month with no replenishment. We had varieties of fruits, vegetables, canned meats, several hams, baking staples, coffees, teas, and cocoa.

It must be nature's way for women to want to give of themselves and to provide nourishment, particularly in dangerous or hard times. I like women. Most of them carry a lot of emotional baggage, but when set aside, underneath is usually a loving, kind, giving person. Women also have a curious need to "fix" things, or make them right. Perhaps this is why we do make such good social workers, nurses and teachers and doctors. And mothers.

We are each the sum of our experiences. We become adults as a product of our basic nature, our training, and our experiences. The early nurturing we receive from loving families allows us to pass this same great gift to the subsequent dear ones who come into our lives. How lucky many of us are to have had parents who epitomized the goodness of the world.

I have now told my own daughter, as I was also told, "You make my sun come up in the morning." Both my daughter and mother certainly have made my sun come up in the morning. I marvel at how lucky I have been throughout life to have the gift of two such extraordinary women. Life is good.

We settled into our cabana, for what we thought might be the duration of the war. On everyone's lips was the promise of the American fleet sailing toward us. It was scheduled to arrive in less than two weeks, and many felt all this nonsense would cease and life would get back to normal. Suddenly, a rumor circulated that the wonderful rescue fleet didn't exist at all. That rumor was true. It was no wonder the military seemed to be preparing to leave us—they were doing just that!

I've always felt the rumors about a non-existent fleet sailing to our rescue hurt morale more than anything. Realistically, there was no fleet coming to our aid because there *was* no longer a Pacific fleet. The great fleet that once had existed now slept on the bottom of Pearl Harbor; it couldn't come to anyone's aid. Yet, for a long time we could not comprehend we were totally abandoned.

It was four long years before a great invasion did arrive. From 1941 to 1945, to survive we would learn to use our own initiative. For four years we scavenged; we lived in constant danger, with little food, rudimentary clothing, no friends, no dwelling, no medical care, no communication with the outside world, and no way out.

We would learn to be resourceful, to take care of each other—and to avoid enraging our captors. Although we could not have imagined it in the beginning we did eventually learn to accomplish each of these things to varying degrees. Day by day, we learned how to survive.

My Nonie accepted our situation no other way. She was determined we *would* survive, though we felt overwhelmingly trapped. Most civilians flew out from the Philippine Islands after the air raid. Others went by boat, and most made it through to Australia—except for us. We went nowhere.

No public means of transportation away from the islands was open to us because the infectious stage of polio was not understood. Nonie tried desperately to find us private transport, but was never successful. Pan American could not honor our round trip tickets since no more Clippers were scheduled to leave Manila. They had already refused us passage earlier because of my polio.

While I waited at our cabana, my dignified, gentle spirited and sheltered little mother *hitch-hiked to Manila, into a war zone,* to find us any kind of transport headed out from the war zone! Terrified, she also searched desperately for transport on small boats, anything safe enough to float. Frantically, finally she exchanged her pearls for passage with a small commercial boat skipper on an inter-island freight carrier. He promised to take us as far as Cebu. She returned to get me, our food, and water supply. Yet when we got to the dock many hours later, he had sailed without us, but with the pearls! He may have thought we weren't coming, since there was chaos all around. We had no money since banks had all been closed since early on Monday when the war started. We had used up our last resource for bribery and were stuck! We needed to deal with it. We were caught in the midst of a maelstrom that refused to spit us out.

Aunt Alice sobbed as she left by submarine on December 11th, under military orders. Tears streamed down her soft, freckled face as she promised to let our relatives at home know all about our plight. We both wrote letters to each one of our loved ones at home and to my new Papa-to-be. We told them not to worry if they did not hear from us often, since communication was dreadful from here, and we anticipated it could become worse. We tried to assure our family we were all right because we had a comfortable cabana to live in, so they should not worry. However, our concern at that time was more for Aunt Alice than for ourselves.

She and other nurses leaving on the sub were assigned to train newer army nurses to handle the large, expected numbers of wounded. Great battles were anticipated. As it turned out, they were confined to islands and at sea, so nursing took place largely on hospital ships for a long time. After permanent bases were established on captured islands where our forces could maintain a foothold, hospital units were set up. Aunt Alice ran the dangerous gauntlet by sub, through the South Sea islands—some of which were not even charted—down to Darwin, Australia.

Japanese subs and airplanes carefully watched for any exodus of people from the Philippines. We didn't know until the war was over if she actually had made it safely through. Aunt Alice did arrive, and was immediately recalled to the United States and assigned to a hospital ship. In the Pacific Theater of War these ships were named *Ernestine Koranda, Mercy, Comfort,* and *Consolation.* Alice later served as Chief Surgical Nurse on both *Ernestine Koranda* and on *Mercy.*

Early in the war, hospital ships sailed with the big war fleets and took part in most major assault landings, like Guadalcanal, Kwajalein, the Aleutians, Saipan, Tinian, Okinawa, Iwo Jima, and Leyte. The ships were bright white, clearly marked with a large red cross on their sides and decks to show they were non-combatants. How brave their ship's cadre was to live and work in such a dangerous position. These ships were also brilliantly lit at night to avoid being mistaken for a warship, but the Japs deliberately targeted them anyway. Eventually they were removed far from the battle fleet, and patients were transferred.

During the war, *Comfort* was severely damaged by Jap dive bombers. Many lives were lost. These included not only patients, but also nurses, doctors, and ship personnel who perished while they tried to help others survive. *Comfort* was clearly seen in daylight as a hospital ship with huge red crosses on her bright hull. Therefore, her destruction was a deliberate act of violence, outside the acceptable rules of war. Thankfully, she did not sink and was later repaired and proudly present at the aggressor's surrender in Tokyo Bay in August, 1945.

CHAPTER 6
LOVING HERITAGE

There is a comfort in the strength of love;
'Twill make a thing endurable, which else
Would overset the brain, or break the heart.
                                        —*Wordsworth*

B less her heart! Up to this time my mother had managed, in spite of herself, to be saddled with an extremely haughty little prima donna. I was raised to believe I lived a bit higher in the pecking order than most other people in the world. I was truly a good girl, gentle, kind, quiet, thoughtful of others, an exceptional student. Yet I was also deplorably outspoken and demanding.

My aunties and grandmother had seen to it that I was educated early at home. Aunt Lucy was County Superintendent of Schools for Musselshell County, Montana. All the sisters were well educated in some professional field. I was foolishly trained and spoiled by the rigid and opinionated triumvirate of my older aunties and grandmother who treated me as an adult, long before I was old enough to have developed the common sense adults need. These relatives held themselves carefully aloof from the rest of the world. Insular and clannish Scots, all of them, none had married outside the clan for 17 generations until Aunt Betty married Swedish Uncle Carl Westine in 1940.

We McGregors had married McKenzies and Finches, Gilderoys, McDonalds, McCallums, Trues, and Scotts who were septs of other highland clans. It's quite a wonder we each don't have three legs and an eye in the middle of our foreheads, since we still inter-marry. My daughter once married a Hume; a second cousin married a Cameron; another married a Kirk; someone else in my generation married a MacDuie; another joined with a Carlisle, and on it goes. We just seem to like each other.

We come from a limited gene pool, indeed. Each person marrying into our family was assimilated and conjoined with affection and encouragement. The extraordinary fact is we have always adored each other. I admit we have let a few blackguards slip through, but they didn't last. Pure strength of numbers eventually sent them on their way. Our family, for a hundred years or more, has accumulated stories about odd and eccentric folks who blossomed in each new generation. That's a whole other book.

Into this bunch of rigidly straight-laced characters I was born as the first grandchild. At the height of the Great Depression my biological father had two jobs. He managed a brickyard and was also a grocery store manager. Of course, neither employer knew about the other. The federal government's rule was firmly: "One job to a family, for the duration of the Depression." Eventually, my father was convinced by Aunt Lucy and her husband, a prize fighter known as Red McKenzie, The Montana Mauler—later turned school teacher—that he should become a veterinarian.

There was money to be made there, even during the depression, they said. When times are hard, people still had pets and they still doctored them. Ladies might need to have their shoes resoled, but still went to hair dressers. Children who may not have winter coats still had hair ribbons and baseball gloves. Luxuries were planned. Doctoring pets followed this line of reasoning, therefore veterinary school seemed like a good idea at the time. Time showed they were correct. Consequently, my mother and father accompanied Aunt Lucy and her husband off to vet school. The two women planned to financially support the men until graduation. To everyone's delight, my mother initially left me with grandmother.

I am told that from the time I could sit up, and after I could talk sensibly, the family treated me with a special fondness. Perhaps it was because for some years I was the *only* grandchild, the *first* grandchild, and *first* niece of the aunties and uncles. Whatever the reason, and whether right or wrong, I had a strange but interesting childhood, treated as a princess by all.

When I turned two years old, my grandmother baked a chocolate cake to be eaten at my birthday party that evening. Aunt Betty had been put in charge of me to see that I stayed out of the kind of trouble little ones get into. She turned her head and I was gone. Found with frosting on my nose, neither of the ladies could scold me. Instead I had my picture taken with Aunt Betty on the new slide Bum Bum made for my birthday present. Life was good. I ruled my own little roost.

Shortly before I was born, my family adopted a lovely Boston Terrier pup, Freckles. In those day, Bostons were called "bulldogs" for some reason. As I grew from infancy into my toddler stage, Freckles, by then grown to be a great big doggie boy, made me the focus of his life. Where I was; there was Freckles.

The day I learned to walk, I slipped away from my here-to-fore attentive family and made my way down the walk and into the street. A speeding car rounded the corner and would certainly have killed me if it hadn't been for my precious dog.

As the car neared me, Freckles screamed out and ran forward knocking me out of the way. Sadly, he took the blow on his head that was meant for me. His cries of pain brought my near hysterical family to us as we lay together in the street. After doctor visits by both of us, we rapidly recovered but ever after my darling Freckles was blind in one eye. The car had never even slowed down.

My pet and I spent joy filled years together until my absence from him during the war years. Years later, after I had gone to college, Freckles died in his sleep at the age of 19. He was more than just my dog. He was my life partner.

*Two years old with frosting on my nose
and loving Aunt Betty*

I was never treated as a baby or a child; instead, I was treated as an equal—at least while I was small and until I began to talk in paragraphs. Since I couldn't participate in on-going debates, arguments, and opinions that were a staple of communication in our family, I was able to stay out of verbal harm's way for many years. I do remember the first time I gave an opinion about a politician and was castigated: "That man's name is never to be spoken in this house!" I learned caution at an early age, but still felt "that man" did *too* have a handsome mustache!

Each auntie vied for my presence, stating she could care for me better than the other. Finally, all the aunties simply moved home. Our problem was resolved by all of us living together with my grandparents in the big house in Roundup, Montana.

Dear Alice, Lucy, Dorothy, and Betty are each gone now. Alice was my god-mother; she and Lucy were quite eccentric, yet so full of love. Lucy was my legal guardian in the absence of my mother due to a strange 1930s Montana legality about a single woman not being allowed total custody of her child after a divorce. Dorothy was my aunt by marriage to Uncle David; she had a compassionate personality and came from a lovely family. Betty was youngest of my grandparent's children and a lifelong gentle, kind, loving companion. She bailed me out of more troubles than any one person should have to deal with in a whole lifetime; bless her. I miss them all greatly.

During the war years, Alice was a busy professional nurse; Lucy was married to her veterinarian. Lucy prayed daily for us in church and cared for my grandparents, having moved them from Montana to Puget Sound in 1938, where by now all their children lived. Uncle David married Aunt Dorothy; they also lived with my grandparents. Betty married and lived only a half-hour away. Professionally, for many years she was secretary to

Supreme Court justices, while her husband was an executive in state government. Each Christmas, Dorothy put pictures under the tree of anyone away during the war, to keep us present with the family. This included Nonie; my new Papa; Uncle Jim True in England; Aunt Alice in the Pacific; Dorothy's brother Bill Taylor, flying the Hump in Burma; and me.

Betty was steadfastly the one who never gave up hope My Nonie and I might be found, and she worked hard to make the day of reunion a happy one. This family was composed of kind, loving, honorable people who grieved for us daily. Later, the family's prayers and our memories of these dear ones played a major role in our will to survive.

Home from boarding school for Christmas. I am five.

Due to this somewhat eccentric but loving background, I had developed an attitude I was owed a level of obeisance by others, simply as a birthright. I started school at age four, turned five in October, and could already read with good comprehension. On my sixth birthday Aunt Lucy gave me a copy of *Gone with the Wind,* for which I had begged. Though I loved it, my most favorite was the wild-west novel from Uncle David entitled *From Hell to Texas.* Aunt Alice and my grandmother were appalled at this and spoke harshly about it to both Lucy and David. I wish I could find a copy of it now.

I was allowed to skip second and third grades and found myself in the midst of students much older and far more mature and socially responsible than I. In the fourth grade, yet barely six years old, rather than being made fun of, ignored completely, or treated with childish disrespect, I was included—like a mascot.

All the ten year olds took care of me and saw to my wishes and needs, unless I acted beastly. Then they immediately thumped me on the head and settled the issue at hand with loud emphasis. I was not allowed to show disrespect to them. I remember absolute amazement at their violent reactions. Only once had someone ever struck me in anger.

That happened when my grandmother gave me an almighty swat on the back of my hands with a wooden spoon for being careless with kitchen knives. She made sure her young helper learned quickly. When I asked why she hit me, she replied she didn't want blood in her food later if I had not paid attention while cooking. She felt her action could make me remember—I think she was right. In the kitchen and at school, I quickly learned to avoid the wrath of my grandmother and my classmates, subsequently causing them fewer problems and myself considerably less anxiety.

We relocated to the southern California area due to the precipitous expulsion from my Northern boarding school. I was already fluent in several languages, learned through the immersion method taught at the already numerous private schools I had attended. Most had asked me to leave because of incorrigible elitism. Administrators genteelly wrote I was "perhaps slightly resistant to school regulations." Not really. Perhaps they hadn't explained things clearly enough. Good grief! Always blame the child. Adults can be so silly.

My Nonie and I both loved the area and were happy to acclimate to Southern California. I had an unnaturally advanced musical talent, and at a young age had the reputation as somewhat of a prodigy in Southern California. During our first year there I appeared as Gretel in a light opera company's production of Humperdinck's Hansel and Gretel. This was the winter before we went to the Philippines.

I was the total creation of my mother and voice teacher, Dr. Andrews, who was beloved by all among the community, faculty, and students at our boarding school. Dr. Andrews, an artistic director with the opera, was a voice of encouragement to the spirit of this star-struck little girl.

Photo used for opera publicity – 1940

Then, Eureka! I met Patrice Munsel, the beautiful coloratura soprano from Spokane, who successfully went on to The

Metropolitan Opera at the age of nineteen. At the time I met her in the summer of 1941, she was in Vancouver, Canada to sing on the radio. She greatly encouraged me. We were there on vacation, as usual. Our families stayed at the same place in Vancouver. I was quite mad about her. I fancied I'd follow her career pattern closely, and Dr. Andrews almost hugged the stuffing out of me when I explained my plan.

Work in the opera was fun; my voice was strong and held up well. During our pleasant performance in the early 1940 Christmas season, to my heartfelt joy, the audience stayed with us all the way. I did my best and wasn't nervous at all, nor were my best friends who were also singers.

Hansel was sung by Laidon Alexander from Britain, a friendly, sweet-faced boy about 11 years old, who was sent to America to remove him from the dangers of the London Blitz. He was a good singer; both leads were sopranos. We had such fun performing. The audience's enthusiasm caught fire within us, and I think the pleasure we exuded excited everyone, including a few critics in attendance. Previously published letters to media editors complained children were exploited for the pleasure of adults at this event. This was ably debunked by critics' reviews and editorial letters from people who attended the operetta, of which I loved being a part. Though we only did one performance, I was willing to perform every night! Critics were kind in their reviews, and I was grateful they hadn't called me "cute," a word I abhorred then, and now. (Another word I can't stand is "dollop." It sounds nasty to me, for some reason.)

Birth of the Canadian Dionne quintuplets created a rage of interest in children during this era. In those days people were kind and indulgent with children and were genuinely interested in their lives. This was pre-Dr. Spock who ruined it for several generations of kids. Children *do* need to be spoiled. I'm an expert on this. Trust me.

Newspaper reviewers lauded me for voice, poise, and acting ability, quite to my mother's dismay. She perceptively thought I was already enough of an egomaniac and told me never to believe my own press. Despite My Nonie's concerns, following these admonitions I acted like the little princess who made others change their ways to suit me.

Sad to say, I was an autocratic little snob, though I honestly did appreciate each kindness. I also expected my every whim would be satisfied—immediately—as they had always been! How was I to know any different?

I can only ask forgiveness of those I may have displeased by claiming in retrospect this behavior was that of a naïve, socially inexperienced child. I was only seven years old at that time. A well-known quote says: "Into each life a little rain must fall." Another axiom is: "What goes around, comes around." True to those statements, not quite a year later, in other countries, I received many huge, life-threatening lessons in humility and personal behavior control.

Difficult as it must have been to be accompanied by an imperious child, my wonderful mother never wavered in her search to do whatever was best for us as a unit. My saving grace was that perhaps by accident, I was a totally obedient child and also a quick learner. To me, My Nonie was not only the most beautiful of women, she was unquestionably the smartest person I had ever known. I adored her. I never outgrew that. I'd do anything to please her.

My Nonie was a small, straight-backed woman of great beauty, with flawless skin, a movie-star smile; a fashionable dresser, she was always turned-out like a fashion model. She felt dressing well was a sign of respect for the people she met, so I was proud to be seen with her at school functions.

I will always remember when she watched me represent our class in a spelling bee. My Nonie was dressed in a form-fitting, red, curly lamb coat and wore a tall black velvet turban, with a finely curled black feather. In those days it was quite acceptable to wear many kinds of furs. She also wore a freshly picked gardenia on her lapel. Completing the look were classic black suede high heeled pumps and long black gloves. She was simply outstanding—as usual.

Other mothers seemed drab and plain compared to my gorgeous and vivacious tiny peacock. I surreptitiously examined other mothers and never saw anyone close to her. I think now, perhaps a great deal of her natural attraction, which people admired, was due to the radiant goodness of her personality. My Nonie was one of the kindest people I've ever known. In repose, her face was striking, with deep chocolate eyes.

Once, we knew a sweet, very elderly dairy farmer. He sought to give My Nonie a sincere and wonderful compliment by saying, "You know, your eyes are as brown and pretty as my Jersey heifer's eyes."

This memory would send my uncles into gales of laughter whenever anyone complimented Nonie about her big, brown eyes, which sparkled with such joy of life. She could have been a movie star. In California, people asked if she was in show business, or perhaps was she a model?

"Oh, no, but thank you anyway for asking. Actually, I have a much more important job. I'm her mother," Nonie said quietly with confidence and flashed a huge, sincere smile, then looked at me with maternal sweetness. Is it any wonder I felt she could do no wrong?

CHILD POW

My Nonie was an educated woman, who spoke softly and kindly to everyone, yet she had great strength of purpose. Sadly, she was also a woman who believed the world was as she wanted it to be, rather than the way it really was. This one flaw caused her enormous mental anguish.

Nonie was one of the "old-fashioned ladies," whom we rarely see any more. Our world is a little shabbier without our grand ladies to civilize us and teach us to pass on a refined manner of living to our children. Nonie's world was one which taught us to always be kind but firm with people who crossed through our lives, while never lowering our own established standards.

Repetitiously, dear reader, I have spoken in these preceding pages about my family and the luxurious trip on the China Clipper. I have done this deliberately, not to bore you, but rather to illustrate how my life filled with love, dignity, and plenty was erased in one stroke on a beautiful afternoon in early December 1941.

Our lives turned upside from our world of grace and benevolence to despair, sorrow, and increasing danger. Our good times had come to an end for a long time.

CHAPTER 7

PROXY WEDDING

.....Til death us do part———

Book of Common Prayer

On December 13, 1941, two days after Aunt Alice left Manila by submarine, a U.S. Army officer in a dusty khaki military sedan drove up the long driveway to our dearly loved cabana. He said American troops were pulling back to the hills and forming a guerrilla army. I misunderstood the word *guerrilla* and thought he meant *gorilla*, like zoo animals.

I begged my mother to go to the hills with the army, so I could see the wonderful gorillas that were training to be soldiers. How smart of our Army to do such a wonderful thing, I thought. My Nonie kept her composure at this request, although the major did not. He snorted mightily then bellowed out in laughter.

"Little lady, I'm not going to forget you. This is the first time I've been able to laugh out loud since the war began," he told me as he grabbed me in a big bear hug.

My mother saw no benefit in this development, regarding our safety; therefore we stayed where we were. The major also told us we would soon surrender to a Japanese tank company, which was gathering prisoners all around in nearby hills. He told us the enemy troops should arrive in only a few days.

On December 14th my mother and I traveled to a nearby military radio antenna station where she and her true love, my dear Papa, were married by radio telephone in what was called a proxy marriage. Lots of proxy marriages occurred during WWII, both in the Pacific and in Europe, joining loving hearts who were separated by happenstance. Many army and government staff people had devised this method to legally unite those who were separated for the duration of this war, including My Nonie.

A physician friend of ours stood in for my new Papa, with Nonie at his side in the Philippines. In California, my new Papa's sister stood in for my mother. In each location, people said an appropriate response, then shouted, "Roger. Over." Then the other couple, five thousand miles away, spoke their part.

My best memory of it is how scratchy and reverberating the voices were, from a large wall-mounted loudspeaker. There was no such thing as international telephone service, as we know it, to the Orient back then. Nonie and Papa had decided to marry this way, hoping she and I had an enhanced protection as military dependents for our future—when, in fact, no protection was forthcoming. The Japanese recognized only passport information from civilians. We could have carried a copy of the entire Geneva Accord from the Geneva Convention—which Japan never signed anyway—and it would have done us no good!

In future years, My Nonie and Papa always celebrated June 14, Flag Day, as their wedding anniversary rather than December 14, for a number of reasons. What I witnessed was not much of a wedding. On the way back to our cabana, Nonie told me that six months earlier, when she and Papa had thought they were married in Canada, they had eaten a wonderful wedding feast in their suite at the Vancouver Hotel. Among other things, for dessert Papa had ordered Baked Alaska for her as a surprise since they didn't have a wedding cake.

Years later, and after I finally became proficient at it, many times I made Baked Alaska for their anniversary. Nonie and Papa would exclaim with great delight, as if they hadn't the slightest idea what they would be served. The looks of endearment they exchanged would fill the pages of many books. What a love affair!

As my recovery from polio continued at our cabana, I received a crutch, and used it for exercise on long walks down our sloping, graveled driveway. At one point near the main road, I discovered a natural archway in the bushes and bamboo; it revealed a sanctuary covered in huge elephant ear plants, with leaves as big as umbrellas. I sat under them in total privacy, even in a rainy downpour. Our gardener kindly carried a small stool downhill to my hide-away, so I didn't sit directly on the ground.

A cacophony of sound enveloped the jungle where we lived, to the extent we could sometimes barely sleep at night. Monkeys, birds, insects, and mammals of every sort screamed, fought, courted, mated, hunted prey, were preyed upon, and established personal territory. Then came an awful day.

I was in my hiding place at the main road coming down from the north when suddenly all noise ceased. Abruptly, there was total silence. Completely stupefied with fear, I could not think or reason or run. In fact I could barely breathe! I was dumbfounded at my feeling of aloneness, and terrified. It was as if every living creature had ceased its natural sounds and huddled in anxious fear from an unseen, but genuinely perceived, potential enemy. I felt as though I was being watched by evil beings invading my place in this jungle. This silence and anxiety continued for days.

We felt quite disassociated from all normal activities of daily living. Our distance from any city, combined with a threatening silence, caused me mental chaos. Ever present was our fearful apprehension concerning an imminent possibility of becoming prisoners of war. We had no life experience to draw from for this situation. How do you learn to be a prisoner of war? The closest information I found in our cabana library on imprisonment was *The Man in the Iron Mask*.

We hoped that would not befall us, but we were terrified. An absence of normal sounds dragged on for two more days. We were jumpy. Even the striking of our only timepiece, an old wall clock, almost scared us to death each time the hour was announced. We kept it wound, however, since without it we could not know noon from evening.

Though I was afraid, each day I trekked down our graveled, winding driveway to my hiding place. There, I nearly scared myself witless, listening intently and imagining I heard enemy troops coming. Years later a doctor explained that when a person is terribly frightened for a length of time, tiny hairs inside the ears actually pick up one's heartbeats, and these pulses are transmitted to the brain as the sound of stomping footsteps.

Would I see them peeking out from behind big trees? Could their tanks knock down our cabana? Would they run over us? I kept listening for clanking metal machines, since we were told they would come for us in tanks, but when?

One day, as I crouched in paranoid fear and expectation in my hidden thicket, I heard a whirring sound from farther up the main road. It remains hard to describe this sound, but it was like a small feather in a fan blade. It was a soft, sibilant sound. Whirr. Whirr. Whirr.

Then suddenly, softly, almost silently, what seemed to be the whole Japanese army came past me quite fast, three abreast, to invade Luzon—on bicycles! Hundreds and hundreds of Japanese soldiers raced by on bicycles, heading for Manila. I could have reached out and touched any one of them. I could have reached out and knocked one off his bike—with my crutch!

Occasionally I entertain myself today and laugh out loud while I'm stopped in traffic gridlock with silly what-ifs. What if I *had* pushed one over? It surely would have created instant mayhem and a gigantic bicycle wreck, yet I was too frightened to move a finger, let alone push over a soldier. Little did I know we were coming ever closer to horror.

CHAPTER 8
THE BAYVIEW HOTEL

Like one, that on a lonesome road
Doth walk in fear and dread.....
Because he knows a frightful fiend
Doth close behind him tread.

——*Coleridge*

Three days later we sat at breakfast and played in the sunshine with the kitties. The precious little things would stretch their necks up for a pet and purr loudly in appreciation. They would groom their soft gentle faces against the side of a stroking hand and loudly exclaim their affection in return.

Suddenly a commotion happened out by the front patio gate. These gates were never closed nor locked as a sign of hospitable welcome. There was the noise of truck motors and the clanging of metal against metal and shouts of male voices in a language we didn't know.

Through the gates stomped a Japanese soldier of some elevated rank with several low-ranked non-coms. The four men pushed their way boldly into our home, banging the large outside door against the wall in emphasis. The officer shouted at us, demanding to know who else was present in our home. We would observe for the next four years that civilians were always shouted at. It was as though they thought their jumbled "pidgen English" would be more understandable if they shouted.

It was also done to demean and dishonor us. My mother told this uncouth interloper that there were just the two of us in residence. Fortunately, Lindia, our housekeeper, had fled very early that morning as my mother told her she should.

The soldier who appeared to be in charge told My Nonie to quickly pack a small bag for the two of us. We had five minutes. I asked my mother what we could do about the kitties. In turn, she quietly and politely asked the officer, "Sir, what may we do with our pets?" He gave a brusque order to the soldiers. They reached out for the little animals who once again stretched themselves up to their full height in anticipation of more affectionate handling. Instead, the men grabbed up the cats whose whole lives had been filled with loving care and as we watched in horror, they quickly snapped their necks and threw them in the middle of our dining room table. I screamed, my mother screamed, and they thrust rifles with bayonets at us and told her to hurry. She took my arm and pulled me with her to pack our bag. I don't know what we packed. I was inconsolable over the deaths of the two gentle, yellow-eyed cats I had grown to love.

It appears that they attacked and killed the cats so viciously to demonstrate their newly assumed total power over us. Naturally, the cats could have been turned loose to fend for themselves. That was not a consideration.

In a few moments, we were shoved rudely toward a truck parked outside our gate. We had finally been gathered together by Japanese tank soldiers to begin a trek which took us to Manila and what later became known as the infamous Bayview Hotel. We were told, in no uncertain terms, our lives had now changed beyond our wildest imaginings.

Our caravan wound down through the hills, loading women and children, until we eventually got to Manila. We saw no men.

No husbands. No fathers. No older sons. No male adults of any kind! I wondered what happened to them. My Nonie thought maybe they had gone further into the hills to fight, but later she said her idea was wrong. None of the men would have left their ladies behind, so they must have already been captured. She was right, of course, as we later found out, to our great sadness.

Heavy smoke from numerous burning buildings filled the air, and oil tanks were still aflame at the harbor. The stench from the burning oil and other fires was all around us. We were stunned when we saw lifeless bodies lying throughout parks and in the streets. Most were men. There were also dead animals, primarily horses, and a few dogs. The dogs probably were killed while defending or accompanying a beloved family member.

Eventually we arrived at the Bayview Hotel. Neither of us had visited there before, so we behaved like tourists and sized-up the area and the adjacent part of town from the back of our truck. There was little to see from whence to make any point of reference. I had the idea that if we could orient ourselves properly, perhaps we could make an escape—the simple plan of a child. Eventually, we were unloaded and prodded toward the hotel entrance at gunpoint. Our new education had only begun.

My mother was taken from me, and I was put with a group of other unaccompanied children. Most of them cried and had runny noses; a few sucked their thumbs. My crutch had long since been taken from me, never to be seen again. I was outraged. I shouted, "Just because I'm a small person, I am not a child! I am a young lady and expect to be treated as one."

We purposefully dressed as though we were invited to tea at the mayor's mansion to show respect for the person who was highest in power at the moment. I even wore my little white gloves and white patent leather shoes—requirements in those days when you dressed-up properly. I held my head erect and stood absolutely as tall as I could, with a haughty, fearless look on my face, showing I was able to take on the world. Instead, I was yanked off my feet and thrown through the air, into a room alone; then the door was locked. The fall to the floor didn't injure me; I don't know why. Perhaps my temper was so intense at the time, I could feel nothing physically. Though my self-assertion accomplished nothing, I remained unbowed.

At this point, the few Asians I had been around, other than My Sweet Friend's marvelous, large family, were cooks, laborers, and people who provided us with daily services. They seemed to be the same as the rest of us. Of course, their skin was darker; after all they lived where the sun shone all the time, so it was only natural. I do know that without the Filippino people, we might have starved to death many different times. They helped us at great peril to themselves, and I remain intensely grateful.

Upon occasion, I have sat down to a lovely meal, only to realize I am alive because many times, in the POW camps, brave Filippino people gave their lives to get food to us. Without their help, I would not be present at any table today. These thoughts still bring me tears and I offer a paean of thanksgiving for the people who cared so much for us. They took chances and entertained great danger to bring us nourishment. The Lord teaches about the special blessing on someone who lays down his life for his brother. These people are surely blessed for their brave acts in helping us.

My racial ignorance caused me to wonder why these Japanese soldiers appeared to consider themselves the equals of my mother and me. Their actions and attitudes showed them to be not at all the kind of people with whom one would normally associate, whereas Filippino people seemed the epitome of decency, grace, and kindness. I imagined my grandmother might call these Japanese soldiers uncouth ruffians—an accurate, but charitable description.

I continue to believe people should be judged strictly by their behavior rather than by the color of their skin. I have held this belief from early childhood, long before Martin Luther King, Jr. was even a twinkle in his daddy's eyes. I have worked professionally since the middle 1950s in the civil rights arena. Portions of this work were deadly dull and other parts of it were just deadly.

I've traveled in Arkansas and Mississippi on school segregation concerns and in Alabama and Kentucky on blatantly offensive voter's rights issues. I was shot at by red-neck law enforcement when I actually snatched a teenager at-risk who had visited a local resort town. She was about to be carried off by the local law on spurious charges and forced into prostitution. We got fourteen federal indictments out of that one. I remain so proud of my work there.

I've testified before the U.S. Congress on behalf of specific civil rights legislation and wrote some of the language for sections of my own state's legal code where it provides protection against abuse and neglect for vulnerable children, the disabled, the ill, and aged citizens. My credo is that we can't afford to be charitable toward abusers. Those who physically or emotionally or economically abuse others are no different than those who abuse others through promulgation of codes, statutes, and laws which leave loopholes for abuse to sneak through. I've paid my

107

dues in many ways. Is it any wonder I became a civil rights advocate in my professional life? The wonder would have been if I had *not* come to this profession. It describes who I am.

Even as a young child, it was clear to me these Japanese troops did not attempt to act like the equals of the impeccably polite, attractive, and gentle Filippino working-class who cared for us. It was only a short time until I discovered they didn't consider themselves equal to anyone. Rather, they believed themselves *superior to* everyone, particularly unaccompanied Caucasian females. They feel they are the original people on earth; their Emperor God sprang from the sea as the morning sun arose. Their battle flags display a Rising Sun to depict this idea.

We grew to hate those ugly, red meatball flags, and the Rising Sun flags with every atom of our being. At that time, flags with single meatballs were for battle, and the ones with light rays were their national emblem, which demonstrate ownership of lands and people.

In spite of their egotistical superiority, they appeared to be very cautious around my mother and me. In most cases, they were not as heavy-handed with us as they were with many others. For a while, we thought perhaps we had been misidentified as dignitaries of whom they should take special care. We never did know exactly why they acted this way. Strange as it may seem, the only idea my mother and I were ever able to conjure is we appeared to be different than the others. Outwardly, we appeared unafraid and were sedately courteous, amenable to direction, and totally non-threatening to the current status-quo. With what could we have threatened them? They simply were not used to this response. We did not beg, plead, or whine. We were two creatures they did not quite understand.

Compared to all the other females, we were well dressed and did not weep or wail. Although we were of small stature, both of us stood erect and tried to display—at least outwardly—dignity and calm. My mother taught me this from earlier days, and children should learn that these rules bring power:

- *Don't make a spectacle of yourself.*

- *Sit still.*

- *Hold your hands in your lap without fidgeting.*

- *Keep your elbows tucked against your ribcage.*

- *Don't chew your lip or make odd movements with your mouth.*

- *Stand straight.*

- *Don't slouch or lean against a wall or chair back.*

- *Cross only your ankles, never your knees.*

- *Never swing your feet or scuffle them about.*

- *Sit straight on a chair with your feet flat on the floor, even if you have to perch on the edge of the seat.*

- *Most importantly, shut up.*

I believe our appearance of composure kept us safer. We did nothing to give offense and did little to draw attention to ourselves, except for one event which could have turned out most unfortunately.

I had been taught by my grandmother, who incidentally was the first woman sheriff west of the Mississippi in 1898 Montana, that when you are faced with a situation that needs changing, you had better get on with it. Following her lesson, now at eight years old I knew I wanted my mother on this day at the Bayview Hotel. It was quite possibly one of the most physically dangerous places in the Pacific theater of war at that particular hour.

I could think of no action to accomplish it, yet I simply refused to be helpless. Then suddenly, thanks to my grandmother's teachings, a wild thought came to me, which illustrates why little girls need keepers and should not be left alone in strange places.

In the middle of the empty room where I had been tossed so unceremoniously, I stood as straight as I could and vocalized a very long, high note, perhaps high F# or G. I imagined Dr. Andrews, my former opera coach, applauding me for breath control, pitch, and volume projection. A wild-eyed soldier with bayonet thrust forward, burst in, looking for all the world like he was about to send me on the road to Glory. I imperiously ordered him to bring my mother immediately into my presence, and we should be given tea.

The poor terrified man who apparently understood English took enormous steps with his feet lifted as high as his knees, looking for all the world like a stand-in for John Cleese from Monty Python movies. He lurched and leaped from the room. The soldier reappeared, still with a terrified look upon his face, in no more than two minutes, with a lovely, full tea tray. It must have been snatched from under someone's nose as they prepared to consume the items upon it.

By this point in my life, I had recently read that, on occasion, the best defense is a good offense, so I had tested the merits of that author's comments. I was not frightened, and I was too naive to be concerned for personal safety. I was, however, extremely worried about my mother's lengthy absence.

Shortly thereafter, my mother was escorted into my room with her hair in great disarray. She had obviously been beaten. Her face was swollen, puffy, and her eyes were shiny bright with old tears. A tiny drop of blood dripped from one ear, and her lower lip was split. I asked her what we were to do next. She replied we had new rules in our lives. A few rules were dictated by the Japs, and other rules Nonie devised as we went along.

Officers told her we must always bend low at our waist and stay there when a soldier passed by or approached us. We must never look them directly in the eye. If we were addressed, we must keep our eyes to the side or toward the ground. We could never speak to a soldier directly. Severe punishment would follow failure to comply to any of these rules. Arguing was punishable with death.

My mother gleaned additional rules we must live by from a monologue given by an officer during the approximate two-hour period she was gone from me:

To remain reasonably safe, we should act invisible.
We must keep a very straight posture.
We must not let them know we feel beaten in any way.
We *must not* laugh or smile at anyone, even each other. They could think we were making fun of them.
We must stay together; we must *never* get separated.

111

Regardless of what we were given to eat, we must eat as much as we could at the time, but we must never hide food in our clothes. We might be accused of being thieves and be treated as such.

We must be diligently well-groomed.

We must try to be as physically clean as we can at all times.

We must be presentable.

We must always act like American ladies.

She understood execution was a possibility—for any transgression. She wasn't sure she believed it, but she quoted the officer as stating it. After the reprehensible way they had killed our pets, anything was probable.

The demonstration of these attributes proved able to separate us from the general group of wailers, whom the Japanese obviously found distasteful, and to whom they were excessively cruel. Soldiers seemed to enjoy making others cry, if they acted afraid. We determined not be like the others, and maybe the Japs might leave us alone, if they were unsuccessful in tormenting us.

My mother had been appalled when the officer who interviewed her said I had done my princess act. She asked me to never do it again and explained I could be killed on the spot. Then Nonie hungrily eyed my tea tray, so I told her how we had come to have it. She laughed, then hugged me and rapidly ate every crumb of her portion.

We devoured many tiny sandwiches, heavy triangular scones with raisins, and sweet tarts. All were served with a lovely big pot of tea, which was—by the way—excellent. Weeks and months later, we often recalled that particular repast on days that were much more bleak when we tried to eat our seaweed and rice balls. Our grand tea on our first day in captivity was our last "normal" meal for many years.

CHAPTER 9

DEATH AT TEA TIME

But weep for them who there remain,
The mournful heritors of pain,
Condem'd to see each bright joy fade,
And see grief's melancholy shade
Flung o'er Hope's fairest rose.

———*Mrs. Embury*

After savoring and finishing our tea, we sat quietly and stared at each other. I asked if she had been beaten. My Nonie nodded affirmative. She told me it was terribly dangerous for us to be here, and it was even worse that we were alone. Just the two of us. Then my mother did something she later repeated every day for the rest of our captivity: She sat beside me on that scratchy wicker settee and took my face in her two hands. She looked solemnly into my eyes and said, "You must believe me. They will come. They will come to take us home. It won't be soon. We are going to get through one day at a time. We just have to get through today." This became our mantra. It saw us through more difficulties than we realized we could ever be called upon to face.

This Bayview Hotel in downtown Manila where we were trucked was a horrendous place, where many war crimes against civilians were committed. Pre-war, it was a second-rate hotel for travelers, substantial, but nothing fancy. We realized within moments we were definitely "across the tracks." This hotel had been

113

confiscated for use as a holding-area for women and children and for the sorting out of the newly made prisoners of war.

Japanese officers, for their exclusive use, had seized the large and luxurious Manila Hotel where General MacArthur had lived in splendor on the top floor. Many more women and children died in the Bayview Hotel than were ever released from it. My Nonie and I were extremely lucky to survive.

Many hours later, we glanced into one room as we were herded to another truck. There were a dozen or more women in the room in terrible physical condition. Most had been beaten to such an extent we could not recognize if some of them were Filipino or Caucasian. Others, including one I recognized as my Sweet Friend's amah, lay naked on the floor in a pile of bodies— apparently dead. At eight years old, I had never seen naked adults before, let alone bloody ones, those I knew, or people who appeared dead. I was fascinated and horrified, simultaneously.

Surely, this was wrong. A mistake had been made, somehow. The injured women screamed when a door opened, and we saw soldiers hit them with gun butts, for silence. For an unknown reason, My Nonie and I were not treated in the same evil manner as Filipino, British, Dutch, and other Caucasian women. Perhaps it was because of my tantrum. Japanese soldiers acted as though they wanted to remove us from their area and not have to deal with us.

We were slowly, but roughly, escorted past an assembly room in which we recognized my Sweet Friend and ladies from her family. We did not call out to them. It was difficult to believe we had visited with them only weeks earlier in happy times. A few appeared beaten into near catatonia. Those women, faces hideously swollen, stared blankly into the distance. A few who faced the door displayed no recognition of either Nonie or me.

My Sweet Friend lay with her head in her mother's lap, but the little girl's face was bloody. Her clothes were ripped. She wore one white sock and had no shoes. Later, as I became more knowledgeable of the ways of an adult world, I realized she had undoubtedly been physically assaulted. Her eyes looked directly into mine, but she showed no recognition. She did not blink nor cry as our eyes met. Her face was blank and her mouth was open and hung slackly. Her tongue had slipped from between her lips. I wondered over the years if she was already dead then. I think she was. Possibly she had been strangled. Poor, poor little Lily.

The other ladies also were bruised, bloody, and obviously harmed. Their clothes, torn or missing, were in a dreadful state of disarray. We felt such sorrow for them but could not help in any way, even after every kind act they had done for us. Before I realized she was probably dead, I wanted to go to my Sweet Friend and comfort her for the loss of her amah. My Nonie cried at the sight and condition of our dear friends. However, we were shoved past their area and put in trucks with other women.

The sorting of prisoners was going on outside the hotel. A long line of conveyances was assembling. Taxis, buses, captured U.S. Army trucks had all been conscripted to ferry prisoners to their new locations. Men and older boys were already separated from the women and all other children. It was pitiful as husbands and wives called to each other. They were struck down by the soldiers who wanted no talking. Men and women were directed into two separate circles and ordered to march slowly around. As the people in the circles passed each other, I could hear voices calling out, questioning, pleading: "George, what should I do now? I'm so afraid" and "Robin, you tell them to let you go, I can't manage the children on my own" and "Dorothy, don't be afraid now. Chin up. Won't be long. Take care of the kiddies." It was all so sad.

Transportation assembling in near empty Manila streets prior to the dispersal of POWs to the camps

When the soldiers saw who was calling out, they would hit those people with their gun butts. I wondered how they could be so brutal when these people were only loved ones being torn apart. Again, it was an exercise of power over us.

A soldier tossed our overnight bag into the back of the truck. He grabbed My Nonie by her arm and threw her up into the truck. I was lifted up around my waist and thrown in also.

As we sat in back of the truck—silent—it seemed as though great life forces had been removed from human history forever. We had never seen nor heard of people treated this way. Numb with disbelief, we felt a variety of emotional responses: anger, disgust, horror—and a bone-chilling fear we might be next.

Surely, our friends hadn't deserved any of this. We decided later that because they were educated, politically and socially prominent, this must be a reason the Japs had treated them so cruelly. We, too, did not deserve to be treated like this, but since reason was not present, we might be next. We must be very careful from now on.

*POWs being separated by gender prior to loading
up for trips to concentration camps*

We sat stiff, straight, and silent in the back of the truck after it finally began to move. We sat in shock at what we had seen inside the hotel. It was the last time we ever saw any of our dear friends again. They were kind, gentle, loving, caring people. They had held out their hands to us in comfort, friendship, and help when we had needed it most. It is impossible to mourn

117

these special people softly. They can only be remembered with a sense of rage at the way they were so cruelly taken from us.

The fine poet Edna St. Vincent Millay wrote,

"I am not resigned to the shutting away of loving hearts in the hard ground. Down, down, down, into the darkness of the grave. Gently they go, the beautiful, the tender, the kind. Quietly they go, the intelligent, the witty, the brave. I know. *But I do not approve, and I am not resigned.*"

We both were heart-broken.

When WWII was over, we discovered our lady friends had all died in POW camps early in 1942 shortly after we had seen them a few weeks before. Their family's men were executed in the first days of conflict, and we never learned to which camps the ladies were taken. After the war, in 1946, I was able to attend a memorial service for My Sweet Friend at our former boarding school. We sang "Abide With Me" and "In The Garden" and "Now the Day Is Over"—all her favorite hymns. These hymns were as gentle as she had been. It made us all cry. Our world today is less lovely without her and her family. Their bright pieces of energy were taken away by those who refused to value goodness or decency or reason.

As I write, I want to scream in rage at these abominable acts. No one can explain to me why it happened. *There are no excuses, and there has been no retribution for these acts of cruelty, which there must be.* If no one speaks against it, it can happen again!

Tyrants are born in every generation, around the globe. Yet we are all demeaned if no one talks about them. Why do good people not demand an accounting from the vermin of the world? Why? I think it's because of money and greed. I think we will see *those devils were allowed to get away with cruelty,* rather than have personal accountability to their fellow man, so it is our fault—some of it. Is it *so* important to be politically correct?

After being sorted as prisoners, we were sent north to a variety of the sub-camps of Camp O'Donnell and Cabanatuan, then eventually to Baguio, the former summer home of Philippine emperors. There were up to seven or eight miserable places operated as sub-camps, within each main, designated area. I'm unsure this long after the fact, but I think I recall O'Donnell had six camps; Cabanatuan had seven ancillaries. Prisoners were transferred back and forth; it depended on the Japs' necessity for laborers and workers. These horrible places would become our home for the next years.

CHAPTER 10
EVIL SWORDS

And then I asked My Nonie, Is it true that there will be no war and all the guns will be made into plows? And she softly answered me saying, Not soon enough, not soon enough. Then she cried. And then I cried with her.

In one camp we had indoctrination into the wonderful world of Japanese culture. Apparently, our captors felt we could be firmly assimilated, probably by force, by the end of the war. They wanted complete victory, and with it the requirement that all conquered people worship the Emperor. Imposed information classes were held frequently—in English! (My recollections and the possible errors are mine alone from the memory of an ill, starved, and terrified little girl.)

The Shinto religion of Japan teaches that The Sun God, Amaterasu, requires unquestioned obedience to the Emperor and his proselytes. The Samurai code of conduct supports this, through Bushido, which is a warrior's way of life and conduct. Its tenets stress mastery of martial arts, frugality, loyalty to superiors and to the Emperor, and the emphasis on death with one's honor intact.

Bushido teaches the fine art of Seppuku, the use of short swords for suicide, but this appears to have lost favor somewhat during the 19th century. Use of the long sword had also come to

121

be discouraged, yet we saw swords flash often! This was at the dire expense of some poor captive who had been a bit too slow to respond or not respectful enough in the eyes of the sword wielder. Sometimes there was no reason at all.

Supposedly, Japanese officers were graduates of military academies patterned after our West Point. However, we found them to be arrogant, supercilious, quick to perceive an offense, quarrelsome even with each other, brutal with underlings, fawning and unctuous with superiors. Common soldiers were brutalized daily by their officers and non-commissioned personnel. Brutality within the ranks seemed to increase, the farther it rolled down through the ranks.

The Bushido code of the Samurai, as it affected us, was basically "Might Makes Right." They seemed to have lost all sense of kindness and decency, which we felt they certainly learned at home. Japanese parents do not raise their children in a cruel atmosphere. Supposedly, the way of the Samurai had been abandoned in the 1800s, along with the habit of wearing swords. However, that was not the case in WWII. Soldiers demonstrated to POWs and to each other daily: might makes right; those evil swords flashed everywhere.

All of the Japanese soldiers seemed a formidable bunch as we got to know them. Therefore we learned to be very, very careful how we acted. The smallest infraction—or perceived infraction—could be punished, far out of scope. We also learned the punishment never suited the crime.

For instance, failing to bow or looking a soldier in the eye might be dealt with by having a toenail torn off, being burned by a lit cigarette, or being beaten insensible with bamboo poles. In the case of angering an officer, a few were beheaded. There seemed to be no standard range of punishments for any specific offense. One of the most frequent outrages for a POW was to have their foot or hand smashed with a rifle butt, which broke toes or fingers.

The operative word to describe their attitudes and their actions is barbarism. Soldiers always laughed when they caused us pain. Over time they refined prisoner executions to the level where they had individual names for each atrocity they inflicted. One execution was labeled "the cheap death" because it wasted no bullets.

For sport, a POW was laid flat on the ground. They would find a door pulled from building wreckage or a large, wide board and place it on the poor soul; then large rocks were piled on top. Finally, laughing soldiers stood on the door, until the person couldn't breath and suffocated. For sport! The Japs' name for it was "pressing," and it was a gambling game. They placed bets on how long the person could last—for sport—pure and simple. These and other "games" were done with malice; the only purpose was to cause pain and terror to helpless POWs. These soldiers were sadists by every definition.

The soldiers would bet on anything. Whether or not a plane would fly over in the next three minutes; how soon until one of them could spot a bird in flight. On a windy day, they would draw out a square of earth about ten feet on each side with the toe of their boots and would bet that ten leaves would land in that square in the next five minutes.

Many of the children were somehow involved in their games. Always in a negative manner. When it came to me, I was small. I was still crippling along on my bad polio stricken legs and I was slow. This gave them the idea to chase me. I would run and dodge and turn and scramble around behind groups of people. It was never successful. I was always grabbed up and carried off under the arm of some laughing and bragging maniac. Who-ever caught me first was the winner of everything "ante-d" in and in turn got to tear off a toenail or snap back a finger until it dislocated or broke. Today, my hands and feet openly display the results of their games. I had been relieved of my crutch in Manila at the Bayview Hotel. How I wished for it now so I could defend myself.

Their cruelty was done with such malice. Their loud and boisterous laughter grated across my ears and I hated them. No officer ever intervened in these "gambling games." They would stand on the sidelines and watch before turning away after I had been "punished for being caught." The officer would shake his head as if to say, "That kid should know better than to be caught." They never intervened.

I would ask my mother why she thought they liked to be so cruel. She would tend to my injuries and cry with me quietly and try to squelch my wrath and temper. "This is not something we can do anything about. We have to be more invisible. We just have to get through today. Just try one more time."

We did learn that if we fought them, they would persist. If we aquiesced quickly, they would lose interest and presume that we had surrendered to them and they would go away. For a time.

How evil they remain in my mind's eye! I still remember each face—soldiers and officers. They remain as familiar to me as the faces of my own dear family. Never will I forget them and I will identify them, if ever we come in contact.

Time has passed now, and if there are any alive, they are quite old. I think their actions during the war must have resulted in each of them growing more mad as they aged. These Japanese officers and soldiers were, and are, if still living, the epitome of evil maniacs. Some nights they continue to populate my dreams in a monstrous array, marching by, doing the devil's work. Hell is surely overpopulated with demons from these camps.

Quite often, defenseless prisoners were nailed, face first, to the side of buildings. This bizarre type of crucifixion's outcome was always death, usually from dehydration and heat exhaustion. Nails were driven through a prisoner's hands and their underarm flesh. The delight with which Jap soldiers committed these acts was indefensible. Again, this was their "sport." Officers watched and laughed, beside enlisted men. Other times, a crucified person was doused with gas and set on fire. Japanese laughter almost drowned prisoner's screams. Jap soldiers absolutely roared with glee, while dancing a manic jig, first on one leg and then the other, mimicking painful writhing movements of the poor burning wretch.

In one sub-camp, the commandant was a horticulturist. He fancied himself another Luther Burbank, propagating seeds. Probably his most bizarre and reprehensible order required a prisoner to be beheaded in his officers' quarters' flower garden, while other prisoners were forced to watch. Imagine how much blood gushes out when a head is severed at the neck. I remember—clearly. And I remember his face as he watched. His eyes would squint ever more tightly closed as his grin became bigger. He had yellow teeth.

Because my mother and I were shorter than many, we were made to stand in the front row at all of these required roll calls. I remember how my shins touched the short wire fence that surrounded the commandant's garden while My Nonie stood behind me. She always tried to cover my eyes, but a soldier always came near and struck her arms down. We were required to face forward, and I never closed my eyes.

In one variation, the prisoner's eyes were covered with a rag blindfold; other times they were not covered. If a POW's eyes were open, and if they looked at me in the front row, I always looked directly back and smiled at them. I folded my hands in front and said a prayer, so the POW could see I supported them.

It was extremely hard to watch. After the first beheading, I remember telling My Nonie that at least the man was now in Heaven, in a better place than we were at the moment. She agreed. Then we cried quietly for him, lying on our sleeping mats. I threw up during the night. Nonie held me tight.

I think we stayed sane by believing Heaven awaited us. I also believe God Himself wanted us to remain sane in order to bear witness in the future.

At a beheading, blood always splashed on our bare feet and ankles. The condemned person was made to kneel in front of all POWs. Then a swordsman took an almighty whack, and it was over. Yet, other times the scene became incredibly gruesome. If a prisoner was praying at the moment of execution, their lips might continue movement for a short time after the head was off, as though their brain had not yet received the message there was no body. At the moment of death, there is an enormous gush from the neck and trunk, then virtually nothing. In four or five heartbeats, the blood is expended. It is extremely quick. Often, I did not have time to get my mind in a properly prayerful mood before it was suddenly over.

If the swordsman was adept at his task, an execution required only one blow to sever the head. If he was not as skilled, many chopping whacks were needed. In the meantime, the poor prisoner was wounded again and again by blows to the head and neck and shoulders without the sweet release of death.

Sometimes another soldier with a pistol delivered a coup-de-grâce to put the poor wretch out of his misery. I always thought of my grandfather, Bum Bum, when this happened.

My grandfather occasionally, to his regret, had to kill an injured mule down in the mines with a single pistol shot. He would hate to know we witnessed these POW atrocities. He had such a respect for life.

After we were excused from these reprehensible executions, I would creep back and surreptitiously grab a small handful of dried, bloody earth. Later, I would take it to the good Catholic priest who ministered to all of us in the camp and ask him to bless the person. He always said a small prayer and took the dirt from me. He never once asked me why I did this, and I couldn't have told him anyway. He was so wise perhaps he knew I wanted God's protection for all the prisoners in our camp. Not understanding God's omnipotence, I thought He might not yet know what was happening in the camp and my prayerful and sincere request for a blessing might bring His merciful attention to us.

Blood always smelled like rusted metal to me. For years after the war, I couldn't wash pots and pans with a steel-wool kitchen soap pad. After use for a while, the pads get rusty, and I became physically ill at the resultant metallic odor.

The commandant who insisted beheadings occur in his flower garden because he thought blood made his flowers brighter colors was a total madman—and we were frightened nearly to death of him! We did our best to be model invisible prisoners, especially when he was around our area.

This evil tyrant did survive WWII. He became a mega-millionaire and was one of the first elected members to their "democratic" Diet (Congress). He was never charged with a war crime. I hope if he grew roses after the war, they all had aphids and black spot! We know what he would blame if they didn't grow well—a lack of nourishing blood.

For years I worried over why he was never punished. I finally figured it out. Our government needed Japanese men to run the new Japanese government. Since few surviving Japanese had the requisite credentials, he was trained and groomed as a business leader in the new Japan. This former Jap officer knew how to manage people and get things done.

No one ever said the world is fair.

CHAPTER 11

UNACCOUNTED FOR AND STARVED

Why should we feed you more? You deserve nothing. You contribute nothing. Food is for the soldiers. Try to die. You won't be hungry then."

——Captain Ishii- Japanese Army

All POW camps were overcrowded; the Japs had no idea the number of prisoners they would be called upon to manage. Consequently, by poor planning—combined with pure evil intention—they starved us. Prisoners got two rice balls a day, infested with insects. Whether that was by design or accidental, I don't know. Each was about the size of a small scoop of ice cream. Men in the camps also got a bit of dried fish everyday with their rice.

To obtain potable water, we were required to stand in line all day to receive possibly a washbasin, a canteen, a tin can—whatever we could lay hands on—filled with water from the one faucet in camp we were allowed to use. In addition, we were allowed to go through the water line only once each day.

With glee, soldiers who saw us carry our meager ration back to our area often knocked it out of our hands. They would kick a foot high in the air and as it came down, it would just happen to knock away a pan of water. Some days, only a few prisoners were allowed to collect water. Soldiers arbitrarily turned the water spigot off and refused that day's ration to all the other people in line, even though there was enough water for all. This was done, once again, out of pure meanness—for sport. Then they laughed. We sucked on rocks trying to create saliva. It seldom helped.

One reason for the way they treated us was their cultural oriental pecking order. Japanese believe they are the Sun God's chosen people. Therefore, people who aren't Japanese are of lesser or no value. Bushido says die, but never surrender. Women are considered chattels, not worthy of legal rights.

An additional problem for My Nonie and me was that we were unprotected by a male figure. We didn't belong to government people, or to traders, or to military men. In effect, we were geographic orphans. Japanese soldiers regarded us with derision as unvalued, unattached, unaccompanied female Caucasians who had surrendered. All prisoners were initially listed under the male head of family's name. Yet, since we had no family head present, our names did not appear on any list. We were only on transport lists when we were moved from one camp to another. We did have my mother's passport, but it was in her maiden name.

As for me, because we had left America so hurriedly I had no passport issued to me at all but was attached to Nonie's as "accompanied by female child." There was not even a birth date to indicate my age. It is amazing Port of Entry officers in Manila didn't question this. Later, a lack of birth information reared its head as a problem when we were shipped to a different camp. The new captors expected me to be considerably older.

Eventually, disease erupted in our camps. Most prisoners were military men who had been through the rigors of battle, were wounded or had malaria and dengue fevers. Many soldiers who had been jungle fighters had elephantiasis. This causes limbs and some body organs to swell to gigantic proportions. The pain is acute. They desperately needed hospital care, but nothing was available.

Our sanitation was egregious. Almost every POW except my mother and me suffered from terrible dysentery. Long trenches to straddle served as latrines. If you were weak, had a bad leg, or were otherwise ill, you needed to take someone with you for balance. There was no way to wash clean after an unfortunate accident like slipping into that filth. Therefore, rather than have a soiled prisoner pollute their surroundings and cause more disease, they were eliminated by our captors while lying in the trench. Basically, if you fell in, you were shot.

A miasma hung in the camp—a pervading, poisonous stench. It *never* left our nostrils. The area reeked like a toilet. It was putrid as a slaughterhouse. Moreover, the odor clearly was making people ill, and if you got sick in a camp, death was almost certain. Also ever-present were indescribable masses of flies. The flies carried disease. They were in our hair, our eyes, in our ears and noses. We constantly breathed molecules rank with death—our daily, invisible hell.

After a time, chronic depression began to plague many prisoners. Rules made no sense. People were punished for no reason. In contrast, there was no reward for cooperation with each other, either. We tried to understand how to exist, how to *not* be a target of the soldiers' wrath. In the middle of this confusion, we focused on the positive goal of staying healthy. We constantly battled the ever present hordes of flies.

My Nonie had already made it a rule for the two of us to never put our fingers in our mouths. Only the good Lord knew what germs were on our hands. Whatever went into our mouths had to be held with a dried leaf or speared on a stick, but we never, ever used our fingers. I did not know where she got this idea for better hygiene, but it worked for us, and we two puny Americans did not get sick like the others. It was a miracle.

Malaria, dengue fever, and a terrible, bloody diarrhea were frequent diseases that decimated many prisoners. More trouble was caused by huge abcessing sores, which seemed to grow on prisoners overnight. These were hard to heal and necessitated many an amputation, which in itself was frequently the cause of death from septic shock. The sores were covered with huge flies. They bit us and they hummed with death.

In general, POW camps were filthy, disease ridden, and unhealthy for anyone without access to medicines of the day. There was no such thing as an antibiotic in those days. Sulfa was still quite new, but we had none there. Prisoners relied on ineffective potions —and hoped for the best.

Malnutrition and starvation had been long words in cross-word puzzles for me until now. Suddenly, for the first time in our lives we experienced deep, agonizing hunger.

Hunger hurt. It ached in a hollow unnatural way clear to the center of my body. My body shook, my head ached, my vision and hearing became more acute at first, but then vision blurred and sounds became less distinct. My back ached and I would cry.

All encompassing, the worst thing about hunger was seeing others with food, in our case, the Japanese soldiers. They would eat in front of us and spoil what they would discard in the garbage by rubbing dirt in it or urinating in it. Then they laughed at us. Sadly, some people were driven to scavenge that food anyway. Hunger humiliates. Hunger makes you hate.

Observant eyes watched us from outside the wire each day. Then at night, kind local people who understood what we were going through and who underwent enormous tragedies themselves, quietly appeared, barely behind the tree line. Carefully and quietly, they lobbed food to us, usually rice with bits of vegetables, rolled in a large leaf and tied with a vine or reed.

At twilight, our fellow POWs strolled the perimeter of the prisoners' yard, then created a reason to bend over to surreptitiously retrieve the food. To overtly accept it was cause for severe punishment. The retrievers were always careful to share the food they gathered. If you got extra one time, you were skipped the next, unless you were ill, a child, or a female.

My Nonie and I often refused additional food, beyond our daily rice allotment, so others could have more. POW soldiers in the camps *always* served themselves last when smuggled food was available. They are a group of heroes who are seldom talked about. I wonder why. Our government later gave the order for extreme confidentiality about what went on in the camps. How could recounting this true heroism have hurt anyone? Why would our government not want the truth to be known about the conditions in the camps? Who were they protecting? Why would they do that?

To our collective horror, every day today *on every continent in the world* people are enslaved, abused, mistreated, and starved. Though we may feel helpless to change this reality, there is one thing we *can* do to help the situation: We can feed our hungry.

CHILD POW

Perhaps we can't help on a world-wide basis, but we can feed the hungry in our own neighborhoods and cities. Please.

If you have ever been hungry or know of someone who has, you understand, so please give whatever you can to a food bank. Each small amount, added with others re-creates the miracle of The Loaves and Fishes. After all, the Lord did tell us, "Feed my people." Please. Feed the hungry. Please.

CHAPTER 12
TRAITORS

Where ever fools gather, cheaters prosper—anon.

We had a ragtag bunch of a dozen or so promoters of various religious cults and beliefs. They made quite a group. There were no Episcopal or Roman Catholic priests, no Methodist, Lutheran pastors nor Jewish rabbis, as I remember. This group of proselytizing charlatans had appointed one of their members as a head-man. They convinced the Japanese upper echelon that they, themselves, could keep order in the camp. In addition, they agreed to bring any unruliness to the attention of the proper Jap authorities. In other words, these pompous men were traitors for the Japanese, against their own people! It still seems unreal, yet it is a fact. It happened that way.

When food was to be distributed, these charlatans assured the Japs they would ensure it was properly divided. I don't know what authority these men thought they had, but throughout my life, I have heard a lot of jingle-jangle about how men should always act like "good Christian gentlemen." In contrast, I remember this group sanctimoniously telling all whom they could coerce to listen, how God had given them "the power to bring us to the Light of Faith." According to them, apparently their God had decided, since we had become prisoners, we impoverished ones must surely be sinners, for only sinners could find themselves in a situation like this—I have a notion they did not include themselves in the group.

The Lord knows we did not want these fakes to get us to "see the Light." We just wanted God's divine intervention and an invasion by the Marines!

One time I watched one of those frauds try to get the attention of a very badly injured Australian soldier. He told the young Aussie he wanted to save him from going to hell. The kid shoved him away in disgust and said, "Aye, mate. Where th' 'ell do ya' think ah been!"

I cry foul to this abuse of the clergyman's collar by these counterfeit imposters. I will also state I know nothing of how ministers, preachers, or men of God—whatever their stripe—behaved in other places.

Never did I see the Lord's comfort and solace offered by any of these quacks. I also never saw an emaciated preacher in that camp. They obviously had cornered some of the food market for themselves. I also never saw one care for an injured soldier, only for each other; it was as if everyone else's needs were invisible. They were not "good Christians" in my book.

However, there *were* other men on whom the Lord surely smiles as He holds them in His heavenly arms. I have heard that in other camps, brave clergy, often with no thought of their own comfort or survival, performed near-miracles and consistently demonstrated great concern and love toward prisoners. My experience is only what I saw in *one* camp where My Nonie and I barely survived.

CHAPTER 13

THE BASKET MAN

Other sins only speak; murder shrieks out.
—John Webster

There were special areas in each camp where POWs were taken, when their lives became perilously short. I have seen dying men, in pitiful condition, wave away their own food to benefit a fellow prisoner who *might be saved* by having more to eat. Many times, American prisoners slowly starved themselves to death as a means of escape.

My Nonie was allowed, as part of her work detail, to spend a lot of time tending these men. It seemed her presence soothed them greatly. She held cool, wet cloths to their heads and rubbed their aching limbs and backs gently. She had a way of touching a shoulder in encouragement and tenderly holding a man's head to give him a drink that gave great comfort. Most of the time she simply talked with them about a thousand different things. She was a real angel, and the men adored her for her kindness.

She would tell them stories of her youth. How she fished with her brothers in Montana's Mussellshell River and how she hunted for arrowheads on the Crow reservation. She told them about attending the burial of Chief Plenty On Top when

139

my grandfather, a good friend of the chief, had a bagpiper play for nearly an hour on a distant hilltop. She told the men about running away to home from her grade school classroom the day she spied a freight wagon bringing the family's new Bosendorfer piano. She would talk about Montana sunsets and the snows of Wyoming and the beauties of Yellowstone Park.

She talked about her younger brother and sister and their funny shenanigans in the mining camps. She told the silly story about the night she and her sisters stole the railroad "crummy," the handcar, and pumped their way from Roundup to Klein so Lucy could visit a boyfriend.

She brought the Puget Sound country to life as she told them about Mt. Rainier and the Cascade Range and the earthquakes that always seemed to happen in March-April and September-October. She talked about animals and happy people she had known. She filled their minds with something other than squalor and pain and deprivation and they knew, as I did, that she had the magic.

She would write down their names on tiny pieces of paper with the hope of someday being able to tell the man's loved ones how bravely he died and relate things they had talked about over that time. She knew this probably wouldn't happen. The men knew it, too. It was like a drama they were all acting out together. As long as My Nonie told them she would do it, they smiled and were glad. It was the least she could do for our men.

Her carefully hidden cache of names was found out and destroyed by the enemy. She wasn't able to be identified as the author so she wasn't punished for this forbidden act. She continued to write down the names and the men adored her for her bravery and begged her not to continue doing it. She would just smile and lift another aching head for a drink of water. She had the magic that made the men feel better. They loved her for this. She was magnificent.

Regardless of nationality or military service group, the POWs cared for and about each other. The tenderness shown to dying men by their fellow companions was both inspiring and heart wrenching. Their compassion, their soft words of encouragement, and the quiet acknowledgment that it was all right to let go of this life—all these were truly beautiful. Prisoners often promised each other to take a final letter or message to a dying man's wife or mother, "When the war is over," or "When we get out of here." Sometimes a softly spoken Hail Mary or 23rd Psalm was shared.

Other times we heard a whispered Pledge of Allegiance. This was as close to a prayer as many could put into words. Then strangely enough, after these exchanges, everyone in the nearby area whispered, "Amen," with deep reverence.

To this day, I continue to say a final Amen when I recite the Pledge of Allegiance. I do this in memory of the fine Americans who died such awful deaths at the hands of our enemies—in any war.

When I think of the brotherhood of man and what I believe God asks of us, I know the Allied soldiers I saw were the "Real McCoy," as opposed to those deceiving men of the cloth we met. Sternly, I remind myself : *There will be a Day of Reckoning*, when each person will stand before the Almighty and will be asked to justify how he has treated his fellow man. Some will be found short in this accounting. They will be turned away.

Stories circulated from soldiers captured on Corregidor Island a fortress laced with inter-connecting tunnels in which people lived and worked. It had a full hospital and many areas to store food and ammunition. Along with Singapore, these two bastions were the "Gibraltars" of the Pacific and were supposedly unable to be captured. Their gigantic guns protected Manila Bay and the coastline, for many miles. At the time this fortress was built, no one considered envelopment by air assault, so when Jap troops landed by parachute, they easily tore down the United States flag and imprisoned the personnel remaining on the big island.

As Jap invaders rampaged through these American-occupied tunnels, they came across wounded patients, nurses, doctors and surgeons operating in this hospital area. The Japs machine-gunned every single person without mercy as they worked or lay in bed recuperating.

In all camps there were soldiers who were grievously injured in battle before the surrender on Bataan. Others' bodies were damaged by the Japs after their capture. All were starving. These soldiers went largely untreated, except for a little help from our few doctors, also camp prisoners, who had volunteered not to be evacuated to Australia. Some doctors who desperately wanted to stay and care for our injured took off for the hills with all the medical supplies they could carry, rather than be forced onto a southbound transfer ship headed out of the war zone.

Fortunately for our wounded soldiers in camp, one of these doctors was an excellent human being, full of compassion. He never ceased to give of himself to care for our wounded. This

142

doctor had purposefully stayed behind during the invasion. He knew he would be captured, but he wanted to be where he was needed most. One particular soldier's leg was shattered below his knee, and our doctor was able to remove the damaged portion. If the soldier could keep healthy and not develop a secondary infection, recovery was possible. The man could walk again one day with an artificial limb. This soldier was called "The Basket Man."

When we first heard the nickname, I thought it might have originated from a former occupation. I wondered if perhaps he had been a basketball player, since he was quite tall and appeared to have been physically fit prior to imprisonment. However, we learned his nickname came about because each day when he sat at the edge of the camp's perimeter fence he always had a basket. In it he carried a few personal belongings and a book to read. With only the one leg and a crutch to move about, he hobbled from place to place, finding shade.

The Basket Man enjoyed watching prisoners toss a ball for a while, then he liked to read. I always wondered if the book was his own or one he happened to find. Entitled *Age of Innocence* by Edith Wharton, I still shake my head in disbelief at the incongruity of his selection. Some days The Basket Man sat quietly and read; other times he spoke with passersby. The scene seemed so totally normal and serene, like something we might see in a town park, back in the world.

Green trees made a pleasant backdrop for these ball games. Primordial fragrances wafted from the earth's rich loam, which nourished hibiscus and bougainvillea bushes, and many others I couldn't name. Small mammals scurried about on the ground and in tall trees, but they were species of which I knew nothing, indigenous to this part of the island of Luzon.

Birds sang in competition with one another, but no species I was used to, like robins or wrens. These avian fliers created a rainbow of red and orange and blue and green. They screamed in raucous abandon, unlike our drab—but beautifully voiced—songbirds at home. This ecological beauty was about to be put in sharp contrast with a tragic display of the Japs power and control—at its fiendish worst.

To pass idle time—and there was much of it for these previously active men—many played catch with balls constructed with scraps of cloth and sturdy leaves, tied with twine or vines called lianas. They tossed the balls back and forth, but on occasion, one went outside the wire, into trees. Quickly, it came flying back, often thrown by a watching local child. Eventually it was tossed to our one-legged friend, The Basket Man, who casually put it into his small basket. Then he picked up his book and continued to read, totally nonchalant. This series of events was repeated, tirelessly, many afternoons.

One day soldiers grabbed the basket and examined it closely. While the leaf balls *appeared* to be innocuous toys, they were not. The Japs discovered all the balls thrown back into the camp were packed with small scoops of cooked rice and vegetables. Our friends outside the fence had tried to support us again, in the only way possible.

Later, we heard that the nearby settlement was raided, and all the villagers, even tiny children and babies who could not yet walk nor crawl, were machine gunned. Then their bodies were casually left scattered to be eaten by wild animals and birds. The deaths of these innocents humbled us beyond imagination for months after. Their only crime was trying to help us survive.

A bit later, the camp commander came to where The Basket Man sat. The officer asked why he had participated in this deception. As usual when talking directly to prisoners, this officer screamed in an insulting and threatening manner.

The POW replied, "Because we are all so hungry." The Basket Man was then asked if he would eat as much as he was given, if such a thing were possible. "Yes," he said. "I certainly would."

Quickly then, he was grabbed, tied upright to a tall stake that was used for whippings and he was stripped naked. A small soldier with a whip of fine wire appeared and literally flayed this brave, injured American soldier. As the skin across his shoulders and back opened, another Jap soldier grabbed loose fragments between a knife and his thumb, then yanked, pulling large strips off the man's back. Then, as if this wasn't horror enough, our brave Basket Man was forced to eat his own skin. The soldiers shoved it in his mouth while his own blood ran down his face and onto his chest.

In derision, the officer screamed at him, "You said you wanted to eat. Very well. Go ahead and eat." The Basket Man, in agony, couldn't chew or swallow, as his mouth could only open to scream.

As the sound of his first screams echoed through the glade, where we watched in stunned horror, My Nonie ran to me from where she had been washing clothes in the nearby stream. She pulled my head tightly against her chest. Yet, even with my eyes covered, I still clearly heard the snap of the wire whip as it cut our friend's skin. These many years later, I cannot forget his screams.

These oppressive tormentors had refined cruelty beyond anything we could imagine. I thought, *What inhumanity can they think of next?* We simply could not imagine.

145

CHILD POW

The Basket Man died, of course, in terrible agonizing pain and from dehydration, after many hours of this continuous torture. The Lord will hold him tightly in His comforting arms. In Heaven I know he has both legs again. He can walk and run!

CHAPTER 14
SECRET RECOGNITION

The joys of parents are secret,
and so are their griefs and fears.
——*Francis Bacon*

In late October, 1941, a large deep-sea tug pulled a quantity of massive construction equipment toward Wake Island in the far, far western Pacific. Wake was a tiny atoll of not much importance except as a refueling stop for ships and planes. Prior to WWII, the Navy set out to reinforce this sand speck, to enable it to be held against intruders and to expand the tiny island as an aircraft landing spot from which, perhaps, to bomb Japan if a war ever came.

The captain of a civilian ocean-going tug was a son of an internationally known tug and barge company owner. This young man was a sterling fellow, youthful, tall, with weather-crinkled eyes from his life at sea with his father. In addition, wonder of wonders, he held a "Master Of Any Ocean" license, which allowed him to take his ship anywhere in the world he wanted. He hadn't been at Wake Island long before WWII began, and the Japanese captured him and all hands.

Most prisoners from Wake Island were moved to Truk Atoll and executed, but a few were transported to Japan to work in the mines. Because these workers could never stand a chance against armed invaders, large construction companies such as Morrison-Knudsen, Teuful and Carlson, and Bechtel lobbied the Navy and Congress for the right to bear weapons. This was approved immediately, so the Construction Battalions (CBs) began, later to be known as the Sea-Bees of the Navy.

When the young tug captain was captured, he gave his captors a false name. Because his father was known internationally, the younger man did not want his family blackmailed to rescue him. The father was Swedish-born and spoke the mother language. Our government was not able to give any information about his son, since the family surname did not appear on any list. However, the son was wise to list himself under his mother's maiden name, so he could be recognized by family.

Eventually, the young skipper's father, Old Swede, heard about a planned prisoner-for-diplomat exchange. He also learned the United States Department of State had chartered neutral Swedish ships for this event. Quietly, Old Swede pulled diplomatic strings until he was personally attached to a Swedish delegation to examine prison-of-war conditions. Sweden, of course, was neutral. In 1943, the father's group set sail for Japan where he intended to search for his son.

Incidental to this, my mother was a friend of one of Old Swede's nieces. He had met my mother and me often during holidays and for occasional summer boating days. He had also known My Sweet Friend—and he was totally unaware we feared for our lives in Asia.

One day, all prisoners in our camp heard the call for routine inspection. This was usually a way to identify prisoners too sick to stand without aid, or those who could not get themselves ready at all for assembly and inspection. Later these unfortunates would be separated from us, left to die unattended. Sometimes POWs simply were executed, often in the rose garden.

We stood in perfect, straight lines that day with our heads down, as required. Abruptly we heard a command to look up. When we did, a line of men chattered away in Swedish while they viewed our camp. To our shock, we recognized Old Swede in the group. My mother grabbed the skin across my shoulders—with her fingernails—and whispered, "Shhhh! Danger."

For once, I kept my mouth shut, but I watched intently with renewed interest. As Old Swede walked near his son, whom he had almost given up for dead, his eyes misted, but neither said anything to the other, for safety's sake.

A moment later he recognized my mother and was obviously startled. Then he saw me; tears welled in his eyes, then silently coursed over his weathered cheeks. Turning away, he wiped his eyes and told the Japanese he was quite overcome at seeing ladies in this situation and to please forgive his emotion. It seemed a logical explanation, and it appeared the Japs did not realize what had occurred, so we remained safe for a time. If we had been identified as acquaintances of the visiting dignitaries, we might have been used for blackmail.

For instance: it was explained to us that if the Japanese had understood that Captain Tug was Old Swede's son, they could have threatened to kill the son, or even us, if the father didn't turn over all his ships around the world to them—or something along that line. Somehow, we understood it was extremely important to remain anonymous while under Japanese control.

However, we did rejoice; at last our family at home would be notified we still lived! Old Swede had identified us, but he did not draw attention to us. He also made a wise decision later not to tell our family the location of our camp, nor that he had seen us at all, except to my grandmother. His only statement was, he had it on good account we were alive—somewhere. He told no one anything else, so we remained free of jeopardy or recognition by the Japanese. Thankfully, it did seem the whole episode had gone completely over their oriental heads.

CHAPTER 15

SERPENTS AND BARBARIANS

A simple child who lightly draws its breath,
And feels its life in every limb,
What should it know of death?

——*Wordsworth*

At one camp women and children tried so hard to survive. I had such a crush on one of the boys named Ari. For many reasons. I thought he was adorable. Dutch-born, the son of a trader. His father was in another camp, while he and his sister stayed with their mother. Blond, tan, laughing, and often naughty, Ari was a regular dickens. Often, you could hear his mother softly calling Ari as she searched for him long after curfew.

Frequently comical, this tall, gawky fourteen-year-old had feet too big for his body. His knees and elbows knocked into everything. He could stand completely still and suddenly almost fall over. Ari was physically growing so fast his coordination couldn't catch up.

CHILD POW

We have all known kids like this who fill up so much of the world with their funny, lanky arms and legs, their feet and hands shooting off awkwardly in all directions. Don't they grow up to be exactly what we had always hoped? You bet they do and Ari was destined for that, too. He had a magic spark about him that makes certain children a little more special.

Ari was a boy whom you knew could take on the world and would grow up to be a fine man one day. We couldn't dislike his pranks nor even his sass because he was merely a sprite with a great big grin. Ari was so smart. He taught all the little kids multiplication tables, poetry, long division, and compound interest. He kept the little ones busy, free from boredom and out of trouble. They adored him, and he had a retinue like the Pied Piper when he walked through camp.

Knowing the little ones would be in dire trouble if they were noisy or got into the idle types of trouble children find, Ari appointed himself the leader of "the band" as he called it. He taught the little ones times tables scratched in the dirt, he taught them songs, some of them quite naughty songs, but they were in Dutch and the other mamas didn't understand. He would march the little kids around, I among them, chanting what must have been many pages of "Evangeline": "This is the forest primeval, The murmuring pines and the hemlocks stand like druids of eld…." He made it all a game and the children adored him.

When this Dutch charmer laughed, others laughed with him, but there was never any malice in anything he did. Ari was a wonderful boy, full of healthy horseplay, yet he lived in the midst of a frightening, challenging nightmare. I adored him and was his abject slave, but he barely noticed me; he had turned fourteen; I was only nine.

One overly hot day Ari and a few other boys accidentally wandered upon a private bathing area where a stream ran from among trees into a knee-deep pond. A small group of soldiers relaxed in the water.

Laundry being done under guard
where Ari teased the guards.

They were aboriginal people from a northern Japanese island who were called the Hairy Ainu. The name was considered a derogatory expletive, much like the "n" word in the United States, for black Americans. The Hairy Ainu descended from a non-Mongoloid race of people who grew excessive amounts of body hair.

153

Mischievously, Ari climbed on a boulder above them, made monkey calls and jumped up and down, imitating apes. The soldiers threw rocks until all the boys ran off, and that seemed the end of it.

Later, after mid-day assembly when roll was taken, we were ordered to stand in formation longer than usual. I still remember feeling the soft, sandy yellow texture between my toes. It seemed we stood an unusually long time, perhaps for an announcement, as this did happen frequently.

That day was terribly hot, and I became extremely tired standing in an immobile position. I wanted a drink of water, and my legs cramped—as they often did during my polio recovery. Still we stood, and we waited.

Scattered throughout our group, little POW children, too young to understand, began to be restless. Mothers hushed them in panic and fear. Soldiers stood guard with bayonets affixed to their rifles. Always with the bayonets—always to intimidate us—and always it worked!

Eventually, a canvas-covered truck backed down a hill toward our group. It parked fairly close to all of us as we stood in our usual "three sides of a square" formation. The driver and another soldier got out and opened the tarp on the back. Then they propped a wood ramp on the truck's rear bed and rolled a heavy, over-sized oil drum from inside the truck, down onto the dirt in front of us, stood the barrel upright, and popped the top off. The drum was filled with water. Next, they called Ari forward and knocked him down, banging his head hard on the dirty yellow earth.

Without warning, soldiers bent down, grasped the boy by the ankles, upended him head-first into the water drum and slammed the lid on top. For a short time, desperate thumps emitted from inside the barrel. In just moments, there was silence, as we all stood at gunpoint.

Ari's mother screamed and ran toward the drum. She called his name, but was knocked to the ground and held there by a bayonet at her chest. Regardless, she fought the soldier and repeatedly pushed away the sharp hooked blade, as she desperately struggled to rescue her child. Another soldier walked up and smashed his rifle butt on her head. She dropped instantly, unconscious. Her hands lay bleeding into the earth, where she had grasped the wicked hooked bayonet.

We all remained frozen, mouths agape, eyes nearly exploded from our skulls, stunned to complete silence. All of this sequence had happened almost simultaneously. It was abominable; it was stupefying. It happened so fast. We had no chance to stop it.

My thoughts raced: *We take care of our children. Don't we? What transgression could ever merit this hideous act against a child? He was part of our future. We always protect children. We don't drown them. He was only a boy—a young boy.* I felt tremendous sadness.

We all lost part of our future that day. To me, the sun has never shone quite as clearly, nor the stars sparkled as brightly since the day Jap barbarians murdered Ari. He was drowned in a dirty, water-filled oil barrel near Cabanatuan, in the Philippine Islands. Ari died September 15, 1942. I remember the date because just the week before, on the 8th, we sang Happy Birthday to Ari when he turned fourteen. I cry silently in my heart as

I retell the event, even today. He was a mere boy. It wasn't his war! He was only a child. He was just a boy!

The soldiers kept us standing another hour in the hot afternoon sun. Ari's mother gradually regained consciousness, sat up, wailed, then fainted. His sister wept quietly in a stranger's arms. Soon after, the soldiers popped the top off the drum and poured the water and Ari's body onto the ground in front of his mother. In accented English, the camp commander sneered and shouted, "There, Mother. Do better with your other child."

Jap soldiers threw Ari's body into the back of their truck, loaded the barrel, and drove off. If any of us had wanted to mourn at Ari's grave site, we had no idea where his body was taken. We never knew what they did with any body after someone died or was killed. We suspected they threw the bodies into the jungle-like forests to be eaten by animals. We didn't know for certain.

My Nonie stayed with Ari's mother all night and gave what comfort she could. Nonie asked her to remember the biblical promise: One day there would be no more sorrow, no more pain, and no more tears. Surely Ari was now in Heaven with His Heavenly Father.

That night, after the Japs murdered Ari, was the only time I can remember armed soldiers constantly on guard, on alert, *inside* the wire of the camp at night. I think they felt as frightened *of us,* and what we might do, as we were afraid of them. They <u>should</u> have been scared to death! The tension and bitter taste of hatred in our mouths was so vivid we could barely speak in a civil manner—even to each other. We vehemently despised them for their fiendish act of cowardice—at the same time, we were terrified!

My Nonie told me that night she felt we had to get out of there: "This is absolutely unsafe for us. I have to find a way!" We knew it could probably be some time before we found an escape, so we continued to live in anguish, fear, and desperation. We walked on eggshells.

The Jap officer in charge of this debacle was never tried for his war crimes. He ran a large American company with a stupendous salary. In the 1980s his picture appeared on the cover of a national magazine. When I saw it, I tore the cover off and tacked it on my office bulletin board. Then every morning for months, when I came to work, and before I opened my office door for business, I stabbed his horrible face with the blade of my key chain Swiss Army knife. With each cut I said, "This is for Ari." Such long-term hatred, even of such a monster, is admittedly not a sign of good mental health. The hatred and the fear of them was still alive in my mouth. It took a very long time to subside. It took more than forty years.

At that time I had not yet been freed from my self-imposed role as a victim. My peaceful world still lay ahead. Eventually my dear friends, whom I had previously told of this incident, loudly protested and tore down the photo in the night. They said it was making me crazy—and I was making them crazy!

We couldn't even grieve for Ari! Crying was not allowed. If we did, the Japs put us in a hut, half buried underground, much like a root cellar. I had no idea—then or now—what it was originally constructed for. It had no windows. It was pitch dark inside. It may well have been constructed to be just that: a cold cellar where food could be kept. Prisoners went five steps down inside, before the door could be shut.

And then there were the snakes. Hundreds of teeming, skinny reptiles nested inside the hut. They probably were not poisonous—as if that mattered! Time spent in this pit of terror was punishment for crying, which our guards despised. Simplicity dictated this method of behavior modification for anyone who caused a disturbance of any kind. A prisoner only had to be in there a few times—and in my case, only once—to determine never to make any sounds at all. I wasn't able to cry for years. And for years after that, I could only cry for happiness. It's only been the last few years, and I am a old woman now, that I have been able to allow myself to cry the tears of sorrow that I was never able to shed since September 1942. Now in my 70s, when I think about those distant times and the loss of the dear good people I knew, I can hardly *stop crying*.

To this day I have a neurotic, psychotic fear of snakes. If it is shaped like a pencil and wiggles, I am out of there in fear. Sixty-plus years after the fact, it takes an extreme effort for me to write this account of that terrible hut.

Snakes writhed everywhere. On the floor. On the stairs. From ceiling boards that held up the dirt roof. The worst part of this experience was being in total darkness, then to feel the sinuous reptiles slither over my bare feet or brush against my naked legs—not knowing which way to step.

If I held totally still, they explored my body. These repulsive creatures tried to climb my legs, they hung down from the roof boards and touched my shoulders and arms. I had to be aggressive to push them off as they continued to try to climb my body. I hyperventilated with fright until I was dizzy. Eventually, I calmed myself. I breathed slowly, deeply. I didn't want to faint and fall in and amongst the eternally writhing mass of creatures. It sounds bizarre, but even the idea of the hut was bizarre.

Subsequently, as an adult, I canceled a subscription to National Geographic Society magazine. Many of their covers, inside stories and photos displayed hideous snakes. I cannot even touch the pictures. During one period of time, after I married, when my husband and I lived in the Sonoran desert, I killed every snake I saw.

Many rattlers lived in and around mines nearby. Shaft work makes miners jumpy enough without the addition of rattlesnakes. I got to be an enthusiastic and excellent shot with my .38 Smith & Wesson. I still have the sales slip that shows the Police Chief bought my pistol for me.

Sadly, one Christmas dozens of years later, my beautiful daughter gave me a gorgeous snake skin purse. Yet, when I opened my gift, I recoiled almost violently and quickly handed it back to her, without removing it from the box. She looked at me with such a look of pain on her face, but I could not bear to touch it. My revulsion hurt her feelings, and I have regretted that fact. However, since I had never discussed the snake hut with her, she had no idea an expensive bag might affect me that way.

I still try hard not to think of that awful place. It has been very hard to write about it, as doing so requires me to recall the memory of those events. Yes, I admit I'm severely neurotic about snakes. So what? I've paid my dues, several times over. As my late husband used to say, "You've been to see the elephant." I am entitled to be as neurotic as I choose.

CHAPTER 16

THE JUMPING FROGS

*I am without charity for the abusive strong, no matter
what their excuse or motive.*

——*A.L. Finch*

I remember the day my mother told me she might have found
a way out of the camp for us. An administrative officer took
her aside and explained a special opportunity, which a few
women might like to accept. We were offered the possibility of
work in an officers' camp. If we performed successfully, we might
be placed on a list with other unattached civilians who would
be sent to the states with severely wounded American soldiers.
This arrangement was in process with the Swedish Red Cross
who remained neutral in the war.

Home! How great the word sounded. We grasped at whatever
straws we could find. In effect, we had a chance to work our
way home—and we felt elated! We could do that!

Nonie did not truly trust the Japanese, yet to stay in this camp
certainly meant eventual, premature death. The wanton murder
of Ari was still in the forefront of our minds. Daily, our bodies
were starved for more nourishment, and I was still recuperating
from polio. Any day we might fall victim to a tropical illness or
a random act of violence.

CHILD POW

Any day I might foolishly say something wrong from habit or in desperation. We simply had to get out of these camps. I was constantly afraid I might knee-jerk react to someone or something, which could cause severe punishment or even death to one or both of us. *I was never ever not afraid.* Terror was my constant companion, and that of my mother.

My Nonie did not fully understand what privileged work was offered. Yet she swore to the Japanese, whatever task they had, we could do it as well or better than any other women, given a chance. The situation seemed an answer to our prayers, and within two weeks, they trucked us to a location near the former summer home of Philippine kings. We were so grateful to be released from the terrible camp we had been staying in. Little did we expect our fate.

Newly constructed road to Baguio

On our way to our new camp from the back of our truck, we glimpsed a POW camp and saw many women and children. We were so happy to think we'd soon be with social and racial peers. We were very wrong.

In this new camp, lovely verdant foliage, rolling hills and a bit of altitude provided relief on hot days. Our camp was near the former summer home of the Philippine emperors. A breeze usually brushed our area. It reminded us of the climate at our cabana. We anticipated we would work as field hands, gardeners, perhaps as a cook, or doing laundry, or cleaning. Yet the reality was, others performed these chores for us.

We could hardly believe the difference in our lives, after only a one-week period. More rice was provided than before; we were encouraged to bathe and wash our hair frequently. We luxuriously enjoyed soaps and lotions. Under supervision, we even had scissors to trim and clean our nails properly! In addition, rather than living in lean-tos in groups on hard ground, we lived alone and were allowed to sleep as late and often as we wanted—on European beds, not straw mats on the floor!

CHILD POW

View through the bars on our hut at Baguio

Our hut at Baguio. At least we had a few books in English.

Then one day the truth was revealed. We had jumped from the proverbial frying pan into a fire. The Japs announced we existed now as their slaves. By accepting extra food, supplies, and privileges, we had inadvertently, nonverbally agreed to personally service the officers who came to the camp for recreation leave, and it was too late to refuse.

My Nonie tried desperately to have me exempted from this disgraceful situation, but to no avail. Japanese officials explained we had no option. My Nonie said no one had described what the new "work" would entail. The officers in charge laughed and said it was too bad. They told her that by her own request for transfer to this camp, she had replaced our prisoner status—voluntarily—and we became slaves. Now if we refused to do whatever we were told, we would be executed. There were plenty of other women to take our places. Neither could we immediately revert to our former POW status.

I was an innocent, young city girl. We had never lived on a farm or had male animals. I had no understanding of the act of copulation, and I had absolutely no idea in the world about human or animal reproduction. One simply did not talk nor ask questions about it in polite society.

I do remember giggling with a group of older girls at a slumber party. Remember, too, that I was three to four years younger than my school peers. As we discussed how babies are made, in a naïve manner, I found no one there knew any more than I did, except for one girl. She had heard talk about a male putting some part of his body into a woman's body. We couldn't imagine what part of his body he might use or where it would fit, but after that night, none of us allowed a French kiss, because we did not want a baby.

We had grown up in such total innocence. We never spoke the word "pregnant." It was reserved for textbooks and dictionaries and was considered "common." To be thought of as "common" in those days was a fearsome charge against one's reputation. It simply wasn't proper.

My mother, my imaginative wonderful 32-year-old mother, then devised the most remarkable idea to help protect my mind. Through magnificent strength and amazing character, My Nonie re-labeled each incident of deranged physical abuse as a stupid activity, committed by men inferior to us mentally and behaviorally. Race had nothing to do it.

Apparently, according to her, these Jap officers derived pleasure from their calisthenic-like gyrations during these acts. My Nonie explained it as activity we had no control over, and consequently we should think of it as totally impersonal. She explained this was the "work" for which we were lured to this camp. She described it, then said each encounter might be uncomfortable; yet I should not be frightened nor worry.

My Nonie explained I should keep my mind on other ideas; if I was patient and accepting, then we would live. We both needed to be extremely careful since their displeasure could translate into our death. Yet if an officer was ever violent, I should scream as loudly as I could. My Nonie felt she had successfully bargained to keep violence out of our situation.

166

She was gentle in her explanation of what would happen, truthful, and honest. I believed her and trusted her implicitly—it was good I did. My Nonie made those months of rapes change from terrifying, horrible, repugnant physical attacks into something more akin to loathsome, disgusting mistreatment. Her biggest gift to me was making it mentally survivable.

Nonie quietly explained these events were more of an inconvenience than anything else. It was easy, she said. It required us to do nothing except just "be there." The activities these men would require us to do might appear ridiculous, but not to worry. She described how foolish Jap soldiers would look; how ridiculous they'd appear, jumping around like frogs; how intense they'd appear, doing these silly antics.

She said we could talk about it later and laugh at them, but I should never laugh in their presence. Nonie stressed important ideas to remember: I'd be completely unchanged by these incidents. Soon we would be home, where these intrusions would never occur again. I would remain the same person I always had been with identical expectations and dreams. I was to remain polite and do nothing to anger the officers. I must remember never to look them directly in their face. (I still have a hard time doing so, with anyone, at any time.)

Most important, she urged me to remember our mantra, which kept us both alive. Each and every day—for four years—My Nonie held my small cheeks in her hands, looked deep into my eyes and my spirit, then whispered: "We just have to get through this day. We just have to get through this day."

We survived sane because of my mother's attitude and how she helped me prepare my mind—and probably hers, as well—for this tragic time in our lives. I have absolutely no shame about what happened to us or to me, personally. I know we existed as slaves without independent choices while barbarians controlled us. We only had to get through each day.

Any rape counselor will explain that the most serious fallout from rape is the residual mental condition of a victim. Years later, I was a rape counselor. People did not understand abuse counseling during WWII, so surely my mother had never heard about this approach. Still, her innate wisdom saved us at the right time, in the right way.

When our new fate became clear, in a small way my mother faded. She became less animated, quiet, sometimes almost mute. It is my belief she died a little inside. She truly felt responsibility for our awful situation. Her own predicament was bad enough; she had been raised in decency and gentility, but to have her young daughter in this situation was nearly unbearable for her to consider.

I often told her, during that time, she had made the only possible choices; totally innocent choices. The Japs set verbal traps, and she had no way to know life as a slave might be different from life as a prisoner. Nonie was not given a description of the type of "work" expected at our new camp. She made the only right choice at that time.

I know if we had not left the other camp, one or both of us could have died. She could easily have succumbed to an illness or even to despair, and I would probably have angered a guard or officer to the point of instant execution. I have a natural knack for irritating people; I believe it developed more fully as a prisoner. It hasn't lessened.

I know My Nonie saved our lives by getting us to a less hazardous area. We endured treatment no one should have to imagine, yet *would* we have been better off to *remain* in the dehumanized, dangerous, completely unhealthy conditions of earlier camps? Absolutely not. My Nonie saved our lives...life a second time. Several times, I have heard perfectly ridiculous and quite pious women profess they would rather die than endure a rape. That is simply an inane and silly remark. The whole point of life is to endure and survive.

Life was not as cruel for us in this new camp—if one can disregard the reason we were sent there. Nutritionally starved, female hormones ceased production, so no women menstruated or got pregnant. I had not yet matured to that point in my life, so it was not an issue for me.

We also did not gain weight, even with special treatment, since we rarely had more than our two rice balls to eat each day, except for an occasional piece of fruit. We didn't want the fruit, after a while. Our starved digestive systems simply could not process it well. Horrendous cramps and diarrhea occasionally kept us from work. When diarrhea disabled us temporarily we were punished. It was better to eat only rice balls than to be whipped for not "working." One exception was when Japanese soldiers provided a lemon now and then as a special treat. It may have been to help us avoid scurvy and other diseases. Even to this day I love lemons; My Nonie loved them, also.

The cleanliness in this camp relieved us of a lot of worry about disease. Dysentery did not exist, nor fevers, except for malaria. Water was plentiful and potable. Japanese officers all wore rudimentary condoms made of animal skin, so the threats of diseases were absent. Extremely strict military laws governed Japanese officers, concerning what happened to them if they contracted what was then termed a "social disease." They always came to us exceedingly clean after ritual bathing.

My mother was treated as poorly as can be imagined, given our circumstances. She was a different race than any woman most of them had ever known. She was regarded as a novelty. Furthermore, because she was a surrendered prisoner, they gleefully attempted to break her spirit.

It seemed physical intrusions in her body were surpassed by pain and anguish in her thoughts. She wasn't given a chance to focus her mind on other things before abuse, as I was. Instead, she was engaged in a question and answer period, which often forced her to pay attention to her attacker. We devised what we called "mind travel." It helped us mentally avoid those men who wanted to practice their English.

Regularly, during abuse, I took my mind to a fantasy world, away from the horror. While my body was attacked and manipulated in a reprehensible manner, I imagined attending a family dinner party. In my mind I created, in detail, words spoken with others, foods served and eaten, clothes worn by each person in attendance, what songs were played and sung. I played with Freckles and sneaked him tidbits of pie crust under the table cloth.

Nonie, on the other hand, did not think about people. She mentally dwelt on her future dream house as her method to escape torments. Room-by-room and board-by-board she built her house. Once, for an entire month, she imagined shingling her roof, and how she set out her chalk lines. Each task was imagined in great detail, while mentally she saw her hands do the work. Later, in her mind, Nonie laid the white maple floors throughout the many rooms of her house.

When we were alone, we told each other minute details of our imaginative trips away from this awful place. I described the clothes every one wore at home, what was served for dinner and how it tasted. She told me about carrying shingles up a ladder a few at a time, since she couldn't manage the whole "square" at once. She said how many she laid that day and how many sacks of nails she still had left, how the hammer felt in her hand, and how the air was so fresh on top of the roof. She explained how refreshing it was to stop for a drink of cold water and sit in the sun a few minutes.

She told me exactly where her house would be built on our land, on the southeast section, close to the fir hedges that surrounded the acreage. The house would have gardens, many patios, rhododendrons and azaleas. It would be beautiful there. Many times she explained the fragrance of newly sawed wood used in the building, and the aroma of cedar shakes.

The more she talked about it, the more I knew we would make it out of this hell. We had goals for the future, and those goals gave us hope. Where there is hope, there is endurance. We clung to our future by the knots at the end of our rope of sanity. The knots held. Our minds remained whole. For now though, we "just had to get through today."

Many years later, her dream house became a reality. Though the roof has been replaced once, under her direction her maple flooring is as light and lovely as when she imagined laying it in 1943. She personally supervised the milling of the inch and a quarter thick redwood siding. All this happened in the house she built so many years ago in her imagination to save her mind. She had the magic. It may have been the caul. Who is to say?

We learned these facts in order to survive: One must refuse to let the mind focus on pain, intense grief, or revulsion. By this refusal, a person can endure physically, to a greater degree. This "mind travel," as Nonie and I called it, is possible by strict thought control. It takes intense practice, yet any person can learn to do it. It can remove pain if you focus strongly enough.

Perhaps this mental detachment could be considered a form of self-hypnosis, but it's a documented fact. Clinical psychologists document cases where people in advanced stages of pain from disease, or former prisoners like us, state they can "mind travel" to avoid the agony of the moment. Upon hearing of others and their means of escaping from torture, pain, or abuse, I am always amazed how much *more alike* our responses have been *than they are different*. This mind travel must be a natural thing. Otherwise, why would so many people be able to describe so clearly about their experience with it?

To accomplish this mental separation effectively, one must find something wonderfully pleasant to focus on, something loved, then totally concentrate on that one distraction, a place or person. Whatever trauma occurs makes little or no impression. It is tremendously fatiguing mental work, but while a physical body is abused, the victim can put his mind in a safe place.

We must be vigilant to remain in control of our thoughts during this evasion. Psychologists and psychiatrists tell us a mind can flee for relief and independence. It is possible that the mind, so intensely used and so injured, may stay away, never to return, as evidenced by those needing to live in hospitals and seclusive facilities.

I believed if I could move my thoughts away from this place of trauma, then my body also could flee from any distress at hand. I felt as though my mind could fly through clouds and passing through them, I could hide safely there.

Using this mental device, abused people are able to survive many kinds of torment. They can and do survive mentally and physically. My Nonie and I did, and in later years, I heard stories of other desperate prisoners using similar mental techniques. Though I hope others never have to apply this technique, any-one can, if they practice hard and keep the same wonderful idea foremost in their mind.

After the war, when constructing Nonie's dream house, my dear Papa and Nonie learned much about the fine carpets and furniture they later used in their home. For years they planned together, until it was finally constructed in the 1950s. They shopped with antique dealers to learn from them as much as to find a specific piece of furniture. They collected and inherited beautiful family furniture, gorgeous silk carpets, paintings, and beautiful silver pieces. Together, they created a home, a haven for themselves and many others, whom they invited as guests, encouraging them to enjoy it too. It has been consistently and continually filled with love, joy and happiness.

It is as Nonie dreamed it, exactly the way she wanted—and I live in it still. I love the night spirits of this place. They are friendly, loving, and teasing. Drawers open by themselves with no breeze, Bellodgia scents the air; plumbing flushes in the night, and music-boxes play.

Great-grand children wake from naps to ask who the man in the hat is, or who is the lady in the lace blouse with the gold necklace who came in their room and smiled at them for a while. Young mamas announce distinctly, "Grandpa, I'm tired, the kids are tired. Let us get some sleep." And then the house goes quiet while the watching shades bide their time once more. It seems the dear ghostly reminders randomly appear to reassure us all that this is a home of a family who loves each other even after death. It's very comforting. It makes me smile in the night.

For this construction to become a perfect reality in the 1950s, many disagreements occurred between the builder and My Nonie. When he told her she didn't need such a heavy beam across one wall, she made it clear he would do it anyway because she had heavy pictures to hang. She didn't really need it, but she wanted it done as she had dreamed it. With sixteen-foot ceilings, marble entry hall, and beautiful chandeliers, she created a small home that might sometimes whisper of a miniature palace, a lovely dream come true.

First-time visitors often sigh and smile broadly when they enter this monument to her planning, her thoughts, her persistence—and her mental survival! Out from a time of appalling abuse and terror grew a thing of beauty because this precious lady discovered how to disassociate herself from cruel abuse. She was supremely special. She was my whole world. I loved her so.

The Jap officers required us to be totally compliant in their presence. If we failed to comply, they jabbed us with their cigarettes. Sometimes we had a finger snapped backwards, until it fractured or became disjointed. A favorite rotten trick was to grab one of us and pull a toenail off. Oddly, it was always the toes. They never came after a finger. I have had fewer toenails since 1945. They never grew back.

Initially, some of these men thought I was a curiosity. Due to my lack of a passport, transport lists did not specify my age, nor even that I was a young girl. While a few officers had nothing to do with me, others noticed me with greater interest *because* I was a child. Quite like people of any race, these Japanese men had a variety of social and sexual appetites—perversion crosses all language and racial barriers.

In general, after the first encounters, which terrified me and hurt me physically, I found this "work," as my mother put it, to be boring. Many officers did indeed look like frogs, jumping about. Some shouted with fiendish joy; others beat me viciously in a senseless rage before they left; a few wept. I found them all to be despicable and pitiful. Even as a young girl, I was aware of psychological issues surrounding social behavior. I couldn't identify these pathologies, however I could recognize that these men were "out of round." That identification made me very afraid of them. To uselessly expend their energy in a futile and truly meaningless activity with a strange, young child seemed to me to be a denial by them of their own self worth.

After an extended time, they tired of us. With little notification, they decided we should be sent to Japan, and other women replaced us. We hoped, but did not know if they'd keep their promise to send us home to America. Nonie hadn't mentioned the possibility to anyone in charge since our arrival at this camp, so maybe it had only been a ploy to get us to transfer here quietly. We dared not inquire again. To do so might bring down severe punishments. We needed to be as invisible as we possibly could.

We returned to prisoner status. This was a tremendous relief. If there was ever a formal accounting—or if they lost the war—the losers were supposed to provide names and bodies of all prisoners. As slaves, we essentially did not exist and could simply have disappeared forever.

Cigarette and cigar burns still scar my arms, legs, and back. Multiple hand and foot fractures healed long ago but were wounds received for my presumed lapses in judgment. Most of these old injuries occurred solely to amuse Japanese soldiers. I was little. I was slow with my impaired gait. I could be caught easily when chased. I was a target. It was a game. "Whoever can catch the little kid can break one of her fingers or tear off a toenail."

It was never ending. What we identified as torment or even torture was a laughing game to them. We had no more identity to them than if we were rocks they would skip across a pond. We were just pawns in their perverted and cruel gambling games.

In the late 1970s I sought elective surgery for joint replacements. When the doctor saw my foot x-rays, he gasped and said, "Where have *these feet* been?" He counted more than 50 healed fractures. They were caused by smashing gun butts, being stomped upon, and other inventive, evil Jap tricks. He told me the bones looked as if they had been "ground up."

I am lucky, for in spite of what those monsters did, I can still walk and I can still use my fingers. Each stitch I knit, each stroke I paint, each penciled letter, each step taken counts as a measure of defiance toward them. I celebrate my life and endurance with a saluting digit to those fiends. The tormentors did not defeat me.

I must tell you that the remainder of my life has been peopled with many wonderful men, including some who appear to have found me a curiosity. They seemed to regard me as one who held an exotic secret. If I do, I'm unaware of it.

My grandson, a seasoned soldier with many overseas experiences, tells me that upon occasion he has seen a look on my face that indicates I carry private knowledge of an undisclosed issue. It is certainly not a blank, thousand-mile stare, but more like: "Been there. Done that." Maybe he is right. Only memories and scars remain.

CHAPTER 17
CHINA TIN MINES

*Now then, as crooked as a dog's hind leg our
musty tunnel runs, until we see the light before....Maxwell*

From the officers' camp, we were taken to the nearby port where ships loaded people and freight. Then we were off-loaded and shoved at bayonet point into a group of about fifty people. During our long wait for transport paperwork, I grew terribly tired and hungry, as was My Nonie. As expected, no one offered us food or drink.

I pantomimed eating to a soldier and made the international sign to beg, with two hands together, pointed up, as in prayer. I bowed to the soldier and repeated my silent plea. He spoke to another man, who walked away toward a group of soldiers. He soon came back with a large rice-ball and a piece of raw squash of some variety.

At this point, as a column of trucks came along the dock, we had to step aside for safety and we became squeezed into a different group of people, against a go-down wall. After this convoy passed, our former cluster of people was gone, and we didn't know what to do or where to go! However, we were soon herded onto a ship and heaved sighs of relief. I thought, *We are*

179

finally headed for Japan and our eventual, promised repatriation to America!

It was a motley group in the ship's hold. Several whispered pidgin Spanish; a few conversed in Tagalog. No one spoke English. One Asian man spoke French. I asked him about our status. He said we were headed somewhere to work, but he wasn't sure. Although we were uneasy about this trip, we found ourselves in good company. The sailors gave us ten buckets of potable water and five empty buckets for sanitary needs. Men among us found a couple of sheets of corrugated metal and rigged a partition for toilet privacy. It wasn't a bad arrangement at all.

After we were at sea about four or five hours, a few large baskets of cooked rice and vegetables were passed down to us. With thanks, we ate, then found old sacks and My Nonie fashioned us a sleeping place. This same pattern continued for days. Though we hated our inability to see outside, all in all the trip wasn't as bad as we had heard people say. We counted our blessings.

Nearing Foochow

Five days later, we felt our ship reduce speed and signal bells rang, and we heard a locomotive whistle, quite close. Soon after anchoring, smaller boats ferried everyone to the port's docks. We wondered what part of Japan this might be? People bustled all over the docks, but most did not look Japanese. I saw a pre-war sign in English on a large go-down, which announced "The Foochow Trading Company."

I asked my French speaking shipmate if we were in Foochow. He asked someone else, and they all replied that this was Foochow. Nonie and I looked at each other, stunned, laughed nervously, then we both cried. We had sailed further *away* from home, rather than toward it. We had landed in China!

Crammed into boxcars, we endured freezing weather on a rackety-back railroad. Eventually, about one hundred prisoners reached our destination, what is today Guanxi Province, in southeast China. In a state of complete confusion, my mother and I found ourselves assigned to work in a new tin mine.

We wondered if the Japs had information about our identities. Maybe they knew we came from mining people. If they did, what difference could it make? We knew nothing about mining yet it was apparent the people who ran this outfit were as confused as we were. They seemed to believe if there was a surface lead, they should start digging and follow the ore—simple.

There didn't seem to be a mining engineer or a qualified geologist among them. No equipment was present to remove any of the overburden; we were expected to do the labor. Our excavation area was examined each day by officials, to identify possible new ore leads. No one could identify for us what the tin ore looked like. My Nonie and I didn't know. Still, they must have known what they were doing. We certainly didn't and who were we to argue with a three-thousand-year-old society?

181

We were forced to dig at a shallow angle downward, thereby beginning an incline shaft. The fact that this mine was new may be a main reason we survived. Because we worked close to the surface, we had more air than if we were deep in the earth. Also, since we did not have lower levels, there was no danger of flooding, as occurs in some mines. All told, in the short time we were there, we didn't dig further than fifty or sixty feet. In the dark, however, it was easy to become misdirected and go off on a tangent, rather than to dig straight. There is no reference point in the dark.

My grandfather had been a miner, a coal miner, all of his life. My mother, her sisters, and brothers grew up in coal camps throughout Wyoming and Montana. I've often thought how glad My Nonie and I were that my grandfather knew nothing of our struggle to stay alive in these conditions.

Soon after we arrived I developed acute bronchitis, which unfortunately lasted many, many months. When Chinese warlords who operated the mines discovered we two females were sent to them as part of the labor force, they quickly intervened. They assured my mother we would be transported back to the harbor on the next return train in about 10 to 14 days. It became much longer than that.

By our garments, they were not able to tell male from female. We had left Baguio in flimsy, form-fitting sheath dresses. We had not worn them long before they simply deteriorated and fell off of us. By the time we were on the ship for Foochow we had scrounged in junk and garbage piles for fabric enough to maintain decency.

We wore ragged men's pants far too large for us. We had no coats but contrived upper garments from chunks of filthy, obviously used blankets, which is probably where we got our first body lice. I could scream just thinking about the vermin. *God, can't you do something about that?*

Everything we wore in the Orient we tied on, since we had nothing that fit. We used torn strips of cloth or found old cordage to hold us together. Whatever worked. For extra layers of warmth, My Nonie had her arms inside the legs of two decrepit pairs of men's trousers, as a makeshift jacket.

Chinese men of the time often wore long queues (pronounced *kews*). Since my long hair fit right in with their style, I passed for a small man. It was clear the Chinese operators of this mine did not want women present. They felt we could be too much of a distraction. It was lucky for us they felt that way.

This area of China was under Japanese control only in part, because it was also commanded by the Chinese warlords, warlike tribal chiefs. These groups had become turncoats for the Japanese in WWII. In return, the Japanese provided them slave labor for their various enterprises.

In the meantime, we were told to "share a rice bowl" with men in the mine. To "share a rice bowl" means you join forces with whomever you congregate for work, food, sleep, and other needs. G.I.s back from the Pacific brought the phrase "gung-ho" from China, which they thought meant battle hungry, battle happy, vengeful, blood thirsty. When we got "back in the world," we also heard servicemen call this battle-ready attitude "going Asiatic." However, in the Chinese languages, gung-ho means "work together for the common good," so we lived gung-ho and survived.

Within days, we learned Chinese people consume anything. They eat anything that moves about on the ground as well as almost everything that grows. One day I watched a group of fellow prisoners as they scurried about on the ground until suddenly one stopped, held up a small scorpion, and put it in his mouth. Thinking he didn't know what it was, I ran to him and told him to spit it out. I told him it was dangerous.

All of the men laughed at me and told me they were only dangerous when they stung you. They thought they were quite edible and offered me one. I recoiled and they laughed again.

After that they would bring Nonie and me bird eggs or a wild radish they showed me how to dig. My fellow prisoners taught me how to forage for food. We were so lucky to be on a major flyway for migrating birds. I was taught to lay very still in the middle of a field for a long time, then jump up yelling and wave my arms while watching to see from whence birds flew up. Then I would run to get the nested eggs before anyone else.

They liked me because I had tried to help one of them, even in my ignorance of their customs. They even taught me to swear. "Pickled lizard!" A terrible epithet. Nonie and I laughed ourselves silly.

Most of what they ate we could not stomach. On the other hand, new wonderful diet supplements for us consisted of leafy greens and strange vegetables, in addition to daily rice scoops. Our food situation was better than at other camps we had lived in, but the work was a nightmare. It required us to work in the dark, enclosed, for our entire time period, without adequate air.

Many people could have *survived* our same challenges *physically*, if they didn't get too sick or too starved; if they remained uninjured; if they didn't die in a mine disaster, like a cave-in, a gas storm, a flood. All these can happen on a regular basis in any mine in the world.

Mental survival is much tougher. At times, help and hope became mere bleak words in our distant memory. Indigenous Chinese people who labored with us were very kind. They had nothing in the way of material possessions, but whatever they had, they shared with gladness. They epitomized gung-ho—"work together for the common good."

For our health, however, soap was one item we keenly needed, but it was a rare luxury. Still, when any existed, we were offered first use—a quite different situation compared with how the Japanese treated prisoners. In a complete contrast of cultures, Chinese people helped those more frail, while the Japanese tormented and mistreated anyone physically less able. And then they would laugh.

Because we put forth our best effort, we were treated with more kindness than ever before. Chinese camp guards seemed genuinely pleased to have us. As women, we two were smaller than any of the men, so they were glad we could push our way into smaller holes in the mine. As these incline tunnels were dug, they turned, sloped up or down, and went almost any direction, similar to the trail of a wild, foraging dog. Therefore, we called them dog-hole tunnels, but I was always terrified in my little "dog-hole in the dark."

We each had a rope tied around our ankles. This enabled rescuers to pull us out in case of a cave-in. We dug with small tools in stagnant air, thick with dust. In our area, we crawled into and through skinny worm-like tunnels.

For light, we only had candles—one to a shift. If one got wet, if it burnt down or blew out due to drafts, we had to continue work anyway, until our time was up. My candle was almost always out because I coughed constantly from bronchitis, and my breath extinguished the flame. It seemed futile to work in darkness, but it was a way to account for each individual. The Chinese had an inordinate need to always know where each POW was located, particularly My Nonie and me, the only females.

Breaks were never allowed for toilet needs, to my frequent shame. I often wet myself since I had to wait each day until I was pulled out of my tunnel at the end of my work time. Then I would run to the barrel and pour water all over myself; I tried to not smell like urine. My clothes were always wet: first from the urine and secondly from my washing up attempts. I hated the wet abrasive cloth against my skin. I was always cold and always had skin scraped off from abrasions.

I had never imagined I might be a miner, let alone one in a Chinese tin mine, so it took me a while to figure out what I could do to ensure greater safety. One way was to dig my tunnel a bit broader and taller. This gave extra room around my body, to move, and a bit more air to breathe. The tin ore we dug was put in woven, bushel-sized baskets. These were dragged from the mine face, where we loaded them, to the surface by attached ropes. Then another basket was sent down to the miner. Since I dug in candlelight or in the dark, I had no idea what I mined. All I knew for sure is I sent basket after basket full of "dirt" out of my little dog-hole, via a heavy rope, pulled by an unseen person outside the portal.

Heavy, humid air seemed to give us many headaches each day. Later though, we deduced this was probably from oxygen deprivation. *Now, I believe we were close to asphyxiation many times, likely a major cause of death in the mines, but we had not realized it at the time.*

I often felt excessive fatigue and illness. Since we worked at a slight downward angle, our noses ran, and our stomachs reacted. Acid and phlegm refluxed into our throats.

One day in total despair, I laid my head down and wondered if this was the rest of my life. Might I ever again ride my black bicycle up and down our lane? Would I feel warm summer rain on my arms? Would I breathe the scent of our tall, Pacific Northwest firs? Would I hug and picnic with dear old Freckles, my half-blind bulldog?

After I rested and cried awhile, a guard or worker on the surface shouted down the adit, the mine opening, for more work. If I was close enough to the surface to be seen, they poked me with long bamboo poles. This latter act was to increase production and also to see if the miner was alive. *I considered a day good whenever their body carts to haul off the dead remained empty.*

Sometimes, undoubtedly hallucinating, I wondered if there were other people who lived in the tunnels and if I would ever dig through to them. Sometimes I couldn't remember any other part of my life except for digging in the tunnels like some errant earth creature endlessly questing for some unknown result.

I was afraid my digging would unearth some foul thing: a snake, a corpse, an unknown terror. I was always afraid. I was afraid something would happen to My Nonie while I was underground. If something happened to her, who would ever know to look for me in China? Would I be forever cut off from the only family I knew just to spend the rest of my life digging in the dirt in the dark? I was continuously terrified.

I wondered if moles and other animals lived in the ground where I was and if they would hurt me. I was afraid of everything—the worms, the large millipedes I would uncover, the dark, the very earth itself. I was always afraid.

In wretched situations, one becomes vague about the passage of time. An hour seems about as long as you can remember. Sometimes, maybe due to oxygen deprivation or fever, I hallucinated and imagined I had worked there forever, and that my life consisted only of digging in the dark—and would be so until I died.

CHILD POW

I never prayed to die like some POWs did. Instead, I invented wonderful scenarios, filled with excitement, wherein brave Allied soldiers and Marines suddenly appeared and told camp leaders the war was over and demanded our release to go home.

After a whack or two with a bamboo pole and a few shouts from above, which interrupted my wishful daydream, I always responded and sent up another basket of dirt. If a prisoner didn't move—and assuming they were dead—the guards pulled them up by the rope attached around the ankles. Yet, with no protective clothing, we tried to avoid this, as our skin could scrape off before too long. Though day-to-day treatment was far above what we had been used to in earlier camps, we still lived like the dregs of humanity—if we were even still considered human.

Sometimes I felt as if I was really home but just having a very bad dream. Then I'd be bitterly disappointed to realize I didn't dream this camp in a nightmare; I was living in it. Perhaps my confusion was from nutritional deficiencies or from lack of sleep or even oxygen deprivation. When I thought about how upset My Nonie was to not be able to protect me or provide more, I felt deep sadness. The world I survived in was completely miserable. I had barely turned ten years old and I wondered, *Will I live to my next birthday?* Can you imagine a ten-year-old you know caught in this type of circumstance?

I often felt oppressive sadness, so I talked to God a lot. It seemed He heard me, and I felt comforted. God was most present in the darkness, in my dog-hole tunnels.

"If You love me, why have You allowed this to happen?" I asked Him one day.

I felt His answer, "Why should you be different from any other little girl, from anyplace else in the world? Why should you be so special to not have problems? You have a place in this world and a reason for being there and you must not be afraid. You are never alone."

It was excruciating and humbling to know I wasn't "special enough" to avoid pain, heartache, and hunger in life. I thought, *In order to grow up, I need these experiences to become a true, whole person. Maybe God means it as a kind of spiritual initiation. Is that what it is?*

Then I put my head down on the hard earth in my tiny tunnel and cried. After a few moments, a great calm overcame me, and I imagined I heard our headmistress at my seminary read the Evening Prayer. I thought I heard our girls with perfect harmonies, singing: "Now the day is over. Night is drawing nigh. Shadows of the evening, creep across the sky...."

My mind was at total peace then, in complete comfort, because I'd had such good, strong teachers in my religious training classes. I understood my experiences—as with all of life—were transitory, and God is always with us.

During this time, my second year as a captive, I invented an imaginary girl my own age as my real-world counterpart and named her Pokumhamburkify. I didn't know why I chose this extravagant title. It seemed most strange, yet somehow familiar. Back in the world, my pretend ten-year-old self went to school, hosted a fanciful birthday party, ate scrumptious meals, and wore beautiful, warm clothes. She slept in a soft bed with a lovable black and white bulldog each night. He barked at strangers to protect her. She lived my life at home as I would have lived it.

The only thing we had in common, while I dug in China and she studied in America, was a mother who loved us and tried her best to care for us. Her mother cooked pancakes and bacon and put ironed pillowcases on her bed. My mother loved me in

China, hugged me, and told me "We just have to get through today," then she would cry because she couldn't make the days move faster toward our homecoming.

Pokumhamburkify went to school, memorized Longfellow, and played tag at recess. I taught my imaginary avatar Mandarin and encouraged her to speak colloquial phrases. Pokumhamburkify could also conjugate French verbs and pronouns. Often, this plethora of mental activity helped speed the time I dug in isolation, in the dark. It also kept me from imagined terrors. I was afraid of everything: worms, bugs, whatever crawled terrorized me.

I mentally recited poems dear, mischievous Ari had taught us in the Philippines before his shocking murder. In my mind, I heard him solemnly intone the opening from "Evangeline."

"This is the forest primeval, the murmuring pines and the hemlocks stand like druids of eld...."

At night we "miners" were hooked to each other at the ankle, preventing escape. Our ankle rag-restraint hooked to a long chain, which attached each person to the next. The theory was, if one tried to get away, they were tethered with everyone else, so escape was impossible, if not comical. I cannot imagine a more bleak place from which to dream of an attempted escape.

Everything in this camp was primitive, totally underdeveloped, even without toilets. We were told the truck road became a slick quagmire in a wet winter. When temperatures turned more extreme, the mud froze and the road became a massive series of rock-hard corrugations, which cut across the landscape. Near the mine site, surrounding hills were bleak, unforested. We saw no vegetation grow during the entire cold blustery month of October we were there. On the positive side, the sun caused the road to dry out; on the negative, dust flew day and night.

All food was freighted in by supply trains. We were "rail-head," the deadend of the line. Although we heard track expansion occurred northwest of us, indigenous groups warred and fought, so little work was ever accomplished. They lived in a totally tribal manner with centuries of enmity and hostility *preventing unification or cooperation.*

Isn't it a paradox that in later years, with joy I married a man who worked uranium and copper mines for years! I often went underground and cleaned parts, while he changed pumps or worked on a hoist-controller. The tight spaces never bothered me while I was underground with him, although several times I spooked myself when he was out of sight.

Perhaps the difference was that the Utah and New Mexico mines were brilliantly lit. They were also huge; large enough to have electric trains on levels as deep as 2000 feet underground. They were gigantic compared with my little dog-hole in Guanxi Province, China. My husband heard about my "mining days" with agony. He asked me never to speak of them.

More than eighty prominent citizens in the Guanxi area were arrested in 2006 and executed for the deliberate flooding deaths of many miners the previous year. Since China has no real due process of law as we know it, there was a short trial. Without question, these crooked officials were found guilty and beheaded.

Apparently, some Chinese union officials, mine owners, and politicians had banded together in 2005 to perpetrate an insurance fraud. Water was kept near mines in holding ponds, to release and quickly smother fires, which are sometimes a natural event underground. Seeping gases, coupled with inadequate air-conditioning or fire suppression systems, are the cause of most underground explosions, fires, or flare-ups. In this 2005 incident, the Guanxi miners could have been evacuated when flooding was deemed necessary, but in China people are expendable.

The whole news story presented an interesting scenario to me because at the time we were there *insurance* in China did not exist, and *trade unions* would have been regarded as silly dreams of a capitalist proletariat.

China is trying hard to move from the 15th Century to the 21st Century. It's happening by fits and jerks. Modernization now entails unions and insurance companies, but on the other hand the irreverence for human life remains. They still kill their baby girls. China hasn't changed much since 1943.

We were eventually put back on a train, each with a pair of padded pants and jacket and a pair of cloth padded-sole slippers. This was far more than we had when we arrived. It was almost like payment for our work. We were grateful for the warmth.

We traveled with a Mongolian mercenary as a guard who laid his head back and slept the entire non-stop eleven hour trip. After the train traveled northeast, we arrived at the coast. Again, we were transported in the hold of a freighter, which seemed in better shape than others we had seen.

A regular shipping pattern seemed to have developed during WWII. From the northern Philippines, ships left for China with a supply of mine laborers and other workers. On the ship's trip away from China, the Chinese exported great quantities of munitions and other crated items we were unable to identify. This equipment followed a circuitous route to Japan before returning to the Philippines then to China and the whole round-robin began again. We became additional—but incidental—cargo.

This was a time of increased anxiety for us. We feared transport back to the large, dangerous, disease-ridden camps we had existed in when first captured. We prayed for anything different! I was more ill now than when we left those camps. We prayed a lot. I didn't think we could survive those earlier camps, as we were in bad condition now. When we had been there before we had our original, albeit fading, physical resources. Now we had none. We were open to disease at this point. We were very weak.

In actuality, we had only a tiny hope to ever reach Japan. We had the hope that as the ship went north, we would be able to be landed in Japan and thus sooner make our way toward repatriation. Did we dare make ourselves visible and inquire about the previous promise to get us there for repatriation? We trusted no one. In addition, we decided any people who sent a couple of females like us to work in a mine—even by accident, as we were assured it had been—had to be out of control in the judgment category!

During the war years, the immense bulk of letters written to and from service personnel overseas almost paralyzed our postal service, so V-mail was developed. Service men used a standard single sheet of paper to compose a letter with an address. After censorship overseas, it was microfilmed, flown to the United States, was semi-enlarged and printed on a small V-mail page, was folded in a special format, sealed, and mailed to the recipient. This efficient idea kept communications flowing between loved ones.

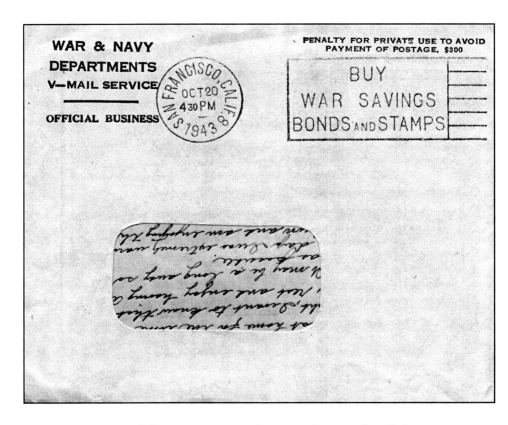

V-Mail from Papa wishes me happy birthday

My new Papa wrote to My Nonie faithfully and often during their long separation, never knowing for sure if she was alive. He wrote sweet letters as opposed to love letters, telling about his work—as much as he could—and about his hopes and plans for their future. He sent these to my grandparents' house and instructed my grandmother to read them, since they were of general interest, but to save them for Nonie. My grandmother saved every one, also not knowing if Nonie would live or ever return to read them herself. Between Papa and all our family a wonderful bond of affection developed in our absence.

One day my grandmother received a V-Mail and discovered in it that Papa anticipated the war to last a long time. He was glad Nonie and I were together. He hoped we had found suitable living arrangements, and he hoped I might have a happy 10th birthday.

That letter was particularly important to me later, since I remember exactly where I was on my 10th birthday. I was digging tin ore in a hole in a Chinese mine, crying and wondering if I'd ever live long enough to be eleven-years-old.

I kept the letter and reproduce it here, an excellent example of writing "between the lines." He was sure we were either prisoners or in hiding, and he was glad if we were together. He hoped wherever we lived was acceptable and said it might be a long time before we could all be together. Papa said the weather is warmer where he recently went. In effect, he tells us he has crossed the equator. October would be warmer south, so he was once again in a South Pacific battle area.

The amazing thing about this letter has always been that he knew in his heart that he and his Nonie would be together again someday. If for no other reason than that he was a good man. I'm glad he didn't know where we were at that time and under what conditions we existed.

CHAPTER 18

LENNIE AND
THE ROSE GARDEN

And God shall wipe away all tears from their eyes;
and there shall be no more death, neither sorrow,
nor crying, neither shall there be any more pain;
for the former things are passed away.—Revelation

Apparently there was a shipping route from the Philippines to Foochow to ports in Japan then back to the Philippines. Supplies of armament, laborers, and equipment were routinely shipped on this round-robin schedule. We boarded in Foochow and followed the whole circular route. At one point, we were off-loaded and sent to a small holding area at Fukuoka for six days. It seemed to be a transit camp of some sort as we met other Americans, some Australians, and even a 'Nederlander', as he called himself. This camp area was almost ignored by Japanese officials. They paid little attention to any of us except for the delivery by the rice wagon once a day. There was potable water from a spigot. Not too good, but basically not a wretched place, either.

We had made friends with other prisoners who seemed both surprised and then delighted to talk to a young mother and child. I think My Nonie and I reminded them of their own far-away families. They would seek us out just to talk and, in the present vernacular, "hang out." One we quickly grew close to was

197

a young Australian fellow named Lennie. He had a sweet sense of humor and coupled with his Aussie, down-under accent we liked him immensely.

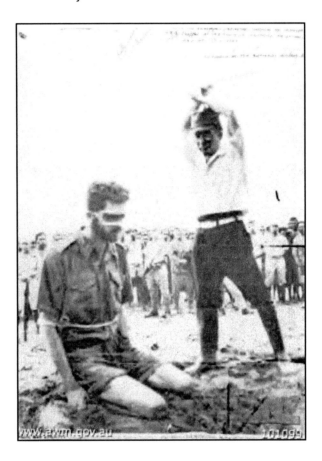

OUR BRAVE FRIEND, LENNIE,
DIES IN THE ROSE GARDEN

By and large this camp was the most benign we had inhabited...until one day we were assembled in the classic prison camp "three sides of a square" formation. My Nonie and I were placed toward the front of the group next to a small fence. In a very short time our friend Lennie was brought forward with an odd sort of blindfold around his face. He was made to kneel.

Someone in the crowd, probably an American Marine, yelled out, "Semper Fi, Mac!" and Lennie called back,

"Don't worry, bonzers, I'll be there before you are."

A camp photographer hastily shoved me aside, knelt down, and just as a soldier swung his sword, the photographer snapped the picture of Lennie being beheaded. Lord, Lord. Why did this happen to Lennie? I wet myself. Lennie's head rolled toward me. His eyes were open.

Many years later the picture was published and when I saw it all the old fears and terrors returned for a moment. It is such a sad picture of the end of a very brave young man's life. *Why had this happened?*

I was afraid to move an eyelash for fear the soldier would turn on My Nonie and me and cut our heads off, too. The sword mesmerized me as it glistened, still held in the killer's hand. He looked at me. My fear surged. Lennie's head was only inches from where my feet had been a minute earlier. I saw blood spattered on Nonie's feet and ankles. My gaze couldn't move away from the blood on her. I saw she had a torn toenail. I wondered when it happened. She hadn't mentioned it. Why was I thinking of such mundane things? I was drifting out of reality. Focus! The sword still dripped with Lennie's blood. For an instant I thought if I could just put his head back on his neck, it might reattach. The sword was so big and dripping I couldn't move. The blood seemed to be congealing while I lay at the killer's feet, afraid for my own life. Why was I such a coward? I must try to help Lennie. No! No! *Oh God! Help us all.*

We couldn't understand why this happened. There must have been a reason, at least in the minds of those devils. Guards with bayonets affixed came and forced us away from the area where Lennie's body and his head lay apart.

We were taken down a road in the camp while I became increasingly more afraid. Their Japanese language was so fast I couldn't understand what they were saying. I thought maybe we were being taken to be killed someplace else. After several city blocks distance we were loaded into trucks and taken from the camp to the coast where we were loaded on another southbound ship.

Our confusion grew by leaps and bounds. Where was the work we were supposed to do in Japan? How were we supposed to get to America? And most important at the moment: Why was Lennie, our friend, murdered? We never knew. The question of his death haunts me to this day. He was a good man. He wasn't known to be a thief who stole food. There was no escape committee so that wasn't the reason. He tried to be as invisible as the rest of us around the guards. Why was he killed like that?

I have many reasons why I hated the Japs for the things they did but one of the most paramount was the requirement to be present, and up front, at the beheadings.

With hearts racing hard in our chests, we sailed off to the Philippines again and arrived with as little problem as possible for the times. We were so quiet on board. We had known all along that the Japanese were manipulating us, just because they had the power to do it. Where were they taking us? Certainly not back to the officers' camp? We finally withdrew into a desperate silence, almost as though we were hibernating animals, waiting for a springtime that would never come to us. I was afraid and very sad. My Nonie cried quietly when she thought I was sleeping or not paying attention. What if something happened to her? I was afraid she was giving up. I tried to get her to play word games with me so to focus on anything else except for our present condition, but she would only turn her head away and shut her eyes. I was so afraid.

CHAPTER 19
THE "HELL SHIP"

*... sleep to say we end the heartache...that flesh is heir to...
for in that sleep of death what dreams may come, when we
have shuffled off this mortal coil........*

— *Wm. Shakespeare*

O ur destination was straightened out by our captors several days after reaching the Philippine Islands again. We camped under guard for almost a week at the same small port from whence we'd left for China. Then, one morning, we were called together, counted off by the guards, and shoved up a gangway on to the deck of a freighter. We climbed down two ladders into the hold and we finally embarked on our formerly scheduled trip to Japan. This was a sea voyage that was the work of the devil.

Only a demon could have planned for nearly 800 people to travel down inside the hold of a large, rusty, old freighter with few supplies! We had *no* food. We had a *tiny* amount of potable water. For sanitary measures, all 800 were provided with a couple of buckets.

In later life, I have been asked many times about what strengths sustained My Nonie and me. Somewhat ruefully, I believe some of my strength came from early family upbringing where I was taught that I might be a little bit "better" than most others, therefore the aberrations of behavior shown by others were something to ignore as much as possible. I was not to dwell on the acts of deviancy, misbehavior, or unkindness committed by others as "they were not our sort of people." Holding oneself apart allows the nurturing of emotional resilience.

We learned to work through situations so we could function with some normalcy. Part of this is built into personality. Part is natural common sense. Part is holding fast to positive attitudes (we will go home some day), setting realistic goals (we will eat whatever we can while we can get it and we will be as clean as possible), and the reliance on others for mutual support and energy (we will never let ourselves be parted).

One needs to examine a situation and decide how much of it actually is in your control. It is necessary to define one's own strengths and find those areas that need work or amplitude. An example would be that we kept a calendar: most forbidden, but not hard to do. We always knew what day it was. Another thing was that we made daily schedules for ourselves. We awoke, we searched for food, we worked. When we had work, we obeyed, we maintained a silent demeanor, we scrupulously obeyed the rules of those in charge, we slept every chance we got, and we ate things for nutrition, not for taste. We appeared submissive to the soldiers, but in fact all of our bowing and kow-towing (kneeling bows) were simply an obeying of rules, not a show of any respect. We loathed them.

The American Psychology Association believes that accepting change as part of living helps build resilience. I strongly concur. Deal with what you have, continually marshal what energies you have to sustain yourself to the next day. By then, conditions may have changed. It is very important to take care of yourself. If you can't survive, you won't be able to help others.

Keep looking for the future. Don't dwell on how great the past was. It's gone. Never whine about your status. Deal with what you're given and don't look back. Only look ahead.

I hesitate in my attempt to describe this voyage because I have deeply blocked the anguish of it from my mind. Pain from these remembrances is almost beyond description, even today. Please turn away if you also find what occurred too terrible to bear. It has taken me an inordinate amount of time to write down these events because I had almost been able to remove them from my mind. Thinking about this voyage still drives me to a level of near madness. I want to shriek at the horror. I continually re-read my words, because if I turn my eyes away, my mind chooses to flee from the material completely. I simply shut down. Please forgive my frailty as I tell you a part of our national history during World War II. You need to know this.

We were broiling in the hull from high temperatures. The outside weather was largely dry with cool breezes, but the metal hull attracted and transmitted the heat much as closed car windows will do on an otherwise average day. Many prisoners were also feverish from malaria—and fear. In addition, I still had bronchitis and continued to try to recover from body-weakening effects of polio. We were unimaginably compacted, upright, like

205

800 asparagus spears packed in a can. Being shorter than the others, My Nonie and I had an extremely difficult time simply catching a breath!

Kind men around us began yelling, asking if there was a place into which we two females could be separated. Others called back. Eventually, we were floated overhead by hundreds of hands to a corner of the hold. A sturdy partition had been built there in the past to hold some kind of equipment. Two other women lived there for many days with My Nonie and me in an area about the size of an old public telephone booth or a modern side-by-side refrigerator-freezer.

Constantly pressing into another person's skin increased our temperature even more, and it was like being locked in the metal trunk of a car on a sweltering day. No drinking water was supplied beyond the first few buckets handed down. That water was consumed within minutes before we ever set sail. The trip to Japan was an abomination, nearly as unbearable as the big POW camps. The heat was excruciating.

A few men went mad; hysterically, they bit fellow prisoners for their blood's moisture. Others begged to be strangled, thinking they could not survive another day. I truly doubt any man complied with that request. First of all, long term POWs seemed to have an almost god-like respect for human life. Second, most of the men had become so weak, from a variety of causes, they did not have the strength to respond to assisted-suicide requests, even had they agreed.

The stench from a lack of sanitary facilities was overpowering, and it was impossible to move about for any reason. The pitiful prisoners urinated, defecated and vomited where they stood, but the odor of dead and decomposing bodies was completely beyond description. Sometimes remains began to exude a waxy material from the skin. It looked a bit like white vegetable shortening my grandmother used in baking. This substance was whitish-tan, malleable and carried the sickening-sweet odor of a body whose soul has flown away. Even as I try to explain, I find there are no words to accurately describe these insane conditions. All the while, continuously, the thick blanket of heat was oppressive.

I have remained claustrophobic since that time. When I ride in a car, a window must be open. In any room, I try to sit facing a window, to be able to see outside, and I'm uncomfortable in narrow stairways or halls, and in elevators. Medical X-rays and CT scans are avoided whenever possible. In theaters and concert halls I always use an aisle seat or I don't attend at all, and I always look for exit signs in public buildings. I never have sheets or blankets tucked in on my bed, nor can I wear tight clothing. Old memories last lifetimes. I have promised myself I will never be trapped again, and I remember distinctly, the heat was oppressive.

For eight days we had no food or water. Occasionally, throughout the interminable hours, the crew turned seawater hoses on us for cooling through steel gratings above on the deck, but there remained nothing to drink except for what we could catch in our upturned mouths. Seawater collected in the hold and sloshed our filth further around our feet and ankles. It was like standing in a septic tank.

One of the women with us was a tall, heavy-set person from British India. To provide more shoulder and hip room in our little metal area, Edna would hold me around her neck like a toddler. I didn't weigh very much then. She never complained and was such nice lady.

Our other companion was a White Russian from Shanghai who wept constantly. Nonie spoke firmly to her about stopping the incessant weeping. She was further dehydrating herself and she would soon be ill if she didn't stop it. She did not stop, and on the sixth day she died, just as Nonie had predicted she would. Eventually, we folded her and stood on her body to avoid standing in the ankle-high filth. We tried to stand as long as we could, then we would arrange ourselves in spoon fashion to try to take some weight from our feet and legs.

I was so sad. Someone had loved Ghislaine. Her mother, her brother, her sister, a lover had been kind and gentle to her and now we stood on her body. I cried later.

Almost all were dehydrated, many to the point of death, and the heat was oppressive. These crates of despair were called "Hell Ships"—accurately named. My Nonie whispered to me that those who died on board would surely go straight to heaven—they had already lived in hell!

I keep telling about the heat so people can understand. But maybe they really should not. It might be too painful. It still is for me. I do not want anyone ever to have personal knowledge of a sea voyage like this. Pure and simple, this was an egregious means of torturing ill, injured, and innocent people.

When my mother and I left the Philippines this second time, we were each given a packet containing four green bananas, indigenous fruit, and four rice balls. We tried to hide what food we had because of the deprivation and desperation of others, and my mother did not let me give anything to anyone else. As long as it lasted, we continued to hide our food.

My Nonie was so wise. How did she know these things? She had been sheltered all her life. Others had always made important decisions and choices for her. Now she said she sensed we needed our strength for what was ahead. I remembered she was born with a caul, indicating extra sense, foresight.

Not many days later, our ripening bananas wafted an enormous odor of their own, but the stench in the hold was such that nausea was the overwhelming condition, and no one noticed our aging fruit. Though we usually did not feel like eating anything, we wanted to survive, so we shared a banana every day and had one bite of a rice ball. We continued to eat, even after our bananas became limp, blackened, and almost slimy. They were simple nourishment, and we determined to eat and stay as strong as we could, for as long as possible. The heat was intolerable.

One of the least comforting things we were told as we had boarded this ship was that U.S. submarines were in the area, sinking freighters like ours. Sayonara, baby, and bon voyage.

We were too miserable and too afraid of the future to *allow* ourselves to be sunk.

Approaching Kobe

After our eighth day at sea, with more than 200 decomposing dead bodies in the hold—200 men and the one dead woman, now gone to meet their Maker, yet who still co-mingled, *upright*, squeezed among us—we finally disembarked in Kobe, Japan. We were taken by "luggers" to the docks. Surviving men went to the coal mines. The three women stayed on the docks. We worked with other groups of prisoners, collected from we knew not where. We landed in Kobe in 1943 on a very cold day. We were hauled up on pallets out of the hold. We were too weak to climb the ladders. The fresh air gave us hope we could survive now we were out of that wretched stinking hold. We carried the odor in our nostrils for days afterwards.

Transfer boats called "luggers"

We talked among ourselves about how the Japs would ever sanitize the ship's hold after our journey to make it clean enough for other cargo. We never knew what they did, of course, but in our eyes, a distinctly preferable possibility was to sink the ship itself!

According to The Center for Internee Rights, 37% of the Japs' Allied POWs died in captivity. Of German Allied POWs, only 2% died. Amazing. Yet, it is clear our government refused to take this fact into consideration after the war was over. No one has ever promised the world was fair. My opinion is, it is our responsibility to make it that way.

CHAPTER 20

KOBE DOCK LABORERS

*With fingers weary and worn, with eyelids heavy and red,
in poverty, hunger and dirt....Oh God, that bread should be
so dear, And flesh and blood so cheap.*

——Thomas Hood

After being directed farther along a dock, we were shoved by rifle-carrying soldiers toward an area near a shed. Before entering, we were given bars of rather caustic soap and told to walk through outdoor showers, to wash our clothes, to put on the diaper like garment we were given that the workmen wore, and that the women should also put on a long sash to tie around their upper body for decency. We were given thong sandals called *zori*.

The shed was about thirty feet wide by fifty feet long. Inside were crude benches, several tables, and a stack of industrial pallets each about two feet wide by six feet long. The cross pieces had narrow gaps at one-inch intervals. They were sturdy; they would serve as our beds. We would be about four inches off the floor. That was good. Too many rats otherwise. I hate rats. Canvas pieces of various sizes became our coverings and supplement to whatever we wore.

We wondered what happened to the people who lived there before us.

It didn't matter that only a few pans were lying about, we didn't have a stove to cook on anyway! For the first week or so, soldiers did bring a brazier every night to cook our rice, a tiny quantity, which had to be divided among us evenly. We learned it was more fair if we divided the dry rice before cooking. It was also faster to cook the rice in tiny quantities. The men were given small pieces of dried fish once a day to supplement their rice.

Some people formed small household groups and bundled their rice together in a pan. The cook was a rotating position. My Nonie and I kept our rice to ourselves and did our own cooking. There were about 50-60 of us in the go-down at any given time. Fellow laborers died and were not immediately replaced. New laborers were transferred in from one of the large concentration camps. Every one was very hungry all the time.

Two people, usually one of the men and Nonie, would carefully count out the individual rice grains into as many piles as there were people.

You might think we would have used a container of some sort to ladle out the rice. In reality there was such a small amount given to the whole group that to assure each got an equal share, grains were counted out and placed into small piles of ten, then combined to twenty, and then eventually to fifty, which was the average of what each person got at each "eating". Most of the time we ate twice a day. Occasionally there was no evening rice and even more occasionally there might be no rice for several consecutive days.

With great trepidation, and displaying what I thought was excessive humility, desperately I approached an officer saying we might load the Emperor's ships more quickly when we were not so famished and faint.

All the while I was being beaten for more than an hour, he shouted at me that only the soldiers should have food; that we were worthless parasites; that we should die and then we wouldn't be so hungry.

We did get more rice after that while he was in charge and in a few days I was recovered enough from the beating that I could once again shovel coal.

I think he was willing to give us the rice, except he had to save face and thus I had to be beaten for him to retain his "honor". Barbarians.

During WWII, the Japanese maritime fleet was largely coal-fired, and we POWs worked as dock laborers on one of the smaller docks. Other larger dock areas had chutes down which coal tumbled, directly from railroad hopper cars into holding compartments. Fancier, larger ships and oil-fired naval vessels earned different and more modern techniques, but our assignment was to feed a variety of smaller ships called "luggers." I never learned what it meant.

Our group of about fifty began the labor of fueling ships. Our routine was ten hours shoveling coal into sacks; ten hours carrying these sacks on our backs onto ships, then dumping wherever told. The work was miserable, exhausting. Hours stretched into longer hours, dependent on the whim of each supervising soldier.

We learned coal dust floats in the air. We breathed it. We swallowed it. We ate it. We coughed, and eventually our breath came out black. It sneaks through fabric and makes skin itch and it develops sores on you that are slow to heal. We had no means by which to bathe. We were always filthy and always trying to find some way to clean ourselves. We had lice. We had intestinal parasites. We were worked hard, long hours by the guards. We were fatigued all the time. We never got enough sleep. We were miserable. We were always hungry. We were always afraid.

Occasionally a soldier actually showed a smidgen of compassion and allowed us rest breaks and fresh water from a nearby pipe. Usually, though, prisoners' thirst was quenched from a barrel with a heavy top-coat of coal dust, floating insects, and dead rats. My mother and I *never* drank from that barrel.

We had extremely short rations at the docks. Lots of seaweed supplemented our daily allotment of rice balls. If we got lucky enough to have a "good" guard at the coaling pit, we were allowed to bag smaller loads, so our partner could carry a coal bag the required distance more easily. Most of the guards allowed this after I was allowed to explain that we could go much faster this way than if we struggled to carry the heavier sacks. By this time my spoken and comprehensive Japanese language skills, although rudimentary, were good enough to be of help to us.

The officers that came around once a day checked the piles of coal the trains had dumped out to see if the guards were bearing down on us and making us work. When we moved faster, the piles appeared smaller as we could carry more over the interval. This pleased the officers. The guards were pleased. We were relieved to be allowed to carry much lighter loads. Many of us were becoming quite ravaged with malnutrition by this time so carrying the lighter coal sack was infinitely more bearable.

One prisoner jumped in the water by our dock. He was shot before even being dragged out. He was dead. I think he committed "death by rifle shot." He knew they'd kill him so he did it deliberately. He just couldn't handle it any longer. Many felt that way because despair weighed so heavily on all of us. It would have been so easy to lose track of time. Luckily, Nonie kept an accurate, but secret, calendar.

*Modern docks at Kobe. Low dark-roofed warehouse
at far lower right is like the one we lived in 12-43 to 4-45.*

After several months, in the spring of 1944, we learned one of the guards at the warehouse where we lived and worked had a wife employed in a wig factory. Since my hair had grown amazingly long, considering my nutritional level, and hung in a braid below my hips, we came to an agreement concerning how much my hair was worth. Nonie cut it off at scalp level. I cried. I was vain about my hair. I hope Fumiko, the wigmaker, appreciated my sacrifice.

Later I received sixteen fishhooks and a large reel of light line in payment. This soldier could have taken the hair from me, giving nothing in return, but he was an honest man. Kazuo, the guard, always spoke kindly to us. In simple English. Kazuo had a brother-in-law who lived in Chicago. Kazuo wanted to go live in Chicago after the war. It was a secret. He was not like the others who ferociously shouted every order and would hit out at us for not being quick enough when they gave an order.

My Nonie and I secretly hung our fish lines off every piling we could reach and managed to catch enough fish to supplement our rice and seaweed—or whatever it was. The fish we caught were very small, about the size of sardines. That was good as we had very small hooks and very fine line. Still, every day we could catch one or two of the little things. It all helped. We saw bigger fish but they didn't come near our hooks. I wondered who wore the wig made from my hair. Hair for fish. It seemed to be a pretty good bargain after all. I could grow my hair again.

When possible, we snatched fruit or vegetables, which rolled off a shipping pallet. These were always a big treat to share—after dark. We never carried them with us, for fear of being accused of being thieves. We would put them in the dark on a low stud in the warehouse. No one stooped to examine anything in the always dark warehouse so it was almost like having a private cupboard.

Today, however, I still cannot choke down a mango. Too many years of eating rotting mangos from the docks has given me a revulsion to them. Nor can I eat any rice, but white rice I cook myself. No fried rice, no rice pilaf, please.

All too often when we were given cooked rice rather than dried rice, many insects—large and small—were stuck in the meager amount. A few prisoners called it "protein on-the-hoof," but it was disgusting. We could not bear it. Always, to us, insects were disease carriers.

About fifty of us lived together in a warehouse on the dock. We few women ferociously intimidated the mostly Asian men, so they always left us alone.

Besides hunger, which was always present, what bothered us most was the cold weather. The summer weather was very nice usually. Even on very warm days we had a lovely sea breeze from the Pacific so we were fortunate never to suffer from the heat. However, it snows and it blows in Kobe all winter, and we spent two winters there.

No cold climate clothing was provided, so we scrounged in garbage dumps for any shred of usable fabric. We found a sectioned-off area where a uniform manufacturer was discarding wrongly cut or flawed garment pieces. We helped ourselves. In other places, usually all we found were scraps from torn signal flags or pieces of canvas. We stuffed everything up our sleeves and tied larger pieces around our bodies. My Nonie and I made use of extra padding against severe temperatures in any way we could contrive.

We found bundles of newspapers that were a life saver to us. A dozen or more sheets of paper tied securely completely cut the wind from our chests and backs. At night we were much warmer wearing all our layers after we found the newspapers.

In sixty years retrospect, the way we treated our rags was actually comical. We exuded pride at our foraging abilities, and we protected our rags fervently, as though we were dressed by

Chanel, Balenciaga, or Mainbocher—famous designers from Paris and London. I often remembered the beautiful clothing my mother had worn back in the world with such elegance and grace; then I wondered how this incredible fiasco happened.

Why had our former world of gentleness been ripped from us by these awful barbarians? Why had they made us their problem? We hadn't done anything to them. Why did they treat us so despicably? Let us go, I thought. *Let us try to survive on our own.* Yet, of course, it didn't happen. We remained on the docks. We only had to get through today.

It wasn't bad shoveling coal—after blisters on our hands and shoulders thickened into calluses with ground-in coal dust—but loading was back-breaking. Our shoulder calluses from the bag straps took years to disappear, and for many years my mother refused to even try on a strapless or off-the-shoulder dress, though eventually her blackened calluses faded. It is too bad our distinct memories of that time cannot do the same.

We had to cross on gangplanks, boards high over water below, to lug sacks from our loading dock onto the ships needing coal. We were given geta, a thong sandal platform on stilts which are good for keeping directly out of water puddles and snow, and several pairs of tabis, which are socks with a great-toe section. Rats stole our tabis. In wet weather the geta were slick. In rain gangplanks also became extremely slippery. Combining the narrow, wooden gangway and slick geta created a frightening situation. I have felt more secure in bare feet since that time.

After a while our feet became numb from cold, which then became as dangerous as wearing geta since frozen feet have no sensation until they warm up. As a non-swimmer, I was terrified I might overbalance with my coal sack and fall into the freezing water. I was always afraid of something. Most of the time with good reason.

Thankfully, I never fell, only by pure luck. We occasionally filled holds in several ships, tied outboard of each other. To accomplish this we had to cross one or more decks before dumping in the final compartment.

There was always a danger of tripping over any item on a deck, or jostling a seaman who might shove us aside accidentally—or on purpose. I was even more afraid a Japanese guard or sailor would shove me off just for fun. It never happened. We knew extreme caution was needed, or an un-survivable event might occur. This was the most wretched work we ever did, due to the danger, weather, and weight of coal sacks.

Before the commencement of the hostilities between Japan and the United States there were quite a few young American-born Japanese men visiting in Japan on family sojourns. They were American citizens by birth and their loyalties were to America.

As the war began, they were denied passage back to America and were conscripted into the Japanese military forces against their will. In this dictatorship, they soon discovered there was no room for self-determination so to save themselves from execution, they became Japanese soldiers. Since they were not really trusted to be good fighters against Japan's enemies, they were usually assigned to situations of lesser importance. One of these jobs was guarding prisoners on the docks.

Fortunately, we were accosted by several of these young Americans of Japanese heritage. They tried to make our lives easier. They allowed us to drink from the spigot, thus avoiding the filth in the water barrel. They made sure vegetables fell off pallets as they were driven past our area. They would leave behind some article of clothing we could use as they left for the end of their shift. Their goodness was only exceeded by the danger they brought to all of us and to themselves.

I remember two of the boys, brothers, had "American" names: Stuart and Randolph. My mother would never let me talk to them directly. She thought I might be seen and punished—probably whipped. On the docks, whipping was the punishment for any misdemeanors. Anything more serious: the prisoner just disappeared.

I think the last name of the brothers was Oneaga, but that could be wrong. It's been more than half a century ago.

My Nonie grabbed one of the kids behind a stack of pallets one day and read him the riot act. She told him they must stop their acts of kindness. If we were found with a shirt they had left behind for us, we could be killed as thieves. They must stop or we and they would be found out and all of us would be executed.

These young American kids, most raised in California, thought it was a lark to be trying to put one over on their enemy. They had never seen the beheadings we had nor the terrible treatment handed to troops by their officers for simple transgressions. Nonie thanked them profusely but ordered them to stay away from us because of the danger. I remember her telling them,

"I haven't come this far through all of this to have you kids ruin it all. Now stay away from us. If we ever all get home, come to Puget Sound and we'll have a high time, but for now you have to realize this isn't some kind of a fraternity game that's going on here. Just stay back from us." After that, the fellows did.

One day American planes bombed Kobe. The Doolittle Raiders, plane 16, had bombed Kobe docks in May 1942. We were at Baguio then, but we heard about it after we arrived in Kobe. Now our Air Force was back and trying to obliterate the port. Incredible damage was inflicted by fire-bombing, but impact bombs seemed to land almost anywhere, helter-skelter, and many of those merely landed in the bay.

We were elated to see American planes fly over on subsequent trips. We saw bombs fall but knew they were "our" bombs, so they wouldn't hurt us. How silly. I think captivity made us a bit irrational. When bombs did explode close, we rolled ourselves into the smallest ball we could, opened our mouths wide, and screamed as loud as possible! It helped relieve the concussive blasts we felt in our bodies, but we still bled from every body orifice. That type of concussion physically blasts one's body, inside-out. Our eardrums were broken and we didn't even care. We loved the hope welling in our spirits, even if we couldn't hear a sound for days, because these were "our" bombs. They were sent from America! Our country was not so defeated that they couldn't get bombs to rain down on Japanese cities. These bombs meant someone, somewhere, had not forgotten us, after all! Our men might not be here yet, but they were on the way. We just had to get through today.

With shattered eardrums and headaches, we smiled and greeted other POWs with hugs after bombings. We reveled in renewed hope! Soon a stronger presence of Japanese ships was seen in the outer harbor, which proved Allied attacks were working. Ha,ha! Our men are on the way.

The Doolittle raid first, and then the subsequent bombing raids seemed to have a tremendous effect on our enemy. In the anticipation of more Allied attacks, the Japs pulled forces back to defend their home islands. This left fewer forces to fight our men in the South Pacific. In turn, our forces had a bit easier time of it than if they had been faced with the full might of the Japs.

All the while, we heard no news concerning the war in the Pacific. Except for an occasional incoming prisoner's update, we did not know who was winning, or if anyone was. We continued, tired and extremely hungry at all times. We just had to get through this day.

We saw our sky lit at night from fire-bombings in various cities. So many, many more people were killed during those than were killed by the atomic bomb, yet today no one discusses that fact. Tokyo and Osaka glowed red at night. To us it was a first and early sign of hope. We just had to get through today. Our men were on the way.

Bombing raids on Tokyo, Osaka, and Yokohama brought more hope and elation, yet we were quite aware that docks such as the one we lived on remained high on the list of facilities our Army Air Corps targeted. Our Kobe-Osaka area was almost totally devoted to port activities, so it was a piece of luck we did not labor at a major dock.

The wondrous tales of pin-point accurate bombing were, in most cases, fiction. The bomb sights themselves may have been accurate, but between the weather, "flak," and plane movement, few targets of any importance were hit. The Air Corps did a good job on things like fire-bombings, demolishing railroad yards and bridges, however. Targets could be decimated at low levels, yes, but from 10,000 feet bombs could miss targets and hit miles away. *Effective* results were achieved by fire-bombs!

A majority of industrial corporations were unscathed, and successful munitions industries were a strangely operated enterprise. We had English-speaking guards who bragged to us about how all Japanese people worked together toward victory, whereas "Yankees," the derisive name they called us most often, were lazy and sat reading Hollywood movie magazines at home while they should be helping their government. We were certainly in no condition or circumstance to argue that point.

The Japanese explained their munitions industry was largely home-bound, which I found quite interesting. As long as there continued to be an adequate supply of brass casings, gunpowder, fuses and primers, the munitions industry rolled along unceasing, due to one fact: The Japanese government had odd-jobbed out all of the manufactory. Hundreds of tiny backyard factories constituted the major part of the armament industry. One factory made fuses in one place, while primers were in another. Gunpowder people loaded shells, others added primers or fuses as the case warranted; then another group finished the munition. This system allowed continuous production.

If one building of powder-loaders was bombed, another was ready to supply from a different neighborhood location. This plan was supremely efficient and seemed to work well for the Japanese, as long as they were provided the essentials to carry out each task. However, later in the war, all supplies began to dwindle, until the distribution trickled to a halt.

I'd have advised more fire-bombings, an effort that accomplished much. It is how American attacks hurt munitions makers more than any other way. Tools crucial for war could be destroyed while they were still in the assembly process in back rooms and shacks of family homes. The rickety structures of that time turned to ash during firestorms from bombings. We truly needed more fire-bombings.

As long as one has the slightest *hope*, there is a better chance of surviving. When hope is lost, a number of things happen. Depression intrudes on an already despairing mind. General health suffers beyond any current debilitation. Relationships feel meaningless. Food becomes unimportant and is refused. *Hope is the one constant* that allows the spirit and body to retain a semblance of humanity.

When major continuing aerial attacks began, it was our first indicator the war might be turning in our favor. The bombings brought our first rays of encouragement, our first inklings of survival. We tied all our dreams for the future on those bombings.

I have wondered how my mother retained her sanity during this time. So many other POWs caved in with depression, became physically lethargic, fearful, lonely. They considered themselves absolutely abandoned. I believe she felt a deep, natural responsibility to care for her child. I was constantly fearful something would happen to her. If anything might impair Nonie's ability to deal with our life situation, what would happen to me? I think she held out, day-by-day, in our surreal world of misery, until acceptance of our situation co-mingled with her spirit.

It was as though she thought to herself,

OK.... Now then..... Here's the situation. This is all I have, so I won't expect any more. I won't fret. I'll simply mark time until our situation changes. I will endure!

The strength of Nonie's entire character was reinforced during this time, and she became the person she imagined she could become, right in front of my eyes.

I also believe, without me, she might have softly succumbed to all the similar conditions others displayed. She was such a sweet, gentle soul, and these were unimaginable circumstances. I don't think she could survive without the necessity of putting her child first. In a way then, it may be that having me around as an irritant to despair actually saved my mother's life. The constant irritation gave her "the grit" she looked for to forge ahead. I believe I became her motive to endure, but whatever her thoughts were at the time, I recognize my mother gave me the gift of life—a second time.

Up to this time, we obsessed over a myriad of questions for which there were no answers: *Was Japan winning this war? They must be, or why were we still captives? Had Germany invaded England? Were the Japanese in Tacoma? Had they fought battles in Canada, too? Was McChord Field still there? The Narrows Bridge had fallen down long before we left home; had another one been built to unite the Bremerton Navy Base with Ft. Lewis and McChord, as had always been planned? What about our big extended family? Had anyone joined the military? Were our older family members alive? Did anyone know we were alive?*

The last news they heard was perhaps from Aunt Alice when she left us in December 1941. This assumed she had survived the submarine journey. Maybe Old Swede sent information that he had recognized us in our first POW camp in 1943.

Then one day I had a terrible thought: *Is it possible we won't ever make it home? Will I be a grown-up by then? If it takes a long time before the war ends, will our family have died by then?*

227

That means there won't be anyone left who remembers us. If we get home, what will happen to us then if they're all gone? I didn't tell My Nonie what I had been thinking about. It was bad enough for one of us to worry.

If anyone in our family found out the slave work we had done to survive, would they accept us or send us away? Would we be treated as criminals when we got home, for living with Japs? Could anyone understand we were never given a choice? Would they be able to understand "slavery"?

What had happened to our new Papa? He was Navy, so was he alive? On a ship?

Where were the battles? Did the Japs capture Hawaii like they did the Philippines? If Japan doesn't win the war and America wins, how will we get home? Would the U.S. government honor the Japanese promise to set us free? Or would they say, "Oh, too bad, that was your agreement with the Japs. We don't know you. You don't even have a passport. Anyway, you're bad for what you did so you can just stay there." Would they leave us there forever?

Does our main house still stand? Does Gram still have a vegetable garden? Do they still raise chickens for Sunday dinner? Do they have enough food? Do they eat macaroni and cheese on Friday nights, and meatloaf with scalloped potatoes when it storms outside? Do they make chocolate cake? Does the house smell like my Grandpa's pipe tobacco? Do they still make bacon and eggs on Sunday morning so the aroma in the kitchen lasts until afternoon?

Does everyone sit around the table and trade sections of the Sunday papers? Does my grandfather still shout at H.V. Kaltenborn and Gabriel Heatter on the radio commentary news program? Does my grandmother still grow a large sweet-pea patch in the spring? Does she still plant it on Washington's birthday? Does she still dry the flowers and put them between stacks of pillowcases in the closet? Is Freckles, my bulldog, still alive? I missed him so much. He was my constant companion from infancy. Day and night we loved each other.

My Nonie and I focused a lot on family relationships. However, by far the greatest obsession we had was *food!* At times we wept at the memory of a favorite comfort meal. Allowing ourselves to obsess on something important from our past made life seem real again. Without it we could have dwelt on our fears, fantasized the worst, and slid into a slimy pit of depression, which we *adamantly refused* to do!

Our fears were baseless in a few areas, but an extreme reality in most concerns: fear of falling off the slick gangplank; fear of disease without medications; fear of being disowned by family; fear of causing worry to family, to the point of their death; fear my new Papa might die in this war; fear we might never go home; fear the Japanese lied about a prisoner exchange.

Bomb raids on the docks gave us hope—the first time we had *any* hope. Yet we knew "we only had to get through that day." We were nutty with exuberance when our area was attacked. People shouted,

"Over here! Over here! Give 'em a good one!"

Someone remembered us! Our bodies hummed with hope! Perhaps it was only a short time until freedom.

One snowy day, as I shoveled coal into the carry sacks, I saw a sailor from a foreign ship watch my mother as she carried her coal sacks. I didn't know what country he came from. *Maybe he is a spy from a Soviet ship*, I thought, since they were neutral to Japan at that time.

When she returned to my loading pit, I told her, so she waved to him. He smiled and waved back. Several times over the next few days we saw him watching her again from his ship which was moored as the second one out from our dock.

One day he stood behind a large crate and pantomimed to her that she should come to his ship at night, swimming through the water. My Nonie was not much of a swimmer. She barely did a sidestroke learned in college, but she could stay afloat.

The whole idea was replete with danger. *If* Nonie could swim that much, as she hadn't been swimming for years that I knew of; *if* she didn't succumb to the icy water; *if* she wasn't discovered by a guard; *if* she didn't swallow any of that filthy bay water in her system. No, no, how foolish this idea was and I was thinking,

Sure. You and the horse you rode in on, buddy. In this filthy cold water? In this weather? Pooh!

However, that evening Nonie told me she did plan to make this swim, and she had a good hunch about doing it. Then, even as I remembered she was born under a caul and likely had second-sight, I still begged her not to go. If caught, she would certainly be executed as an escaping prisoner. Then I thought, *How do they think she could escape from Japan? Swim all the way to Hawaii?* It had been impressed on us strongly never to attempt escape. We had seen the one prisoner shot for just being in the water.

Late that night, nude, shivering with cold, she climbed down the ladder onto a lower dock, where we were forbidden to go at any time. The water was so cold, she gasped and caught her breath as she slipped into it. In the somber, murky water, she swam out of my sight. We were in near complete darkness in our blackout area. Ever so silently, she slid around the nearest ship and was lost in the reflections on distant ripples. This frigid, blustery night, I was afraid My Nonie might succumb to the temperature and drown from exposure. *What if this man planned a trick? What if he raised an alarm and she was discovered? What would I do without her?* Still, I was so scared for her.

Then to my complete surprise, in just minutes before much time had passed at all, I heard soft splashing and My Nonie came back into sight from the other ship about a 100-foot swim from our dock ladders. Freezing and absolutely exhausted, she lifted a large package up to me, wrapped in oilcloth, tied with twine. After we got back to our warehouse—no warmer, but out of the wind—we crawled under our coverings and hugged until she was warm enough to move.

Opening the package later, we found two pair of men's wool socks, two men's wool shirts, a sleeveless pullover sweater, fishing line and hooks. Multiple layers of used newspapers wrapped portions of tea, uncooked rice, fish paste, meat paste, dried fish, and a large package of uncooked noodles. We immediately dressed Nonie in the warm woolen shirt and pullover sweater and one pair of the socks. I put on the other shirt and pair of socks and my skinny little body felt such happiness and joy as we both began to warm considerably. I chafed her legs and feet and hands with my hands until she began to warm a little bit. We were so happy with our new gifts. What could have ever possessed that man to have such compassion?

We were able to cover our new gifts with our old rags. No one ever accosted us about the clothing. Apparently we had pulled it off. We blessed the heart of that sailor from some foreign shore and wanted to at least nod our thanks and acknowledgement to him, but in the morning when we went on to the dock his ship was gone. We never saw him again.

We put the newspapers to immediate use as linings inside our pitiful clothing. Our old newspapers had been stolen while we slept one time during the warm summer weather. If we didn't wear things, we had no way of securing them against theft.

Eventually we felt warmer if we remained out of the wind. Our gratitude to this stranger was immeasurable. He could have been setting a trap. Almost immediately, someone stole our wool shirts and sweater. We were afraid we would be found out but there were no repercussions. Most other prisoners were as pitifully clothed as we were so we could barely find fault with them for the theft.

We did have a hearty laugh later. What I thought our secret pal had included as fish bait was in fact Russian caviar, meant for our nourishment. However, in the following days, what caviar bits we could not get to stick on a hook as bait fell into Kobe Bay. I don't remember if we ever caught anything! I still believe fish eggs are fish eggs, and therefore, they are bait! My mother never ate caviar, nor do I. The thought of it brings working the docks back to vivid memory.

Working on the docks was such hard work. It would have been hard work for a healthy man to do but we were so starved and I was so sick with that terrible chronic bronchitis all the time. We tried everything we could think of to make our lives easier and even healthier. I think we succeeded as witnessed by our survival. However, I am sure if we had remained on the docks in Kobe for very much longer, one or both of us would have succumbed to the effects of illness and malnutrition.

CHAPTER 21
A LONG ROAD HOME

Perhaps the self-same song of Ruth, when, sick for home,
she stood in tears amid the alien corn; the same...charmed
magic casements, opening on the foam
Of perilous seas in faery lands forlorn
——John Keats

One very rainy day, when the rain mixed with the coal dust and stuck to us like library paste, an officer and some enlisted men came for my mother. I immediately ran to her so as not to be separated. We were told to gather our belongings. We were to be moved. Befuddled, My Nonie and I barely grabbed our precious newspapers, our fishing hooks and lines, and our wool socks, before we had to run along behind their car. Most everything else was already in layers on our bodies because we worked in perpetual cold. The wind blew at us right out of the north Pacific Ocean. It was enough to make your throat ache and burn raw if you breathed in directly without turning your head away from the wind.

The dockyard guards drove slowly, then turned in at another dock area. Shortly after, we caught up. We could hardly believe our eyes as we rounded a very large warehouse. There in the water, in all her glory, sat a beautiful ocean liner. Apparently she had docked during the night since we had not seen her or even heard a rumor that a foreign ship had arrived. We

233

were not working nights any longer as we had established a self-policing system of prisoner seniority. Late-comers to our go-down worked nights while we slept out of the cold.

This beautiful ship was marked Drottningholm/ Sverge (Sweden) and Repatriation in big letters on each side, as we found out later. She was stark white and had black letters and flew a blue and yellow Swedish flag with the Rising Sun flag at her stern, as is proper when visiting a foreign port. She brought to mind the pictures of liners in story books. She was gorgeous.

The guards and officer stepped out of the sedan we had followed and motioned us to follow several hundred feet along the dock, toward a single gangway. We were accustomed to the anchoring, tying-up and sailing routines of ships. It was apparent this beautiful, immaculately clean ship was about to leave port. Short lines were still attached, but shore power and freshwater lines were disengaged. Only the one gangway was still attached to the dock. Though obviously an older ocean liner, she looked in wonderfully seaworthy shape.

I wondered, *Is this dock a new place to work? Would we be loading on this ship?* Holding out to the last minute, we were afraid to even *think* this ship might be "our" ship to take us home. I was scalded with the sudden flooding of memories of home. For a long time I had tried not to think of home. It was too sweet in memory.

As the guards prodded us with bayonets, we clutched our insulating newspapers ever tighter. In our haste, and because I had been carrying coal sacks barefoot, I had left without my geta. I often went barefoot even in the coldest weather to assure better footing on planks between dock and ships. My Nonie wore her geta and tabis, and she stumbled as she tried to approach the end of this beautiful ship's gangway.

A blond sailor at the foot of the gangway stepped forward and grabbed her arm to help keep her footing, but she was startled and squealed in fright. He froze in place and looked up the gangway for direction from his officer. An order was given, then the sailor said to Nonie, "Gut flicka. Gut flicka, OK?" We understood, since my Swedish Uncle Carl had taught us simple phrases. "Good girl, good girl. OK?"

Yes, very OK. We were so excited. These events were more than we could comprehend. Yet we were struck mute with fear! Our first fear was these *were* our rescuers, and we would be found lacking in some way. They could turn us away at the last minute! We looked at each other. Who would want to help anyone who looked as wretched as we did? Second, at this final minute of succor, might the tormenting Japanese cruelly say it was a big joke and not release us after all? Third, our thoughts were crammed with apprehension and anxiety. *What if there was a test we had to pass to be allowed on board? What if we needed passports?* My Nonie had last seen hers in the Philippines, and I never had one. As far as anyone knew, I was listed only as: "accompanied by female child"; no name; no birthday. Just an added line on Nonie's passport. This could be our undoing. *Maybe they'd make My Nonie go and I'd have to stay behind.*

Lord, please help us! Don't leave us here. Please God. If they can only take one of us, let them take Nonie. She can't last much longer. I'm littler. I don't need so much to survive. I've tried to accept what you said about not thinking I was more "special" than any other little girl. Please, God. I know you can hear me pray. You told me You were always with me when I was in the tin mine. Please, God. Help us. I'm so afraid all the time. I'm so cold. Please, God, be here with us now.

Two sailors gently pried our pitiful belongings from us: our reel of fishing line and hooks, folded carefully in crumpled newsprint; our extra insulating newspapers; and our three wool socks—one had unaccountably become lost. We thought a rat might have carried it off in the night while we slept.

We always took turns wearing two socks on our feet and one with both hands tucked inside, like a muff. Sleep often came more easily when our hands and feet warmed. Whoever warmed first acted as a radiator for the other. We needed our newspapers and socks as cold-weather survival gear, so we made it clear we didn't want them to hold our "valuables."

With big smiles, the sailors gently turned us to face the ship and whispered, "God bless America. OK?" We nodded our assent, then slowly, almost as though hypnotized, we followed them up the steep, cleated gangway. The tide was very high and the ship was sailing light as though she needed to be refueled. The sailors walked backwards, ahead of us, holding onto our possessions like carrots in front of balky mules. When I stepped onto the deck, I felt the ship's engines running under my bare feet.

Two blond, husky male nurses appeared and began to usher us down a passageway. Suddenly, My Nonie stopped, turned to the officer on deck, apparently the person in charge, and said, "Thank you for coming for us. Thank you so much. You've saved our lives. Thank you."

I remembered a little phrase and thanked him in Swedish, "Tack så mycket." I could barely get out the words I was so overcome with gratefulness.

He folded his hands together in the universal sign of prayer and peace and he replied, "Var så god," (You're welcome), with tears in his eyes—it must have been the wind.

We followed the nurses down many passageways. It was so warm! *I hadn't been this warm since last summer.* Apparently, we were the final travelers to board since the ship was now moving away from the dock with loud horns blaring and bells signaling.

Later we learned nearly two hundred other wretched souls like us had also been taken aboard, first at Osaka, then at Kobe. Most were severely wounded soldiers, plus a few repatriating families out of China, missionaries or teachers, who had also been swept up as the fighting overran their areas. Yet My Nonie and I were the only single females.

There was an established hierarchy for repatriation. It appeared that My Nonie and I, and others like us, were at the top of the list of people repatriating. The categories went something like this: First were people specially nominated by the State Department. None of this category was present on the *Drottningholm.* Secondly, and here we fit the category, were unaccompanied women and women with children, then seriously ill men, then men over sixty-five and so on.

We always wondered what had happened to the teachers we had met on the China Clipper. They had our postwar family address but even years later we never heard from them. Perhaps they were among the multitude of people in China, only wanting to do good for others, who were slaughtered by the fiends.

We met a child, a Caucasian boy about ten years old, who had been raised by his Chinese amah and spoke absolutely no English. His parents had wisely tried to camouflage his nationality when he was tiny to protect him. He had been hidden away with Chinese children in their settlement and had gone unnoticed by visiting Japanese.

He professed, in Mandarin, to be quite baffled to leave his Chinese home, the only one he had ever known. The four of them were on the way to Cincinnati, Ohio, to their missionary headquarters. Luckily, they were able to have their amah accompany them. Little did the boy know how happy he would be, later in his life, to have been rescued. I practiced his English with him all the time, every day, all the way to Australia.

The nurses took us to a cabin that had tightly made-up snow white bunks—two of them! We stood in horror at our predicament. We dared not step into the room or even touch the doorway. We were filthy! Fearful thoughts came fast: *We will surely be punished if we get anything dirty. We might even be turned back to the docks. Maybe we might be accepted if we told them we could clean the floor if we made any mess or got anything dirty.* These concerns were unfounded. They were well prepared for us.

Nurses, wearing rubber gloves and surgical gowns, brought large sheets of paper for us to stand on as we undressed. Soon we were divested of our rags and guided into warm showers. Our hair was washed and cut to the scalp for us, then our heads were shaved; we were deloused and given medicine to de-worm us. All our filthy, old possessions were rolled up in the papers to be burned. For just a moment I felt a pang at the loss of our newspapers and wool socks. We had guarded them so carefully.

I had forgotten the psychological comfort one can get from a warm steamy shower. It had been four year since either of us had a bath or shower. The soap was a plain white bar of castile soap. It was a true luxury. It had been so long since we had been clean and warm and away from soldiers with bayonets pointed at us that we quickly became stuporous from lack of sleep and from the warmth we felt.

Grateful, we relaxed for the moment, in thick, warm bath-robes, then slept. *I had a hot water bottle in my bed.* The luxury of it! The nurses understood when we had to be encouraged to sleep separately in single beds. They told us that it wasn't unusual for mothers and children. For far too long sleeping stuck-together was one of the ways we assured each other of a maintained presence. While we slept, our habit had been to interlock our arms at the elbows so neither of us could be spirited away.

As I slowly slid into slumber, I thought of My Nonie's mantra: *"We only have to get through this day"*—which flowed into months and turned into years. Yet we had done it! We had made it through to the day of rescue, as my precious mother had always promised. And it was true. They *had* come for us! As I dropped off to sleep, I thought I heard My Nonie softly crying tears of relief and gratefulness. I was too.

When we were well enough to come out of our stateroom, we began to meet other refugees in the passageways. We kept to ourselves, not knowing how we would be received. Most of them seemed a garrulous bunch always playing cards or trying to dance to a Victrola in the dining hall. Most of them were Americans. They seemed like foreigners to us. They had normal clothes they had brought with them and they weren't cadaverous looking like we were. We were badly out of touch and we rejected their friendly overtures.

One woman, the wife of a missionary, asked us to join them at their Sunday worship service in the dining room. Lord, Lord, forgive us. We coldly declined to participate. The remembrance of those hooligan preachers in the camps was still with us. After that time, they left us alone. I'm sure they thought we were the deepest heathens. Maybe we were.

Surely, there must be a special magic in a person who can make any dream come true under those incredible conditions. My Nonie was wonderfully special. She and her sister, Betty, had been born under the caul as had I, and as my daughter Jeannie was, many years later. Old Scottish witches swore this gave an adult special qualities to foretell futures, read omens, and have extraordinary good luck. These are ideas barely recalled in this day and age and even then regarded only as folk history. What do you think? Perhaps the old ways work only if you believe in them. There's been far more than coincidence there in my life when I think about my extraordinary good luck.

We had long and often dreamed about "freedom food." Comfort food, like macaroni and cheese, pot roast with potatoes and carrots, meat loaf, fried chicken, apple pie, trifle, chocolate cake, all food enjoyed when one lived in freedom. Green beans. Milk in a glass.

We were disappointed to have a restricted diet of clear broths and gelatin for several days. Out of kindness and wisdom, our liberators said our stomachs probably could not handle anything else, but after the abominable substances we *had* survived on, who knows. It's also possible that after ingesting the poison to kill the worms we had, that any substantial food would have made us very sick. At any rate, for a few days we ate fruit gelatin, ice cream, and clear soups. To us, it certainly was far from a hardship diet. We didn't complain. I still had a hard time not leaping out of bed in the morning to forage on the dock for fire to cook our little bit of rice, but the movement of the ship and the vibration from the engines quickly brought me to my senses each day.

Before too long we were sauntering around in our bathrobes, being gently teased by crew members. They laughed and remarked how we seemed to eat everything that didn't move and was small enough to fit in our mouths. The ship's cooks were marvelous; they prepared selections we had long forgotten. They cooked four full meals a day: breakfast at 6:00 a.m., lunch at 11:00 a.m., dinner at 5:00 p.m., and supper at 9:00 p.m. In between, juices were provided to each passenger: orange, tomato, and apple. When Nonie took her first sip of tomato juice, she gave a long sigh and smiled like she had in the old days. I dunked buttered toast into my tomato juice and thought it must be manna.

The bakers worked around the clock it seemed. There was a continual offering of pastries, tiny tarts, cookies, even fatigman after I asked once if they had any, since it was a Swedish ship, after all. We had small potato dumplings introduced into our clear broths, then lefsa and fatigman came to the table, then finally all dietary restrictions were lifted and we ate what everyone else had.

These cooks were gracious in so many ways. Pork chops greeted us one morning at breakfast. I'll always remember my confusion over what they were. I had actually forgotten; I sat and stared in wonder. Thinking I did not like pork chops, one cook in a tall, white, pleated hat came from the galley. He told me if I didn't like any particular item, I was to let him know and he would make me some food I did like. Good grief! I must have fallen in love with each member of that crew—forty times a day! What a treat to have someone cater to my needs.

241

CHILD POW

For many years after our return, my mother sent and received Christmas cards from a few of that crew. And I do love pork chops. I eat them today, and each time, I remember the loving words of that cook with a tall, white hat. Bless his heart. His hair was nearly orange-red, and he showed a grateful 11-year-old where he had carved his initials into the ship's railing in secret—I never told on him.

When we were eventually, officially, released from bed rest, we each received two bright sweaters, a short-sleeved pullover, a long-sleeve cardigan, and a pleated, heavy cotton twill skirt. My sweaters were pale blue and navy. My Nonie had rose and chocolate brown. Our skirts were both navy blue. We were also given clogs to wear. These were leather on top, with inch-thick wooden soles. Their foot-beds were carved into the soles, which made them very comfortable, although quite noisy when we walked until we got on to it. When we went on deck we wore our ship's bathrobes for coats. Outer wear was something we'd have to wait for. What we had was more than we'd worn in years so we were very appreciative.

We handled our various new undergarments with great tenderness, afraid our rough hands might snag their soft knit. Nonie was given a beautiful slip made entirely of heavy cream lace. The lace was re-embroidered so thick and it was so heavy it was like a lined dress that could almost stand by itself. She kept that wonderful creation for many years. It was more than a souvenir. It was like a hall pass that allowed her to go to a different place freely.

I still often give a silent blessing for the unknown individual (a man, a woman?) who chose that slip for a freed prisoner. It made my mother extremely happy; it was restorative. My Nonie had always loved and worn beautiful undergarments. This gift was both the first step in allowing her to resume her persona and a sign to her that she was accepted "back in the world"—she had finally sailed away from Hell. Years later, when I noticed it was gone, I never asked her what happened to it.

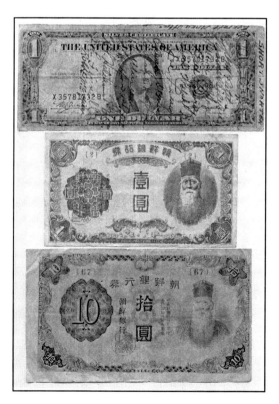

Three pieces of signed currency called Short Snorters: An "I Was There" momento of WWII.

243

On our trip home, a number of soldiers had fun signing and passing around paper currency, which they called a "short-snorter." I'm told this practice originated early in the war when American servicemen, primarily aviators, crossed the Atlantic. Ferry pilots who delivered planes to England made many round-trips. They devised the exchange of signed money as an interesting way to brag about how many trips they had made, getting an ink signature on a bill as documentation. The fellow with the most signatures won and others bought his drinks as the prize. Then they'd all sign each others' "short-snorter" and on it went. Many people had numerous bills. Some men taped them end-to-end, and the longest naturally won.

Soldiers on our ship also used Chinese money for their currency across the Pacific. In the midst of war it was a way to say, "Yeah, buddy. I was there too!" After WWII I met veterans who collected these as souvenirs, which I considered better than matchbooks or cocktail napkins. I'm proud to own three as keepsakes.

One morning while underway I went to the rear deck to watch a sunrise. It had been years since we had felt or smelled such an expanse of fresh, free air, nor had we moved about, independent of each other. My senses were intoxicated!

Sailors speak of a phenomenon in which one who stares into the moving sea from a deck can experience a self-hypnosis, which causes them to suddenly leap over the railing to their death. Sailors on sailing ships in days gone by said it was the Siren of the sea calling them home.

I certainly had no such urge, but the captain, also an early riser, appeared by my side quietly and put an arm around my shoulder. He smiled and wished me good morning. As the sun rose he said, "Morgenstunn har gul i mun."

He explained it can have numerous translations including "morning has gold in its mouth" meaning "The sun will shine on you and bring you good fortune." I snuggled deeper under his arm and realized this was the first time in four years in which I had been touched by an adult man in a caring way. He was also the first Caucasian man who had shown me affection since our long imprisonment began. I felt I had just been given a gift. My emotional world improved a thousand-fold, and I have carried the memory of his blessing with me every day since then.

Some years after the war, I visited Heidi, a childhood friend. On the wall of her Norwegian grandmother's kitchen was a simple embroidery of a house, several trees, a path and a sun shining brightly. Beneath this quite primitively drawn colorful embroidered work was the embroidered motto, "Morgenstunn har gul i munn."

Isn't it just such a small world?

During the preceding four years, we had gone from living comfortably in the heart of a loving family to desperate fear and hopelessness, to horror, to hopefulness, and now we headed home. I wondered what adventures were ahead, though it didn't really matter. As long as we were together, My Nonie and I could handle anything! After all, if our return to America did not come to fruition for any reason, "we only had to get through today."

From nearly the moment we embarked onto the ship, we asked about notifying our family that we were not only alive but returning home! Access to cable or radiotelephone was under severe restriction to most people on board and totally denied to all of us freed POWs. We imagined it was due to radio traffic being restricted to military only, or to those who held government priorities.

CHILD POW

What we did not understand at the time was that this denial was on orders of our American government to protect *future Japanese* relations. No consideration was given to freed POWs, and it would not be the last time any of us were disregarded in this way in deference to monsters who had tortured and harmed us for years. My heart still aches with pain at this betrayal committed by my own government.

As for being a General, well, at the age of four with paper hats and wooden swords we're all Generals. Only some of us never grow out of it.
——Peter Ustinov

A strange historical footnote was about to occur, which affected us deeply. After all we had lived through, we were coming home to a country that, with nearly Pentecostal fervor, had fallen under the sway of General Douglas MacArthur. The general who held immense personal property in the Philippines, strangely, was about to install himself as the American pseudo-emperor of post-war Japan. He was a Medal of Honor winner, the son of a Medal of Honor winner and a man who epitomized everything America yearned for during the war years. He was a strong military leader yet he was both revered and openly disliked by those who served under him and with him. He was a man who could speak directly to the hearts of the common man yet, reportedly, was an inveterate snob in his personal dealings with others. He was an enigma and was now about to become in charge of dealing with the gravest enemy America had ever fought.

Our nation's people who had sacrificed so much for the war effort, including their best and brightest sons, were now told the bad Japanese warlords would indeed be punished, but we must be all-forgiving of the rest of them. They were "religious, clean, friendly, industrious people" who needed us to restore their country because we had destroyed what they used to have.

Why should we? They started it; we won! That's the natural process of things.

We didn't restore the property or fortunes of American *citizens* of Japanese ancestry *whom we had imprisoned* so grievously. Why should we protect anything on the Japanese mainland? As a first-hand witness to what these people did, it remains my opinion the entire Japanese archipelago should have been nuclear-bombed back to the Stone Age. In attitude and social behaviors, they are barely beyond that now anyway.

Barely a few months after the war ended, Professor Benzuo Koro, Professor Yuichiro Nambu, and Professor Kika Kigoshi, a student of Nambu, were all brought to the United States in 1946. They had worked on the Japanese atomic bomb before and during WWII. They settled in as immigrating physicists at the University of Arkansas in 1949.

These Jap scientists were under the protection of our government as were physicist Werner Von Braun and others from Germany. This was all kept very quiet, although there are archival drawings that support the knowledge of Professor Koroda's atomic research. Incidentally, the Japs were not close to having a functional bomb as they had no plutonium necessary for the exploder.

Why are things like this kept quiet? Unless there is something dishonorable and cagey about the action, the information should be open and discussed. Why create secrets where none need be?

Only a fool would think the Japanese would have held back from using the A-bomb if they had it first. All of this nonsense about the poor Japanese people this and the poor Japanese people that is just a media-taught form of national liberal political guilt because we were lucky enough to develop the bomb before they did. Believe me, there would be no recriminations and no one in Japan would chastise their government if they had dropped the bomb first. It's the way of wars. People win and people lose. They lost. We won. Let it be.

MacArthur saved many Japanese from prosecution who should have been hanged, and this folly will always remain precisely that to me, a folly. I was there during the blackest days. He was not. I know what occurred. He knew the sanitized version of what he had been told.

For all his grand "speechifying," he did not have the right to talk for me or my mother. He did not have the right to speak on behalf of anyone who was there without their permission. Because of his actions at that time, adults who survived the torturous Jap imprisonment were denied the right to speak out about it later, by being forced to sign confidentiality documents. Whose Bill of Rights is it anyway? Ours or the Japanese? No one asked *me* to sign anything because I was child at the time we came home. Adult crimes were committed against me and I will continue to talk about those crimes until my dying day. I will never forget. And I will never shut up.

I had the actual life's blood of innocent soldiers splashed onto my feet. MacArthur did not. The Japanese commander who relished fresh blood from beheaded POW soldiers to water his flowers was designated the American head of an immense Jap electronic corporation, which MacArthur helped establish. Why was this maniac, former torturer even allowed into our country? He should have been hung as a war criminal! But no, we could not do that. We needed these villains who knew how to run their new country that we were building for them. Somehow our economy depended on it. Indeed? Tell it to the Marines... the ones who didn't come back. If you dare.

The next two paragraphs are totally unrelated to each other. I just have some questions that I can't seem to find the answers for.

One question occurs to me, over and over: After his retirement from the Army in 1951, MacArthur and his family lived for many years in a tower penthouse of the Waldorf-Astoria Hotel in New York. At that time, the Waldorf was one of the four greatest hotels in the world. Where did he get the money to afford this? His Army pension certainly wasn't enough. Was he the recipient of a charity established for that purpose? Did his family have money? Where did they get their money? I have my own ideas, but one isn't regarded as quite "all there" when attacking a demi-god, so I rarely bring it up.

Secondly, and unrelated to the first one, my question is: What happened to all the Philippine gold bullion? I've heard no one ever found it. I've even heard the U.S. submarine *Wahoo* transported a great quantity. General Yamashita, the Tiger of Malaya, got blamed for its loss, but he's not likely responsible. He was merely handy at the time, then he was hastily hung. You can't ask a man a question after he is dead, can you? It is interesting that the *Wahoo* was reported to have had a hand in transporting gold but the *Wahoo* was lost on patrol. She was discovered and identified in 2006 in Japanese waters north of Hokkaido and south of the Kurile Islands. Yet I still have never heard the gold discussed. Everyone somehow keeps disappearing or dying. Oh, well.

Our government fed the media the idea we must somehow create a new Japan, one more modern than it was before WWII, for future trade relations. Does this make any sense? Not to me. For just one example: I have been told incessantly our economy gained advantages by funding Japan's total industrial rehabilitation. *If so, why is it most of the cars sold in this country are not made here, but in Japan, and thousands of our auto workers are now unemployed?* If this helps our economy will someone please tell me how it does? It sounds very much like the children's story of the Emperor's New Clothes in which a lie, if told often enough, is finally supposed to be believable. It's not!

I guess, in my darkest moments, I do realize any country that loses a war to America is lucky. However, we still should punish the miscreants.

Japanese interests have bought out and shipped to Japan complete steel works and foundries for reassembly. Isaakson in Seattle is one example. They have purchased our banks and real estate, and bought many of the holding companies of our Northwest wood products corporations. They log here, ship the timbers to Japan, then sell finished wood products back to America at a much increased price. They buy our sports teams, computer industries, public utilities, and vast mining enterprises.

Look what they did to Kennecott Copper: Closed it down. Mines, mills and smelters all gone. Many large corporations bought by the Japanese put American employees out of work, even to canceling retirements. Japan could not beat us in a shooting war but watch out for our economy. They'll try it another way.

Recall how they always plan many years in advance. Remember the march into Manchuria was in 1931. Pearl Harbor wasn't until 1941. Now after 60-plus years the Japanese will attempt to win an economic war with the us. If they succeed, rest assured, we will be a sorry nation. There is such a thing as retribution.

The modern day Japanese Self-Defense Force (SDF) has a nuclear *powered* submarine force. They deny they have nuclear weapons. Okay. Just so you know. Make up your own mind. It makes me very, very nervous. These are not trustworthy people. They are people led by a current Prime Minister who blatantly denies that prisoners of war were ever forced into slavery or prostitution by their captors. He advises us that what women were in "comfort camps" were there by choice and were well paid for the privilege of working there. How can these people be trusted? Good grief!

Our country's altruism and kindness baffles me sometimes. Japan saw our goodness as passive naivety and weakness so in 1941 they attacked. Will they presume, once again, we are soft? I think they will.

CHAPTER 22

THANKS,
DOWN UNDER!

And he sang as he sat and waited till his billy boiled,
'You'll come a-waltzing, Matilda, with me.'
—Andrew Paterson

We began our long trip home. First we traveled to Australia for medical triage. They had begun a form of socialized medicine, which was eventually adopted by the entire Commonwealth. They created a system similar to our present HMOs. The idea was to staff a large hospital/clinic complex with nearly every kind of medical personnel one might need: dentists, orthopedists, dermatologists, neurologists, psychiatrists and psychologists, cardiologists, ophthalmologists, and every specialty available.

In Australia we were assessed. A tag was tied to us with a list of problems which needed professional, medical attention. We'd be treated and released by each participating specialist, and our tag was marked-off. It was quite well-planned and totally efficient, but there was no feeling of a medical "mill." Each practitioner had a smile, loving hands and heart. We were treated wonderfully.

One who stands out in memory was a pediatrician who assessed me. This gentle soul was exceptional and compassionate, but it took all his courage to complete the examination. He was flabbergasted by my scars, unhealed wounds, torn skin, and violated tissues. After a while, I saw on his face the look of horror I had seen on some of the soldiers My Nonie had nursed. The look that showed an inability for the brain to acknowledge what the eye has seen.

I couldn't do this to him any longer and I asked him to check off my tag. I told the doctor I didn't want to continue my examination; I dressed and left the room. Almost immediately, I realized I had left our possessions sack, so I quickly returned and opened the door.

The doctor, bless him, stood beside the exam table, head bent, with hands folded and such a grim look of sadness I couldn't disturb him, so I took my sack and tiptoed out, silently. Bless his heart. He had seen the results of unchecked evil.

Bravo, bravo, many times over to the Australians for being warm, generous hosts and healers. They did their best for us in every way. Their lightness of spirit and quick, happy teasing and their laughter was contagious. Eventually, former POWs smiled at each other. Smiles had been in short supply for so long. We were taught—by paranoid beasts who had controlled us—smiling was an affront. They thought we made fun of them, personally.

At the start of our incarceration, a smile was regularly punished by a violent "reminder," so we quickly learned to keep a poker face or pay a painful price. In freedom it was hard for us to learn to live and act without fear of violence on a daily basis. Here we were, well-trained to expect atrocious punishment for a mere smile, and now we were asked to show our pleasure. Although they realized re-training takes time, our kind helpers often asked with genuine concern why it was we didn't smile.

We civilians, according to our gender, each received a good-sized box of personal items like facial moisturizer, popular Dr. Lyon's tooth powder, toothbrushes, brushless shaving soap, a bar of Pears soap, and deodorant, which was especially welcomed. Now that we ate real food—in quantity—former prisoners began to perspire again. We weren't given shampoo since, on our arrival at the ship, our heads were shaved to get rid of lice.

Adult ladies also received simple make-up items like Tangee lipsticks that changed color on each person, several safety pins, a tiny bottle of inexpensive cologne, and even some gold-tone earrings. Later, we learned elastic was gone for the duration so the small safety pins were to attach a sanitary napkin in underpants. Women would surely begin to menstruate again as their bodies changed from a state of starvation and became more well nourished.

My Nonie's cologne smelled of roses and jasmine. For years after our imprisonment, she almost always wore Caron's Bellodgia, which reminded us both of the first little bottle on the ship. It certainly wasn't a designer fragrance by any means, but it may have been a distant, fragrant cousin and in any event, it was actually the thought that counted.

Men received a harmonica and Vitalis hair dressing, which smelled of bay rum and a comb, but until their hair grew they did not need it, though again, the thought was nice. We all needed to learn how to live normally again, and they taught us by awakening our senses to pleasant odors and normal activities. The men were given backgammon sets and cribbage boards and the ladies received decks of cards and American movie magazines.

Children received very special, small boxes of appropriate items. Since the war had not yet ended, it should be noted this wonderful collection of people who had fought hard to barely survive in Australia had—in the midst of their own chaos—the kind foresight to gather together a box of special *gifts* just for the newly freed children. Six and seven-year-olds were young enough when taken into captivity they couldn't remember ever receiving a Christmas or birthday gift. This gift business was absolutely new to them. They were surprised, puzzled, and overjoyed! They didn't understand the phenomenon of gift-giving.

I was given a Tonette, a clarinet-type plastic musical instrument with an instruction book and beginner's songs. It had a sweet, hollow tone, but I wasn't really interested in musical instruments of any kind. In my box there was also a sack of Jacks, a ball, watercolor paints, and a sketch book.

The most important gift to me was a five-inch china doll. She was beautiful! Her arms moved. Her hair was long like mine—or like mine would be when it grew again. She had an apricot satin dress, a lace petticoat, and painted-on shoes. A tiny gold paper bracelet wrapped around her wrist, telling me her name was "Princess Mignonne Minette." Her tiny crown had a gold feather, and a white woolly dog was attached to her wrist by a gold chain. I thought she was the most miraculous gift I had ever received! I gave all the other gifts away to other children. After seeing my doll, I had no eyes for anything but her.

It's hard to fully describe how appreciative I was at this incredible kindness. At this very moment, she sits on my kitchen counter with a freshly laundered dress, which is waiting to be pressed. She has no woolly dog, nor crown, but in my mind's eye, she is as gorgeous as the day we met in the early summer of 1945.

All the kids were given hairbrushes and combs. We didn't need them yet, but looked forward to future days with full heads of hair. We were each given a bar of scented soap. It was such a treat. It had been so long since we even had soap. Our soaps were pine and carnation scented. We nearly washed ourselves away with the pure joy of it. It was fine to just be clean!

Everyone relished the fresh, clean fragrance of the pine scented bath soap. I think Nonie and I were reminded of home with the scent of Douglas firs after a rainstorm when the air is like crystal. Did you know that Douglas firs are not fir trees at all, but members of the pine family? The soap was a continual reminder of our homeland. Now that we were no longer prisoners, we felt tremendous urges to speed on our way to the Pacific Northwest and our loved ones.

In Australia, we observed the free world with disbelief. Our eyes were unaccustomed to such visual richness. Tours through the surrounding area helped acclimate us back to real world normalcy. Once again, the Australians led the way, first in 1941 with Sister Kenny, the wonderful nurse-physical therapist, and now with this thoughtfulness toward returning POWs. They understood about our need for re-acclimating to the real world.

Positive psychology just had to have been developed in Australia. Of all the places we traveled through, they seemed the most sensitive to who we were as formerly civilized people and what we had suffered. We had forgotten about such disparate things as traffic lights, variety stores, neon signs, lunch counters in drug stores, and cars of varied colors. Cats on leashes fascinated us as did decorated windows in department and specialty stores.

I saw one woman waiting on a bench at a trolley stop—oblivious to the rest of the world—knitting a bright blue sweater! Vast fields of fall-winter vegetables amazed us, as well as the many different styles of closures on peoples' clothes; some buttons so artistic, they resembled jewelry.

Australia experienced a late, unseasonably warm fall that year. People still sun-bathed on beaches. While the month was late March, it was also fall-winter season for them below the equator. Weather there was similar to Southern California beaches in September, still warm, but with a cooler forecast.

Blind people with white canes navigated streets alone and ladies wore real stockings. Pre-war varieties had been cotton, rayon, silk, and even a few of the new nylon stockings had begun to appear. There were few bare-legs and *everyone* was fortunate enough to wear shoes! At first it seemed odd that no one had bare toes, or more to the point, no one had bare *feet*. After four years as POWs, covered feet were a novelty!

Music students played accordions in a music store window, and on a street corner a musician bowed and fingered a Bach partita gloriously on his violin with his case propped open. Wonder of wonders, people dropped coins into his case and *no one* stole from him. One woman led two apricot colored Pomeranian dogs on leashes. The dogs wore silver collars and had painted toenails! I burst out laughing right there on the street. I couldn't remember when I had last laughed out loud. My Nonie almost shouted,

"Do you know what you just did? You just laughed out loud!" Then she hugged and hugged me and we were so happy. It was the dogs that did it for me. I love dogs.

Children with an older man we thought might be their grandfather were up on a hill near a park, flying kites—yellow sails against a brilliant sky. They reminded us of the Puyallup Valley Daffodil Festival at home in south Puget Sound. The huge flower farms along the Puyallup River would be a massed blaze of golden yellow and then the enormous fields would turn the valley to red, blue, white and lavender near Sumner when the tulips and the hyacinths bloomed. What a memory.

Though it was a warm fall in Australia days were beginning to cool, recoloring the leaves on trees. We hadn't seen such wonderful, natural trees in years. In addition, they were painting a spectacular autumn March landscape in Australia! We never forgot it.

Many adventures ensued between Kobe and America. In Australia we again boarded the Drottningholm–next stop Laurenco Marques.

While on the Gripsholm, our liner from Laurenco Marques to America, one night after showering, we were being very silly. I had wrapped a towel around myself and was attempting a very poorly done Balinese folk dance. My Nonie said, "Turn around to me" and I did. Still being silly, she hung a coat hanger on my jutting hip bone. We laughed and laughed until we actually fell down on the bed and then laughed some more. The laughter was almost an acknowledgment that now we were allowed to laugh and that we could laugh because we were free.

Years later, as we remembered this frivolity, we would be brought to tears as we recalled the hunger that caused our incredible malnourishment.

CHILD POW

Our voyage home from Australia was via Laurenco Marques, Portuguese East Africa, the Azores, and to Norfolk where we were quickly boarded onto a train with windows painted dark green. Five days later we arrived in California for a cloistered existence of many weeks until we were finally released to go to our home.

During this time, we were still not allowed to make personal contact with our family, and it was not only us, but all returning civilian prisoners of war. Unfortunately, we had no items to bribe anyone with to make a call for us. The explanation was that long distance calls required a priority, and officials had applied for one for us, but it was not yet in effect.

It was a lie. They had *never* applied. They merely wanted to shut us up with hope.

We returnees were in such terrible physical shape, our government did not want the American people to see what the Japanese had done to civilian POWs. Those supposedly "religious, clean, friendly, and industrious people" must not to be exposed to our immensely patriotic—but naïve—nation, as the incredible villains they were.

I asked myself, why? Or better yet, why not? The answer is simple: No support would come from American citizens or from Congress to rebuild Japan if the Japanese were shown as maniacal, murderous heathen, who committed dastardly attacks against innocent civilians during the war.

Atrocities committed against the innocent Manchurians or the Chinese in Nanking were "different," we were told, with a snotty tone. Those people were "Asians, not white Americans"—as if that made it OK. Good grief!

By refusing to expose the criminal Japanese behavior of both the men who commanded it to happen and those who carried it out, our country betrayed us—the POWs who suffered. I will always ache in my heart at this fact. We freed prisoners should have been treated with a welcoming spirit by our own country. Not by media coverage, parades, film crews, or the like, but we should have been treated with kindness, with an understanding of—or at least the attempt to understand—what we had endured for four years! Yet it was not to be.

Instead, we were hidden away as soon as our feet touched a shore outside of captivity. In order to protect the future reconstruction of Japan, we were treated as though we had done something shameful. The government wanted us "fixed up" before we were returned to our families. They were very concerned about the civilian populace's reaction to our physical appearances. As well they should have been. We were ghastly. What really needed to happen was that we should have immediately gone to our homes and be allowed to "fix up" ourselves under the care of our families.

The newly-contrived excellent reputation of the murderous Japs was an overnight media invention by our own country, and our precious America became "those bastards who fire-bombed Japan." The world had turned upside-down! How could we survive in this political climate? Might we too be blamed for some act? Yet, could we do it? Maybe it would be better after the war was over. We hoped so. Again, "we only had to get through today."

CHAPTER 23

TEARS, MEMORIES, AND JOY

'Tis too much proved—that, with devotion's visage
And pious action, we do sugar o'er the devil himself.
——Wm. Shakespeare

We were kept as near prisoners until our skin sores were somewhat healed, our teeth were repaired, and our hair grew out and looked like whiskers. It took weeks for our parasites to be presumed gone and for us to be found clear of any communicable diseases. Finally then a clanking bureaucracy declared we were safe for release at large among the general population. This was simply a matter of a government that did not want citizens to see what vile, vicious damages occurred to our bodies at the hands of the Japanese because this enemy was now courted as a future partner in trade. Money and greed always speak with loud voices!

There is no legitimate explanation why we were kept from contact with our family. We could have at least, at the *very* least, been allowed to telephone them or even send telegrams. The

263

pseudo-reason given was national security. Yet, what, in the name of common sense might we tell anybody? How I sold my hair for supplies to catch fish off a filthy dock in Kobe because the Japs refused to give us food? That was the *truth*, not national security. Did they fear we might expose how to keep wooden-soled geta from slipping on ship gangways as we were forced to load coal for the Emperor? That nightmare was also *truth*, but it was not a national security issue. Who would have been harmed if we had told anyone the road to the officers' camp had recently been repaved? It was the *truth*, but who would care? It certainly wasn't an item of national security. We had nothing of value to tell.

Except the names of the murderers.

Daily we both continued to wear two sweaters and the skirt we were given. At the convalescent center Red Cross workers gave us each a pair of "slacks," as they were called. We had never worn trousers of any kind, although My Nonie had seen them on women in the movies, worn by actresses like Carole Lombard and Paulette Goddard. We were told slacks were good for travel, and they might be fun if we wanted to vary our wardrobes a bit. We didn't want them, but they were sent to our room via a nurses' aide who thought we should try them on, at least. This was the only contact we had with the Red Cross, that almighty bastion of altruism.

My dear Papa told stories, during post-war years, about Red Cross people charging a fee for the coffee and doughnuts they provided to service personnel on foreign beachheads we landed on during WWII. Did they make the doughnuts on the ships? I always wondered. Surely they couldn't have brought them from America. How could our government *allow them* to charge our men in a battle area!

Papa always became angry discussing the Red Cross. Since the soldiers did not carry money into battle, they could never receive any of these goodies during a lull in battle, and Papa did not consider it just or fair.

It wearies me to think what money-grabbers they are, yet how desperately they talk of need. In the late 1990s, the Red Cross national executive director was paid more than one million dollars a year—in a *volunteer* organization. All of the little school children who gave their dimes and quarters must be proud they helped pay her salary, a woman with a veteran husband, handicapped in the war in Europe. Politics is a nasty game. Shame on her. And shame on the Red Cross for allowing it.

They never helped My Nonie nor me in any way. They could have asked if we wanted a book to read. We saw them daily with their book carts and their coffee wagons in their sweet little uniforms, waltzing through hospital halls. Five or six of them often drove in long DeSoto sedans or station wagons. They wore long, grey "first-communion" type veils; they were called The Grey Ladies. They knew My Nonie and I were there. Yet, we were invisible. They avoided looking at us. If we noticed them, they abruptly left the area. They were far too grand to acknowledge a couple of impoverished ex-POWs who didn't have a penny to our name or anything more than the one suit of clothes on our backs. We were definitely not in their class of society. Every single thing we owned between the two of us fit in a tiny paper sack.

One lady knelt in the hall to tie her shoe. Since she was unable to quickly escape, I asked her why they avoided us, "We're Americans, like you. Why don't you talk to us? It would be so nice for my mother, if you did. She's been a prisoner of war for such a long time." As soon as she stood up, the woman fled.

Donate instead to the Salvation Army or St. Vincent de Paul—groups who *really* help people.

It was difficult for some time to convince us, a couple of ex-POWs, to lay down any precious possession, leave the room, and be assured no one might take it. What a joke. We had learned during our four years in captivity: "Out of hand means gone forever." Yet we thought we had moved past this particular paranoia.

Eventually, we were convinced by others that it was common place to keep items in one's room and we accepted the slacks. No sooner had we tried them on than the gong rang, announcing the evening meal. We folded our slacks with care, put them away, and then left our room for the dining hall.

At the dinner table we enjoyed describing our new acquisitions and hearing the ensuing discussions, both pro and con, about women wearing trousers. After an interval, we adjourned to our room for the night, planning to happily read current magazines.

Imagine our surprise when we discovered our room turned upside-down, apparently by thieves. It was preposterous, primarily because there were no items to steal, except our slacks. Obviously, someone needed them more than we did. They got no gift. The slacks were cheaply made of an inferior fabric.

From that day on, again overly-cautious, my mother constantly wore her beautiful lace slip, and we continued to wear our Swedish skirts and both sweaters at all times. However, we felt no bitterness because for so many years we had possessed nothing but rags and newspaper for warmth and fashion. In fact, we felt sorry for any thief who could stoop so low as to steal from anyone as poor as we were. Cynical as I am, I always wondered if the Red Cross women reclaimed them because I had put the one old gal on the spot.

We shifted back into our prisoner status-quo actions, which meant we carried all possessions with us, absolutely everywhere we went. Inside our sack was a still unneeded hair brush, Nonie's lipstick, two spare under panties, two toothbrushes, and Dr. Lyon's tooth powder. That was it, everything we owned. I carried my beautiful, petite china doll in my hand. To us it seemed like an overabundance of wealth to each keep a second sweater so we refused to complain about the theft.

There was much ado about finding me shoes other than my Swedish clogs, which had been taken from me at our first exam in California. Although it was summer season, and the first plastic sandals we had ever seen were in vogue, the straps were molded in such a way that the shoe could not be cinched up. Regular oxfords or tennis shoes could not be found, and nothing available in my length stayed on my skinny feet.

Even on the ship, sailors had teased me about having tentacles because my feet and fingers looked so thin in comparison to normal. A lovely girl in my high school class, Debbie, had the most beautiful fingers and hands, which I always envied. However, my hand joints had healed large and clumsy after being repeatedly smashed and broken. There's no point in wishing for something that will never happen, like slim, graceful fingers. I was lucky to have fingers that worked.

When I was measured for shoes in California, I was size 6 in length, but AAAA was the narrowest available and it was much too wide. I really did have merely bones for feet. Eventually I was given a pair of moccasin-type bedroom slippers to wear with a pair of socks over the top. It made for a most peculiar fashion statement! The socks held the slippers onto my narrow feet, but I much preferred nothing at all—too many years of bare feet or geta.

My poor feet have always felt like such *old* feet. About fifty healed fractures criss-crossed the landscape of my feet after they were stomped and hit at with gun butts for punishment. Yet the most ridiculous fact is, I have never even had a blister. My Nonie and I used to tease each other and say we'd never be tried for collaboration with the enemy since we each had too many broken toes and fingers to show for our imprisonment. These feet used to love to dance, even after WWII. It has always seemed dancing was a way to feel free and I've had some splendid dancing partners.

To travel we had only the clothes we wore, my moccasins, and our small sack of toiletries and extra underwear, but we were certainly ready to go home. We guessed no coat or jacket was needed since it was middle-to-late summer in California, and our weather was likely pleasant farther north. Like a couple of barney horses, we strained at the bit for release, to race for home. It was a definite obsession for us both.

Faces of our dear ones became more distinct in our memories, the more we thought about them. We could hardly imagine touching each one again. We had always been a family who expressed love with kisses and hugs of pleasure and gratitude. We were a family who could verbalize our feelings. We could say, "I love you" and even "You disappointed me." We were so open with each other. It was comfortable.

Finally the day came when we left that military installation, bound for Puget Sound country and our glorious Mt. Rainier. My Nonie who in pre-war life weighed about 115 pounds, now weighed 87 pounds, *after five weeks of nursing and good food* at hospitals in California! I weighed 45 pounds the same day, a gain of nearly 20 pounds on my 11 and ¾ year-old frame. We both were still so thin we were peculiar looking.

In retrospect, a most pitiful fact about our return to America is we made no objection to the way we were treated by our own government: their refusal to let us contact our family, the compelled isolation from our family, the scornful bravado of those in charge of us, and the disdainful treatment and demeaning attitudes we were subjected to.

As former POWs, we were completely inured to disrespectful or mean-spirited treatment. Yet it is difficult and strange to realize, after incarceration by the Japs, that we saw our own country now do the same things. By teaching us instant command compliance, each country made their world revolve more smoothly—for themselves!

Where, oh where, was our Bill of Rights? I jest, of course. We all know in 1945 the Bill of Rights applied only to affluent, white, adult American males. My grandmother was an early suffragette. She stood at the governor of Wyoming's side when he signed into law the bill which gave women in that state the right to vote. She was appalled at our stories. Good grief!

Eventually, we realized things had changed while we were gone, but our mantra was still with us: "We only have to get through today." We did it before, and we could do it again. If such a thing exists: this might be a prime example of how one becomes strong through adversity. My Nonie said it four years before, and it was almost as if we challenged whomever presented a new roadblock: "All right. Bring it on! We've been there and back again. There is not a single thing you can do to us to weaken our resolve."

CHAPTER 24

OLD HIGHWAY 99

The flowers appear on the earth;
the time of the singing of birds is come,
and the voice of the turtle is heard in our land
                                        —*Song of Solomon*

After what seemed an unusually long time, we received a voucher for two bus tickets, a five-dollar bill each for food, and we were ready for our trip north. Ten dollars may sound like meager funds to sustain the two of us for such a long trip, yet we checked at the bus terminal and were advised that at most diners and bus stop cafés, we could order a fried egg sandwich and a bowl of bean soup for thirty cents.

In those days, a universally known "Blue Plate Special" was always available at bus stop diners and at drug store lunch counters. It consisted of mashed potatoes and peas, a slice of tomato, with a hamburger patty, applesauce and a roll, all for sixty cents. Unfortunately, a hamburger patty was a thing of the past, for the duration of the war. Blue Plate Specials seemed to have become a "Vegetable Plate Special," with mashed potatoes, extra vegetables, usually creamed corn and squash, or Lima beans in addition to the tomato slice and the green peas; maybe coleslaw; and the addition of a large, hard roll which we couldn't eat because our teeth were still tender. I was enchanted how it was served on a heavy stoneware plate with indentations to hold each individual food. I always admired efficient planning.

We figured we each could eat one "special" every day at a bus stop. Then since our trip should take about three days, our calculations showed expenses totaling $3.60, leaving a balance of $6.40. This meant we could also have a noon meal, like a sandwich and a cup of soup for thirty cents, multiplied by three days, times two of us, equaled another $1.80. That still left us $4.60 from our original $10.00 meal allotment. We were rich! We even had enough for proper dime tips to our waitresses.

After four years of eating only one meager meal a day, on our return trip home we planned to eat peanut butter sandwiches and a cup of milk each day for breakfast, in addition to whatever we chose at the bus station cafés along our way. We knew we were going to be just fine.

Before we left for the bus station, we bought a loaf of white bread for twelve cents and quart of milk for ten cents at the hospital commissary. The clerk kindly didn't charge us for a small jar of peanut butter, which cost nineteen cents, but instead he winked and said, "Good luck, you two. Don't take any wooden nickels." He was so funny.

In a military sedan, a sailor delivered us to the bus station with a grand flourish of brakes and squealing tires shortly before 4:00 p. m. one Monday afternoon. I felt completely free for the first time since we left Kobe. No one was in charge of us. We had made it! We were finally on our own!

I teased My Nonie: "What if we don't go home, but instead we could fly to Paris?" She laughed, said it was a great idea, and told me about the fun we'd have when we finally did go together in a few years, after the war was over and France was put back together. Sadly, My Nonie and I never went to Paris together, but the initial discussion was heady. Nonie and Papa went many times, and she told me it was bittersweet that I couldn't share the experience. I had always dreamed of going. I still dream of it.

My Nonie explained days later how we could actually afford to go. A hospital finance officer had checked her Social Security number and Papa's military identification number and discovered a dependents' allotment had been sent to our family's address each month since their proxy marriage in December 1941. Apparently my Papa had signed papers to allow my grandmother full access in this account at a local bank. By the time Nonie heard about it, her account had grown to almost $8000.

In addition, my grandparents had sold Nonie's car years ago, along with all our clothing except a few keepsake pieces, and all our household goods. From these proceeds, my grandmother had added $2,000 more to the account, which now totaled over $10,000. Nonie was amazed at this largess. It would help to build our dream house. She told me repeatedly that she felt we had earned this money by being good and faithful Americans who supported our country, even as POWs.

We showed our vouchers to an agent at the station; he gave us our tickets and pointed us toward the proper bus. Arriving late from the hospital, we had nearly missed our ride, which was loaded and idling in the driveway. At our approach, the driver who stood talking with relief personnel turned to us and curtly asked for our luggage. In those days, a relief driver drove while the main driver slept. In this way, a trip was faster and safer and we had the same drivers all the way. We politely replied all we had were our paper sacks of food and toiletries, and we'd prefer to keep them with us.

CHILD POW

The driver wanted to look inside so we showed him our simple toiletries. Then he looked in our grocery sack at the bread, milk, and peanut butter. We were quite frightened at his brusque manner. When we asked him politely if it was permissible to eat on the bus, he acted like something was amiss and stared at us intently. I wondered, *Had we said the wrong thing to ask if we could eat on his bus? I could tell him we would throw away our food if he wanted us to. We needed to get on the bus.*

Next, he wanted to know if we had been ill or were sick now? Simultaneously, my mother said yes, and I said no. She meant yes, we had been ill; I meant no, we weren't sick right now. Admittedly, we did look like cadavers. We were dramatically too thin with pale, yellow-gray skin. Almost no hair had grown back, and I had some big scars on my head. In addition, I had a limp, a crutch, and wore my socks over my moccasins. We were a proper sight. It's not any wonder that the bus driver questioned us. We must have looked like aliens landed from Mars!

My Nonie explained we had recently returned from four years in Japanese prison camps, and we were headed home to our family in Puget Sound. Then the driver looked at us with a fierce intensity; he seemed furious. He explained later that he was trying not to cry. Men, regardless of the reason, did not cry in those days if they could help it. We were afraid he was considering revoking our tickets for some reason we didn't understand but then how could we get home? He looked us over carefully and shook his head, negatively.

God, help us get home! I thought he meant we couldn't ride his bus, but in contrast he made the whole world open up for us. The driver held his arms wide, and with tears welling in his eyes said, "I lost my son at Guadalcanal. It's an honor to have you aboard. I'll take good care of you. Come on here. Let's get you loaded up." With that he helped Nonie up the stairs, then lifted me and my crutch onto the uppermost bus step.

The driver climbed up behind us and announced, "Now folks, we have some pretty special people with us. This lady and her little girl have come home from being prisoners of the dirty Japs. They're headed north with us, and we'll take good care of them, won't we!" (In those times, "dirty Japs" was no more an expletive than if you said "Yankee Doodle". It was just something people said during the war years with feeling.)

Passengers cheered and called out encouragement in a deluge of support, like a rill of sparkling water softly tumbling, cascading over small rocks and collecting in a crystal pool. Then I thought of the beautiful koi pond I had loved at our Manila cabana.

From that moment every passenger made us his or her short-term relative. Most of them had family members in America's military, a few in the Pacific. Later, we cried with them in their worry about dear ones. We tried to reassure them whenever we could, though there wasn't much we could say to give comfort. We had only known bad places—the POW camps. We told them how supportive servicemen were to each other when times got tough, and how needed supplies were now flowing in abundance through Australian ports. It wasn't much information to dissuade their worry, but it was all we could think to say. We didn't want to share the bad places.

Most travelers were ticketed through to Portland or Seattle, and it seemed like everyone helped us one way or another. They all shared food, since Godfrey, our driver, told everyone it was OK to eat on his bus. Quite a few had brought fried chicken from home—collectively, there was lots of it, actually! People brought potato salad and macaroni salad, which we devoured the first night. A few had deviled-eggs—strange and delicate things—which should have been called angel-eggs. Other passengers had fruit cocktail in screw-top Mason jars.

At one stop, the driver bought glass mugs of root beer for everyone. We had to return the mugs, but it was fun, because the mugs were iced and the frost stuck our lips to the mugs. I couldn't remember ever tasting it before, but My Nonie reminded me that Uncle David ran a Triple-X Root Beer stand in Roundup during his high school years.

One person had wisely thought to bring a huge stack of paper plates and cups. Yet no one remembered forks or spoons, so we asked the root beer stand owner if we could buy a few from him. Graciously, he gave us a whole box of wooden spoons, meant for small ice cream treats called Dixie Cups. (Dixie Cups were filled half with vanilla ice cream and half with orange sherbet and had the picture of a movie star under the lid for kids to collect.) Picnicking had definitely grown into a normal activity among bus travelers during the war. People who previously went by car now took the bus and prepared food enough for themselves and for others. I was amazed how everyone came with provisions to share. *And the Lord said, 'Feed my people.'* And they did.

These dear, good people passed notes behind our backs while we slept. They organized more help for us with a "Welcome Wagon" spirit. People pooled money and resources. They bought My Nonie makeup at a gas stop in Northern California, including lipstick, rouge, and an eyebrow pencil.

One lady I remember, Brenda Jorgenson, was a beautician, traveling to visit a new grandchild in Albany, Oregon. She showed Nonie the latest fashion trends in magazines, and parted with a bottle of nail polish and an emery board. She even gave Nonie her small, personal bottle of Jergens® hand lotion. We hadn't enjoyed that fragrance since 1941. It smelled like *heaven*, and My Nonie cried. Then of course, I cried, in chorus. Lots of things made us cry lately. It had been years since we were *allowed* to cry. Now that we could, tears seemed to spurt from our eyes at most inappropriate moments.

A dear older lady traveler was crocheting slippers and caps for Navy Relief to help pass the time, and she crocheted long shoelaces for me. Then a gentleman passenger punched lacing holes along the sides of my moccasin-style slippers, so I could come home with custom-fitted imitation espadrilles, instead of slippers held on by a pair of socks on top. I threw the socks away that day, but I kept those special laces. I intertwined them with a pale lavender velvet ribbon and hung them on the side of my dressing table mirror for years.

It's wonderful to remember things from the past—several passengers, in particular. They're surely long gone now, yet I'm certain I could identify them today: Mrs. Charlotte Evans, crocheting her way north; Mr. Sterling Shortland, whose knife and awl punched lacing holes in my moccasin slippers; Godfrey Archerson, our dear, soft-hearted bus driver with the grumpy face; Rex Polson, the kind relief driver who could whistle like a canary; Jack Fitch; Dorothy; twins Millie and Ginny Rollofson; Delores Cannon; Lloyd and Evelyn, owners of a small used car dealership in Marysville, Washington.

Lloyd and Evelyn explained that until a cessation of hostilities for the duration of the war no new cars would come from Detroit. (In those days *all* cars came from Detroit.) Dealers now sold only used vehicles; that's all there were. They were all wonderfully good to us, helping in many small ways along our trip.

There is an adjective that often describes an organization, a method, or an attitude. In this case it personifies our small group of lovely companions: *humane*.

Jack Fitch bought Hershey bars at each stop between San Diego and Portland, simply to share with all of us on the bus. Candy bars were newly introduced back on the market as the rationing process tapered down. Sugar had supposedly been rationed during the war; it was used to produce ammunition. When I noticed he never ate one himself, I asked him why? His reply was he had "sugar" diabetes. He could not eat candy, but he liked to make people smile, and candy bars always did it.

Mr. Fitch was a traveling salesman for the Remington Rand Typewriter Corporation. He and I found mutual fascination; I of him, awed by his huge diamond pinky ring, and he of me, because I said I had received a new Remington portable in a case on my seventh birthday. (I still have it. In pristine condition, it still has the original ribbon, and types beautifully although, after all these years, the print is faint.)

Delores Cannon gave Nonie a manicure, then polished her nails with Brenda's gift. Twin Ginny Rollofson, a dietitian, tried hard to teach us how to improve our nutrition now that we were home. She was devastated when we told her our lowest weight when rescued only two months earlier.

Millie and Ginny were headed north to their brother's wedding in Seattle before he was shipped overseas from Fort Lawton. They cried when they spoke of how he was probably bound for the invasion of Japan, which was anticipated to be extremely dangerous. We cried with them.

Millie showed Nonie how to set ladies' hairdos. She couldn't pin curl My Nonie's hair. It wasn't long enough. Yet she gave Nonie her own bobby pins and told her laughingly to guard them with her life. They were apparently nearly impossible to find in stores since metal was also diverted to the war effort.

We were so blessed that all these people would go out of their way to involve us back in the daily world of Americans.

They kissed and hugged us, and took our snapshots. Each person gave us his or her home address with a firm demand that we visit them for any length of vacation we'd like. Many asked: "Do you have a place to live? Do you need money? Do you have funds to support yourselves? Do you need a job?" Such kindnesses left us frequently weeping tears of joy and gratitude.

They were real Americans—not like the government officials who had been nasty snots. Not like those too bored to leave us with even a tiny bit of our dignity intact!

When My Nonie and I both worked in various levels of the government years later, we made sure no one could ever accuse us of being bureaucrats, acting unkind or nasty. We remembered who paid our salaries—the citizens we served. The responsibilities of citizenship were always important to us.

At one roadside vendor we bought fresh orange juice from the orchards. They also sold freshly cooked and buttered—or oleo-ed—corn on the cob, wrapped in waxed paper. Heavenly!

279

It was sweet, like an exotic, new food developed during our absence.

What really awed us was the fact none of the people in line grabbed or fought for food like in the camps. They waited politely in line. We had to realize no one *needed* to push or shove. Also in contrast with our incarceration, no one here used a club to shoo people away. No one yelled, "There's no more food for those in the back of the line." These farmers smiled and talked with us instead of snarling and acting impatient.

I looked at My Nonie while we stood in the bus shade with oleo smeared from ear-to-ear. She had an odd, far-away look. Remembering old times of trouble, I quickly picked up on her mood and asked what she was thinking.

"I was thinking this is so good, and it has a familiar taste. I was trying to imagine what it tasted like. Do you know? It tastes like *corn*!"

We laughed so loudly our fellow passengers wanted to hear the joke, which we shared. Then they laughed too. But softly. It was okay. They just didn't understand.

Old habits die hard, likewise, old memories. To protect ourselves and each other, we had learned to live and act like prisoners. Our challenge now was learning to be free people again. We determined to get through each day with joy, rather than with terror and fear. Rescuers had come for us just as My Nonie had repeated for the last four years.

Eventually, over our several days of travel, we probably ate more than we had during an entire month in a POW camp! Our fellow riders treated us to our first real hamburger, which tasted like a miracle on bread.

Over the ensuing years, neither of us lost our taste for a good hamburger. Never! Before WWII we had never eaten a hamburger. Since our large family always ate at home, we had never tasted this restaurant delight. In those days the only drive-ins were A&W and TripleXXX, both of whom were largely there to sell their root beer. It was the beginning of an industry.

On our bus, nutritionist Ginny Rollofson and Delores, a cook at a school in Centralia, told us about a new idea in nutrition. They taught healthy eating habits by placing items into food groups. A person is supposed to eat certain things daily, in specific amounts, in each food group, to maintain a healthy body. Ginny patiently tried to teach us this method, but in vain. I never did get Ginny to tell me how many calories seaweed had. She almost gagged when we mentioned it so we quit teasing her.

As we talked about food groups, we eventually digressed to memories. I thought about the scorpions the miners ate in China. We remembered eating our meager catches from lines which hung off the Kobe dock. We recalled the smell and taste of kelp and rice balls, infested with "protein on the hoof." Then we would begin to cry once again.

It seems extremely important today to tell about our food. About how it felt to have good American food after such an extended time with none. About people on the bus who shared and were patient and giving in our need.

Please remember to help the hungry every day. In your area, in your city or town, there are famished people—every day—whom you can help. I have been hungry. I hope you never will be. Please give regularly to your nearest food bank. It is one way an individual person can make a difference in someone's life. Please.

Hamburger discussions were a good diversion. We decided a hamburger has every food group in it. As we laughed and laughed, one conclusion we agreed on was that pickles count as fruit. We knew pickles are really cucumbers, and cucumbers are vegetables yet we ignored that and swore they must be fruit because they are far too *tasty* to be vegetables! However, we *didn't* understand why there was meat available, since we had been told meat was rationed and we were proud owners of new ration books. People in California had taught Nonie how money must be accompanied by "stamps" for certain food items like meat and butter, and luxuries like leather shoes and gasoline.

Most passengers called the hamburgers "ersatz meat," though we never did find out what that actually meant. Some people said it was a lesser grade of meat with oatmeal or barley added. Others claimed it was horse meat, or goat. Yet it tasted fine to us. We didn't care! We simply chewed away in delight and gratitude.

Our companions sang every new song they could think of for us. "Mairzy Doats" was a funny song that made me laugh. Nonie wondered if Papa had heard "I'll Be Seeing You" and "I'll Get By." We considered "White Christmas" particularly lovely. On the trip we learned the words to the war songs "Praise the Lord and Pass the Ammunition" and "Coming in on a Wing and a Prayer." We cried when the passengers tried to teach us

"Sentimental Journey." The emotional meaning of those words was understandable to us on our own sentimental journey home.

Later, I learned this was an especially favored song of Aunt Dorothy. It reminded her of Bill, her dear brother, who was lost flying The Hump over the Himalayas. Unfortunately his two-motor DC-3 carrying cargo and gasoline to support American troops in China had never arrived at the proper destination. He had begun his war service as a nineteen-year-old tail-gunner on a B25. His loss was immense. He was one of the best of them all. Our family, our country, all of us—lost a part of our future when Bill Taylor went down in China.

Our trip took hours of continuous bus travel and more layover hours in large cities like San Francisco, Eugene, and Portland. Progress was interrupted only when diesel trucks did not arrive to fuel bus stations' tanks. Sometimes tankers were delayed in the mountains, but usually we never found out why they were late.

Maintenance parts were also difficult to obtain during the war; some delays were undoubtedly from mechanical break-downs. New trucks, buses, or cars weren't even available. Our driver, Godfrey Archerson, also told us fuel trucks had been hi-jacked on California and Oregon mountain roads. The fuel they carried was sold on "the black market." This illegal consortium of gangs—for the right price—could provide almost anything in short supply, without ration stamps, including gasoline, ladies silk and nylon stockings, meat, and shoes.

We didn't want to hear about these gangs. They reminded us too much of the Chinese warlords. Apparently they operated quite freely in spite of laws proscribing the black market. People who need things like gasoline will often do almost anything and pay any price to get it.

We left California at 4:00 p. m. on a Monday and arrived at our Pacific Northwest stop at 5:00 p. m., the following Thursday. We traveled on two-lane Highway 99, which ran from California to Canada. (Old 99 has since been supplanted by Interstate 5, in most areas an eight lane freeway with limited access.) In most places, during the war days, the speed limit was an enforced forty miles per hour in the interest of gas conservation.

Comically, we noticed that when going *down* long grades, speed limit signs often posted five miles per hour faster than going *up* the same hill from the opposite direction. Godfrey, our driver, explained it was so people wouldn't wear out their car's brakes going down, or burn too much fuel going up.

In places like California and southern Oregon, Highway 99 had actually been expanded to a four-lane road. North of Portland, however, the road was quite dangerous, back to two lanes with many logging trucks impeding traffic on hills. This encouraged careless and impatient drivers to attempt to pass cars and buses. Godfrey or Rex had to blow the horn long and loud at those imbeciles whose close calls scared us to pieces. After everything we had been through, we certainly didn't want to die in a traffic accident due to some idiot on the road.

Our weather was beautiful, as expected, but cooling this late June as we drove through a lovely, short rain spell south of Olympia. And then at the top of the Nisqually Hill we saw our mountain. There, in all her snow-capped glory, rose Mt. Rainier, sunlit against the blue sky, rising from sea level to over 14,000 feet of unobstructed beauty. Nowhere in the world is there such a glorious mountain. She makes Mt. Fuji look like a pimple. It felt so good to be home.

Mt. Rainier is 14,400 feet from sea level. Photo taken from Fireman's Park, Tacoma by My Nonie c. 1990

Descending the long Nisqually Hill toward the Nisqually River delta, we could smell tidal pools in the estuary on the Braget Ranch. Clam and oyster beds were exposed at low tide and the salty Puget Sound aroma was intoxicating and unique. My Uncle Carl used to take me fishing there. Though we had been exposed to the Pacific Ocean for a long time on the Kobe docks, there was no comparison between these two bodies of water. The Kobe seaport was filthy with pumped bilges, raw sewage, industrial runoff, and the ever present coal and coal dust. Finally home to our loved Puget Sound, our senses were now nourished by the tidal pools, this kelp which smelled of

285

iodine, and the briny odor of the clam and oyster beds. It's such a life-giving fragrance.

We were amazed at the growth of the huge fort we drove past. Many miles of rows and rows of large tents housed soldiers, assembled to ship overseas. At one place we had to wait while a troop train crossed the highway, then wait again while another long train, loaded with tanks, also entered the military reservation. We were immensely impressed with what we saw, but also sad at the anticipation of potential casualties. (Please God, some day, may we all quit killing each other?)

Eventually we reached our road near home where drivers Godfrey and Rex had agreed to drop us in our rural area, ten miles south of the city. The men acknowledged it might be hard for us to find a way back from the downtown bus station, so they sensibly suggested an informal stop at the side of Old 99. It isn't as though we had a lot of baggage to unload and cause delay with only our paper sack of personal possessions: a hairbrush, toothbrushes, a washcloth, two panties, and our two extra sweaters. By the second day of our trip, we had eaten all our peanut butter and bread, so our stop by the side of the road was only a quick hiccup on Godfrey's drive north to Seattle.

As we stepped off our bus everyone cheered us on our way. Many shouted: "Remember to write before long! Tell us how you are doing." I think My Nonie was a little self-conscious with only a paper sack to carry our few possessions. This was June 29, 1945.

CHAPTER 25

WE COME HOME

.......and every reunion is a type of heaven——Edwards

As we expected, it was a cool, clear late summer afternoon in the Pacific Northwest with deliciously scrubbed air. Heat doesn't come here until late July or August. Even in our excitement and trepidation, we could have found our way home from the highway—blindfolded! Rain lay puddled beside the tarred and graveled two lane arterial. A worn, yellow line down the middle was like a guiding ray of happy sunshine, leading home. Yet I wondered, *Would our family accept us, when they knew our story? They were all so decent. We used to be but maybe our imprisonment had marked us somehow. Would they be able to tell?*

We sang "Follow the Yellow Brick Road" as we walked, having seen *The Wizard of Oz* in 1939. We also talked about Uncle Jim who as director of highways in Wyoming back in the early 1930s was the first to order a dividing-line painted down the middle of paved roads in that state. It seems no one had thought of it before that time. After a trial section of road was painted with the yellow line between Cheyenne and Laramie, and when cars no longer ran headlong into each other at night the idea was declared a success. Accident rates dropped overnight, and the improvement spread nationwide.

We walked two miles toward our home and gloried in how beautiful our homecoming day was, and how quiet. It had been so long since we had enjoyed silence. In our travels home, although America was quieter than war zones, we were quite accustomed to machinery constantly grinding, people talking, mechanical apparatus clanking, bells and whistles.

We reveled in this serene, long slow walk and reexamined our own precious part of the world. Since we were physically a bit stronger now, slow walking relaxed rather than fatigued us. I still needed a crutch, yet I was fortunate to receive a French model, which supported weight on my forearm rather than the underarm. It was infinitely more comfortable.

Shift employees at the nearby air field had come and gone so we missed the normal change of shift traffic. Everything was as we remembered, except the trees seemed taller, our road seemed narrower, and the few houses in the area seemed familiar but also smaller than we remembered. Towering Douglas firs cast long summer afternoon shadows. Clover Creek ran pristine and gurgling under the bridge as we crossed. Before too long an ancient Hupmobile car, heading for the air field, wheezed to a stop near us. A young captain driving asked if we cared for a ride.

My Nonie replied, "We don't have far to go. We aren't going onto the base, only nearby in the neighborhood, but thanks anyway."

Since traveling and being socially accepted on our bus with friendly, wonderful fellow riders, we no longer felt great trepidation about our relatives' possible response. Now we knew we could handle it. We were tremendously fortunate to have come north with this group of dear, new friends.

It's too bad we weren't allowed to make contact with our family while in California, but we couldn't have called during our trip north. We were never in one place long enough! Long distance calls weren't private or quickly dialed in those days. One dialed an operator who attempted to find a circuit through to the called party. Calls would have been relayed from San Diego to Los Angeles, to San Francisco, to Portland, to Seattle, then back south to our town to a local operator who would dial our home. At each "ring down" or city, there might be a delay of a few minutes—or many hours. It usually took the better part of a day, and calls were put in a priority register.

We wanted our family to know we were coming, instead of shocking them with a sudden arrival, yet the forewarning was just not available to us. We continued walking and we enjoyed our final few minutes of quiet together. Even after all we had survived, all the places we had traveled, and all the people we had met, I still preferred to be with My Nonie more than any other person on earth. She was so special.

As we neared home, I could look through the small forest and see the home of my dearly loved childhood friends. They had loving parents and aunties and uncles in the neighborhood just as I did. They also had a dog who terrified me, but in adulthood I realized Sparky was only lonely and wanted our attention when he lunged at us on his chain. They also had a mysterious and enormous black cat named Ammie who hissed at me. I wondered if Joanne and Gloria would remember me. Maybe I was gone too long.

In the officers' camp when I "mind traveled" to flee from the ongoing abuse, I often went to my friends house and saw their pretty polka dot wall paper and pink chenille bedspreads, their new Nancy Drew novels—so many good memories. I hoped I hadn't been gone too long. Would their parents let me be friends with them again? So many fears.

Patriotic cousin Chuck with the anti-aircraft
tower and guns across the street.

As we turned the last corner nearing home, we noticed a three-story wooden anti-aircraft tower had been built directly across a road from our property. Since Uncle Jim True firs bought the acreage in 1938, our neighbor across the street was the enormous military complex, including an Army Air Corps base, adjacent to the huge army fort. This combined reservation ran for many miles, north and south, east and west.

A nice benefit for us when we were children was learning to ice skate on the Army's little Lake Milburn, directly across the street and only 100 yards from our home. The military was always indulgent with us, sometimes even joining us as they allowed our picnics and forest exploration. Whenever we asked at the Main Gate near our homes, after a few telephone calls, permission was always granted.

Our family's home c. 1950
Nonie, Papa, a bulldog and a Doberman

291

Since those pastoral years, the lake was destroyed when the fort built *an obstacle course* in 1990, which they only use twice a year. It is an ecological disaster. Can you hear my anger? Wetlands were destroyed; Lake Milburn was filled in. All the red-tailed hawks are gone, as are herons, woodpeckers, smaller eagles, red-winged blackbirds, the dragonflies, and many other species of wildlife we enjoyed for sixty years, during my youth and after. No frogs sing their songs, nor bull-frogs shout out chug-a-rum. Deer, foxes, mountain beavers, and raccoons can no longer co-exist. For a nothing.

How silly. How like the military to thumb their nose at the wetland rules in this state. After all, *they are the army*. How grand and mighty. It isn't as though they didn't have thousands of other acres in which to put their damn obstacle course. How can I love them so much when I'm always so mad at them?

On this bright June day, not a soul in our family knew we were alive. They didn't know we were in America.

We each took a big breath then walked through the gate-posts. We walked past the big hedge bordering our property and our family's houses. We walked slowly up the long, rocky driveway.

It was June 29, 1945. It was 5:00 p.m. We had been gone for four long years.

We had finally come home.

Aunt Lucy was forty-three on that day. I was eleven and three-fourth years old. Many years later I joyfully married the love of my life, also on June 29, at 5:00 p.m. in memory of the day we were enveloped back into our family unit.

I giggled, wishing we had some sort of drum-roll we could create and then strike a pose and yell. "Ta da! We're home. It's us. We're back." There was no drum-roll.

In the dining room window, we saw a few heads turn toward us. Aunt Lucy, at the back of the table, stood up to better examine who these two strangers were, so boldly walking in the front gate. At first glance, because we were so peculiar looking, they thought we might be beggars asking for a handout Remember how thin we were: Nonie still under ¾ of her normal weight and I was just under half of my supposed normal weight for my age.

Our skin was a faded yellow-gray and we still had no hair. We were dressed like females, but we actually looked more like half grown skinny boys dressed in skirts. Additionally, I had a crutch and we had just a small paper sack. We certainly appeared pretty forlorn and indigent. We were forlorn and indigent.

Then suddenly, Lucy turned and ran out the back door. She screamed as she ran down the driveway with wide-open arms. She was my god-mother. Several little ones had never met us: Eleanor, Jim, and Johnny. They were born after we left for Asia. Chuck, the oldest, was now seven. Just the age I had been when we went to Manila. Family members whom we had carried in our hearts for years dashed outside, screaming, crying.

"Is it you? Is it you?"

"I can't believe it! How can it be?"

"We thought you were probably dead!"

"Why didn't you let us know you were coming?"

293

They cried and shouted over each other. Everyone tried to be heard. We are *such* a family of screamers. Everyone was over-talking one another. It was pandemonium! It was wonderful. They told us we didn't look the same. We told them they *did* look the same. We stopped and then we all laughed at our own exuberance and it started all over again.

My grandmother wanted to know, "Have you eaten?"

"I prayed so hard you weren't dead!" Aunt Betty explained.

"Why are you so thin?" young Chuck asked us.

"Where are your bags and do we need to go someplace to pick them up?"

"Did you come in to Boeing Field? We could have picked you up."

"I missed you so much!!"

"Have you had your dinner yet?"

"It's Lucy's birthday. We were just sitting down to eat."

"Where did you come from? Did you just land?"

Uncle David wanted to know, "How long have you been in the United States?"

"How did you get here? Where's your luggage?"

"Quick, come and sit down. We'll get you some dinner!"

"Child, be careful. Don't hurt yourself with that crutch on this rocky driveway."

Freckles, my bulldog, had recognized me. He barked and barked, frolicking like a young dog between our legs. He almost rubbed my skin off, licking and kissing me. Freckles lived another eight years, to nineteen years old. He was my first pet in the whole world. I've always had a dog since then, most often more than one at a time. Right now there are three pugs.

There was more hugging and screaming until finally all the generations from inside the house reached us.

"You're both so thin. We need to get some good food into you."

"Let's eat first; then we can talk."

Lucy wanted to know, "Are you sick or are you just getting well from being sick?"

"You look like those pictures we saw in Life Magazine of the prisoners in Germany. Were you prisoners, too?" Chuck asked.

During our noisy reunion, soldiers from the anti-aircraft tower across the street jumped the two-strand barbed-wire fence along our outer hedge and ran over to ask if there was trouble. Did someone need help? They heard people screaming and were ready to come to the rescue, if needed.

It felt so good to know these young fellows looked after my family. They were mere kids, away from home for the first time. My uncles briefly and excitedly explained who My Nonie and I were and from whence we came. The boys stood there with mouths agape, as though we had landed in a hot air balloon from Oz. They promised to help if anything was needed, then went back to their tower, and we went on with our meal preparations and conversations.

We saw much of these young enlisted men after that day and enjoyed their company immensely. They often asked me questions about the Japanese, since they imagined they'd soon ship out and invade Japan. They were worried that when the time came, they might not be brave enough because they'd be too scared.

Though much younger than these young men, I felt so much older, so I gave them the benefit of what I had learned already about feeling scared. I explained that being scared or being afraid are two different things. Scared means shivering in anticipation, but willing. Fear indicates being numb with terror, and helpless. The first gives a person motivation to stand and be counted; the second makes one flee, like a coward. One is the act of a man; fear is childlike, immature.

Our boys, despite their youth, climbed their anti-aircraft tower every night as men, real men, with determination to do whatever was needed. Several days later, one soldier brought a five-gallon can almost full of gas for Uncle David's car so we could go to a doctor for a check-up. Uncle David declined the gift of gas. It was a sweet, caring idea, but of course we didn't need to see a doctor. We had recuperated in a hospital for almost six weeks, though I am sure we looked like "death warmed-over" to those hearty soldiers. We never heard from them after their reassignment, but we remembered them often as years passed, and hoped they fared well.

Dinner was hurriedly served, then I scared everyone and myself as well because I began to sob. I cried so hard I nearly threw up. Then my sobs caught in my throat; I couldn't ever swallow.

Why? Good grief. The meal was *meatloaf and scalloped potatoes and fruit salad and chocolate cake.* It was all our "comfort food!" Food we had dreamed of—for so very long! Food, at one point, that I thought I'd never see again.

I remembered weird things we did in the camps, attempting to prolong what enjoyment we tried to have in the food we ate. We held food in our mouths for as long as possible, tasting each molecule before swallowing. We also chewed and chewed each bite until we had extracted any possible remaining flavor. After four years, tens of thousands of miles completely around the world, and life in four foreign countries, I could barely believe we were home, eating family food with our loved ones.

My Nonie explained how we had often tried to blunt our hunger by devising menus and remembering specific dishes we called "comfort food," like this meal's food. We tried to imagine smells and describe how each morsel tasted and felt in our mouths. We imagined the texture of cake or cornbread; we'd remind each other how great it was to gnaw on a fried chicken wing; how sugar crystals on oatmeal looked right before milk dissolved them; the bite of pepper on a tomato; the crunch of a fresh baked bread crust. Sometimes we didn't have any food, but we had memories of tastes and textures. We would try to convince our stomachs we had just finished eating, but our stomachs didn't comply with our imaginations' requests.

Hundreds of times we tried hard to blunt our hunger by focusing our minds on the idea that we had eaten and still had the food's taste in our mouths. *Food.* It passed the time and occupied our thoughts—year after year. Our only real tastes were fish and rice—but little of either. The only other thing we ever thought about obsessively was home.

CHILD POW

Lovely, sensitive Uncle Carl with his sweet big grin laid his cheek on top of my head as he held me on his lap. He wanted to hold my plate while I ate, as though I were a small child, instead of eleven and three-fourth—going on thirty. His gentleness of spirit and action was healing to me. He intuitively knew exactly what I needed most, to calm myself and to begin fitting back into my family.

David Gilderoy and Carl Westine, my uncles I loved so much.

The past few years had made me far older than I should have been, in many ways. No child should ever witness what I did or have my experiences, yet each day, someplace, in countries all over the world, children are experiencing the same things I did: hunger, slavery, abuse, back-breaking work. I ask myself what I can do to stop it? What will *you* do to stop it? We *all* feel helpless about lots of things, but we can help in one way; we can feed the hungry, locally, at the very least. Please. Please feed the hungry.

CHAPTER 26
LISTENING

....Naught shall disturb our cheerful faith...that all which
we behold is full of blessings
—Wordsworth

M y family wept, and then sobbed when we told them
of our long separation from them. They were also
full of questions about where we had been and how
we were treated. They wanted to know what had occurred in
our lives to have put us in this horrendous physical condition
they observed.

When Old Swede had returned from his Red Cross trip to
POW camps, he had surreptitiously let our family know we
were alive at that time. For him to say anymore could endanger
his son. If someone else learned we were alive, it would surely
make life more difficult for his son and probably for us as well
if they discovered the information came from Old Swede and
his trip to the camps.

He wisely kept his counsel, but my grandmother was pro-
foundly grateful to him for his efforts and for telling her alone,
what little he could safely recount. She, in turn, never told a
soul except my Bum Bum, for our safety's sake.

Our family's direct questions were often painful for us to answer—causing us to relive those awful times. Many of our replies were met with stunned silence, as though what we said was too unbelievable to be true.

"No! We don't ever talk about things like this in general conversation," someone said, repelled and shocked when we told them about the rose garden and Lennie's death.

My Nonie explained that the real world of war, outside our country, was much different than they could possibly imagine. She added that our stories would soon be corroborated by other POWs and soldiers returning from war zones. She asked them to be extremely patient with us since life had not only changed abruptly *for us*, life had *changed* us, and we still had a hard time to accept and adjust to those changes.

I thought she spoke impressively, with passion, unlike her usual role in the family before the war. Her brothers, sisters, and her mother were astonished by her eloquence, as they had regarded her as the "Brownie" of the family with a soft manner and one who rarely gave an opinion or made a strong statement. This was a new sister talking to them now. They listened intently.

She told them my experience with pork chops on the ship to Australia, and how I had forgotten such food existed. She told how amazed we were to see people act polite and caring as they stood in line to buy food, rather than frantically, selfishly grabbing. My Nonie explained that going from a free person to a prisoner—to a slave—then back to a prisoner—and once again to a free person—was mentally an incredibly taxing process!

She asked for their understanding on early mornings when rapidly dressed and went outside. Eventually, as I re-acclimated to the normal world my bizarre routine would disappear, bu for now it was a throwback to our POW daily routine. Our lives had depended on my early morning activity. If we were to survive, we had to eat. If we were to eat, I had to carry out my responsibilities in the morning. Our lives depended on me.

At Kobe I had to get up, rush outside, find fire, and search for combustibles before we could cook our three or four tablespoons of dried rice with whatever fish might have been caught during the night on my fish lines. I had to check our lines on the dock, gut the fish and cut off the heads and get them in the rice water to boil. We never ate heads, ever! I used them for bait.

Our family sat silently, frozen during our narrations, like petrified mummies. Their eyes darted from My Nonie to me and back to her.

Aunt Lucy wanted to know what I meant by "finding fire." I told her someone, someplace along the docks, always had a brazier lit, often with coal. Lots of tiny pieces of coal were scattered around so it was easy to gather for our cooking fire, if I could find a starter flame from someone.

A few sticks could start a small fire for a few hours, but the process took a long time so we scrambled each morning. I was always on a dead run to get us fed, then hand our fire off to someone else who needed it.

In the meantime, My Nonie searched for longer wood pieces for our fire base, and as scavengers do anywhere we needed to be fast and be early before someone else found the coveted scraps. There were many pallets like the ones we slept on, which got banged around. I would find wood chips from these, along with matchstick-sized dock splinters. I had to be quick, or someone might shove me to steal what I already had, or they might rush to an area where there were usually plenty of fragments before me. It sounds like an awful job, but it actually wasn't too hard to make a morning fire if I moved right along. The fire needn't be big; a tiny fire as small as a tea cup would do it.

We were now back in the world, yet the pattern was firmly established in Japan as a necessity. In California, ward nurses thought I was psychotic because I was so driven to get outside in the morning. They were so snotty and taken with themselves! We never explained to them. It was none of their affair. Though home now, I would continue to find myself later, still half asleep, yet trying to grab a sheet or some such to wrap around myself and hurry outside, to keep us safe, at eleven years old.

This habit was hard to break, and our family was appalled by it! As Nonie had asked of them though, they were very patient with me. Uncle Dave would hold out his arms to me in the kitchen as I began to hurry by and give me enveloping quiet hugs and tell me it was going to be okay and I would relax and get my breath and fully come awake.

"'We only had to get through each day,' so that's what we did to survive—every day," we gently explained.

We recounted how fellow travelers had nurtured us on our bus ride from California. We shared how passengers bought makeup for My Nonie. My grandmother laughed, then asked about our short hair.

"We had fleas and lice. They shaved us bald on the ship bound for Australia. I'm sensitive about my appearance without hair so I'll stay at home a lot for a while," My Nonie said.

"No. You need to get out. What you have to do is to put on a bit too much rouge. Then people will say to each other, 'Look at that woman. She has too much rouge,' and they'll never notice your hair at all!" my grandmother replied.

Over the years I've used that technique a time or two, and you know, it works exactly as my grandmother said. In addition, My

Nonie wore attractive turbans of soft, drapeable fabrics, to which she would affix an attractive pin of costume jewelry. As usual, she was gorgeous, even though she was still so thin. Eventually, after we went to California she was fitted temporarily for a nice wig but her hair soon grew in and she no longer needed it.

We told stories about sharing food on the bus, the job offers, and other kindnesses from other passengers. My grandmother and Aunt Lucy and all of us later wrote to all the people who had given us their addresses and thanked them for being so kind and attentive. Uncle David sent each family a huge box of Washington Red Delicious apples from the grocery store he recently opened. Letters came back, telling how grateful they were to receive his gift for only doing what was right at the time. Each also said they regretted not being able to do more for us.

See, now! That's what America is all about! You do good because it's the right thing to do, not because you expect anything in return. I believe this sets a great many people apart from all the others. I find it particularly true among Americans. Americans of any race or ethnic background. We are somehow blessed at birth and raised in goodness. How wonderfully lucky we are.

As for My Nonie and me, we had decided early on, after landing in California, we would be open and truthful about our wartime experiences. This may not have been the best choice, but at the time it seemed the only right choice. We were used to living totally *inside* our experiences. While not normal or natural events at least they seemed *familiar,* and our family members deserved to know what our lives were like, no matter how painful the hearing—or the recounting.

"How can you trust me so much?" My Nonie once asked when we were prisoners.

"Because my name is safe in your mouth. When you say it, you make it sound so pretty," I replied. In the same way now, we thought the memories of what we would tell our dear ones would be safe in their keeping.

Regrettably, we were wrong. Our family was completely unhinged by our recitations of prisoner life abroad. My Nonie asked if they truly wanted to listen, or if they preferred we remain silent about our time in Asia? Thankfully, every person wanted us to continue with honesty, even as they became more horrified as we went along. Nonie told them that we agreed to be completely honest with them about our lives for the past four years.

I told them how POW soldiers loved Nonie for her many kindnesses. We explained that most of those very ill men were executed before we ever left for Japan. The family was aghast. Surely, even the Japanese could not have done the things they heard from us. They asked more questions, which we patiently answered:

"What? You had lice?"

"Yes. And fleas and parasites."

"What parasites do you mean?"

"Mother, I mean worms. Worms."

"Why did doctors allow that?"

"*We never saw any doctors.*"

"What kind of a place was this? Why didn't you complain?"

"*This place was Hell on earth. If you complained you would be killed.*"

"Dead rats floated in a water barrel, and no one cleaned it out for you?"

"*The worst was when the men, a few of them, skinned the rats to add to their food. Also, if we complained we were punished, usually whipping with a rope or a bamboo rod for causing dissension.*"

"What do you mean, you cut off your hair to trade it for fishhooks? Whatever possessed you to do that?"

"*It was a way to live one more day, until someone might come to help us get away.*"

"You used newspapers to stuff inside your rags? Didn't you tell them you were cold? Why didn't you demand appropriate winter clothing?"

"*If they had known we even had the bits of newspapers or signal flags, we faced swift, severe punishment for theft. Then they would also confiscate the rest of our meager belongings. Theft was punished by cutting off a hand or arm or by beheading. We didn't want them to know we had contraband of any kind!*"

We had lived in constant fear. It was hard to leave it behind us and far harder to explain it.

"Surely now, really. How could you have survived this kind of treatment?" they asked many times.

"*We survived as a result of will, to come home, and so we could tell other people what vicious tyrants the Japs were!*"

Then they cried, again. Even the uncles this time.

After a time, our loved ones' tears ceased and they frowned in disbelief at our fervent answers. They looked at each other with questioning sideways glances, to affirm a mutual consensus that no one would dare do such things to their dear ones. Incredibly, these adults were totally naïve about what happens in a war zone.

I make them sound like a group of dummies. They were not dummies and I apologize, first to their memories and then to you, if I've led your thoughts that way. Their personal and family group identities were so decent, so kind, so altruistic and so honorable that what we told them was nearly incomprehensible within the framework of everything they knew up to that time. In a way, we were glad they *were* naïve. They were far too decent to be able to imagine humans could treat one another these ways. My Nonie and I talked about it later. We agreed we were sorry we had exposed them to such evil.

After a little time, the uncles carefully, tenderly asked if they could hug us. I quickly understood their quandary and explained I wanted my family to hug and kiss me! I told them I had often dreamed of this day, when they could be near, to hug me tight. It was part of being a family again.

I told them how Nonie would regularly reinforce to me that, "When we get back in the world, you will be the same person they knew before. We need their love, their touch and their questions, to heal. We need to cry, and we need to have them cry with us. By this, we will heal—inside." My Nonie had constantly reassured me of this.

At this, the men scowled as we sat talking and drinking our after-dinner coffee. They said they couldn't remember when they had last cried. The women said nothing, but those immediately nearby hugged us. Those across the dining room table reached out and held our hands.

"When you cry with us and for us, we'll know it is a sign we are loved and worthy of affection—no longer simply numbers on Hell's transport list," My Nonie had explained.

It bothered the uncles, the aunties, and my grandmother to hug us too firmly since we were excessively thin—they said they thought they might injure us. When they said this, Nonie laughed and replied, "Thin? Ha! You should have seen us two months ago! But please, don't take us to an oriental café for dinner. I've eaten all the seaweed and rice I'm ever going to eat!"

She thought it was lighthearted and funny, so did I; we felt we were demonstrating we had regained a sense of humor. However, much later we found out it broke their hearts to hear us bravely make light of our horrendous treatment.

Burns on my back, arms, and legs from officers' cigarettes and cigars still hadn't healed from their infliction three years before in the officers' camp. Nonie used to put salt water poultices on them in Kobe but I had previously become so infected while working in the dirt in the tin mine that any non-medicated treatment was quite futile.

The physicians in Australia had begun to treat me with sulfa, a new drug invention. It was applied as a powder and I also took sulfa tablets daily. Due to the condition of the wounds and the manner in which they had become further contaminated in China, I was checked continually in Australia and once again in California to determine if I had contracted leprosy, also known as Hansen's Disease. Leprosy was endemic in the part of China we went to, as was tuberculosis.

For several years, it was assumed I had TB and I was medicated for it. Later it was found that my condition was not tuberculosis after all but only severe scarring and bleeding throat lesions from the bronchitis I had for so many months. I was never diagnosed with either terrible disease. Perhaps we weren't there long enough. I was lucky once again. It's the caul.

Again, although sulfa was the recommendation in America along with the addition of a new drug, tetracycline, yet my body's healing would take a very long time. The greater barrier to healing was my own basic physical condition. My body was still so malnourished, it didn't have the ability to repair itself. When my grandmother saw the supperrating burn wounds, she immediately wanted to know how and why I was burned. Then, without waiting for an answer, she set about treating me with a salve called Unguentine. It was quite soothing, though not particularly healing.

I explained the burns were several years old. I'd received them from the camp officers at Baguio, when I displeased them. Uncle David asked what I had done.

"*I didn't obey fast enough, or I wasn't as cooperative as they expected.*"

"Oh, honey, they couldn't have *meant* to hurt you. You're only a little kid. It must have been an accident," precious Uncle David said. He was such a sweet, almost innocent soul, and only two years younger than Nonie.

I looked at My Nonie. She took a deep breath, closed her eyes as if for a quick prayer, then she gave me an affirmative nod and softly said, "Here it comes."

I understood this as permission to talk openly. I looked at their questioning faces and told them, "I hate telling you this because I have nightmares after I talk about it. Something bad happened to me in one of the camps." I paused and looked around. I met only loving faces and Uncle Carl hugged me tighter. Aunt Dorothy stroked my arm and gave me tiny squeezes. Everyone tried to help. My grandmother sat looking down at her hands.

"Really it happened to both of us."

Aunt Lucy held her mouth tight and said, "Go on, honey. We're going to do this all today and once and for all. We're ready. Take your time. What happened?"

I took another deep breath and started to cry and then said, "I'm afraid you won't love us anymore. The Japs used me as the toy for the sexual deviants in one camp. I didn't want to do it but they were going to kill us if I didn't." They gasped. The silence was so profound, I needn't raise my voice over a whisper to continue.

I cried when I told them how repugnant the soldiers were. A few were excessively hairy; one had an enormous ugly mole on his chest; another never cleaned his jagged fingernails, and I hated him to touch me. Most of the officers ate a pungent relish or condiment that gave them such terrible breath it incapacitated me.

Some were so heavy, I thought I would be crushed. They were disgusting and filled me with revulsion. I was so repelled by them that many times I nearly threw up. I knew they would kill me if I vomited on them, and that fact terrified me because I didn't want to die.

Sometimes the officers' fat bellies would push against me so hard I couldn't get a breath and I thought I would suffocate and die. When I struggled they liked it more and it lasted longer. I became so afraid that most of the time I remained silent when they were with me. I would leave them and flee to the safe place in my mind. I knew I was safe there and I could calm myself. For months I fled in my mind.

I cried as I spoke, huddled in Uncle Carl's arms because the telling of it was over.

"We were so afraid you'd send us away when you found out. We had to do such bad things that we thought you'd hate us and wouldn't stand to have us around," I told them. A throaty murmur arose around the table. Interspersed were sharp comments of, "Those bastards!" and "Damn those Japs." This from a family of people who never swore over anything. Then I saw everyone's tears and knew we were home to stay.

I couldn't hold back then. My tears were those of a little girl who finally felt safe in the arms of people she knew would die for her. I knew my loved ones would never think of me in any way but with love and kindness. It was simply too much strain to recount the horrible memories, then to try to remain composed in the face of this loving support. I kept trying to act as I thought a grown-up would act, but I couldn't hold back. In spite of my effort, I was still only eleven years old. I was still a little girl.

The room was pregnant with silence and shock, as heavy as any load of grief imaginable. My grandmother spoke through her tears, "I'm only glad your grandfather didn't know any of this. It would have broken his heart to know his Babby and his Brownie underwent these atrocities."

Dear Aunt Betty laid her head upon our dinner table and wept. Dorothy and David clutched each other and their tiny, youngest child. The babe was named Eleanor after my grandmother and also after My Nonie who was her aunt Eleanor, and who was missing in Asia at the time of her birth. She was such a good baby. She has brought great joy to all of us over all the years of her life. She grew to be a lovely woman.

Like carved stone, My Nonie sat, tears streaming down her cheeks. Aunt Lucy tearfully left the dining room. She returned in a few minutes with warm, damp washcloths. She handed one to Nonie across the table and then reached around Carl's shoulder and wiped my face and eyes. She kissed me and gently said, "There. Now no one will ever hurt you again. You and your mama are home now, for good."

Soldiers had wandered back over our fence and through the hedge and played ball outside with the smaller children. One pushed a child's swing, another rolled a ball and someone walked around the yard with the newest baby showing her the blossoms on flowers in bloom. They were extremely helpful and sensitive to our family's need that night. Sunset had come and the light was golden through the firs as

John Henry Gilderoy,
my grandfather.
My grandmother called him
Jack and I called him
BumBum

the young men sang folks songs to the little ones while they pushed the swing gently. "I gotta gal in Baltimore, Little Liza Jane....street car comes right by her door..." ; and "..and I went downtown for to see my gal, singing Polly-Wolly-Doodle all the way.." The little children were smiling and happy. Their eyes

313

were drooping with sleep but they didn't want to leave their new friends. Soon the boys brought the children in and mamas began the bedtime ritual for each of them.

My grandmother told us how she often cooked fried chicken for the boys in the tower and made her special donuts for them. She cooked because it was better than having her chickens stolen in the night—as had happened. She said the men broke too many eggs, fumbling in the dark for the poultry. When off duty, these same soldiers were lonely and visited us often. Most were mere kids from farms in the Southeast.

My Nonie and I continued to talk with family well into the night. Children went to bed, and the babies were tended.

The house grew quiet, somber, as if it also waited to hear what had happened to its people. There is a strength and wholesomeness about this house. The house has held lovers and some who hated, mothers, fathers, children, and grandparents adored by all. It has seen sickness, sorrow, and death. Romantic affairs, broken hearts, birthdays, and holidays galore. To this day, the house remains..... Bethesda........... a haven of comfort and help.

CHAPTER 27

POKUMHAMBURKIFY

My other self; my sister; my avatar, my friend.
She helps me plant May-flowers
and she sings sweetly to my heart.

——*Swinburne*

W e told the family about Pokumhamburkify—my avatar in the tin mine. They didn't really understand at first about the wonderful support I felt from my imaginary, invented companion. By believing her to be present with me, my mind was able to block out whatever was happening and I could dig in my tunnel in the mine without overwhelming loneliness. I explained how I taught her to speak Mandarin.

The family immediately asked me to verify if I really spoke Chinese. They knew I learned languages like dogs pick up fleas, so I responded in Mandarin, "Please love us. We need to be with you." Relatives scrutinized me, then Nonie, nonverbally asking if I was faking.

"She kept us alive all the time in China. She bartered everything she could find in exchange for more food. She even robbed birds' nests. Yes, she speaks the language," Nonie said with solemn assurance.

This was as great a shock to our loved ones as was recounting abuses in the officers' camp. Once again their faces paled;

then they all talked at once—over-talked each other is more like it. A cacophony!

"China?" they asked. "What do you mean, China? You said you were in Japan!"

"Yes, the Philippines, China, Japan, too, but it was no vacation. We were made to work hard in the tin mine tunnels."

"A tin mine? What could *you two* do in a tin mine?" Scornfully, disbelieving.

"Absolutely everything we were told to do."

After we related the saga of our life in China, Uncle David stood and said, "I've cried so much, I have a headache. I didn't think I could cry any longer but this news is really something to hear about. I'm getting an aspirin. Can I bring one for anyone else?" Everyone nodded in unison, so he returned with the entire bottle, then, abruptly, he took a pencil from the kitchen counter and wrote "Pokumhamburkify" on the woodwork beside the refrigerator. My grandmother and Uncle David began to laugh through their tears, and she said, "Shades of Cheyenne." Then everyone laughed, even I, because I finally remembered where Pokumhamburkify came from! We all did.

When I was only three years old, recovering from a near-fatal car accident in Cheyenne, I invented Pokumhamburkify as an invisible friend. I was a lonely little girl living on a horse ranch with no one for a playmate except my bulldog, Freckles. This imaginary girl became my constant companion, to the point that I eventually took her name as my own and never answered unless that name was used. Uncle David, my grandmother, and my grandfather couldn't remember its convoluted pronunciation, so my Bum-Bum wrote the name with his carpenter's pencil on the fresh, painted woodwork.

I realized now that in a time of stress in China, I had come full-circle. I had needed my friend again when I was lonely and desperate there. I didn't even recall the name's origin, but Pokumhamburkify rose from my subconscious to provide a needed, comforting memory from a *gentler* time and place.

Except for these few times of serious discussions, My Nonie and I did try to speak lightly of our experiences to spare our family great despair over our captivity. Light-hearted bantering worked most of the time, but once in a while a question was asked that pulled the proverbial rug right out from under our controlled emotions.

"What did you do on Christmas Day?" was a tough question, yet Christmas was one of the few good memories we had while prisoners of war. It was a time of tremendous nostalgia. My Nonie was not particularly a formal religious person. She had been raised in a family who called themselves "Dancing Methodists." She was quite dissatisfied with various major religious denominations, however, her faith was solid and true. She prayed to God and worshiped Him and she lived His commandments daily.

My Nonie understood I was inclined to embrace the religious focus I had received at Episcopal boarding schools. Therefore, we celebrated and honored Christmas and made it a religious, ceremonial occasion. Quietly, apart from others, secretively, she hummed the Advent hymns with me, and we tried to recall the Gospels' language of the Christmas story from Luke.

One year we made a three-piece Nativity set of our own with sticks and small round rocks. After roll-call that day, we came back to our mats in our shed and found our Nativity scattered all about. But it did not matter. The holiday was still in our heads and hearts.

317

"Where were you on your tenth birthday?" asked Aunt Betty.

At this question, I forgot to be circumspect and I rapidly blurted, "I know exactly where I was. I was sick, coughing, I was lying face down on my chest in a tiny, cold, wet tunnel in a Chinese tin mine. I was scratching at dirt in the dark, gasping for breath. Then suddenly I remembered it was my birthday. I laid my head down and cried a while, and I wondered if I would be able to live long enough to be eleven." Tears began anew even though we were all exhausted from crying.

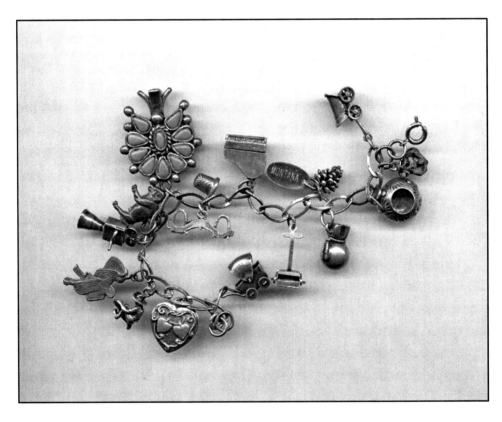

MY CHARM BRACELET

Aunt Betty cried as though she had been there as a witness. Then she said she had a special gift for me in my grandmother's dresser. It had waited there all these years. She immediately retrieved it—my first charm bracelet! From silver links hung pretty, intricate charms. A copper buffalo from Montana celebrated the state where I was born as well as the immense copper mines there. Each charm was a special remembrance, and some were commemorating trips Betty and Carl took while I was gone and places they wanted to take me now that I was home. They also found delicate charms for each birthday and Christmas I was away. There was a doll buggy, a miner, and even a grand piano. How special! What a happy thing to do.

I have worn the bracelet many times since then. I've added charms on special occasions. A tiny piece of copper ore from the '85 Mine in New Mexico, several others from my dear Southwest, and of course, a pine cone for our Northwest forests. It is carefully protected in my jewelry chest and grows ever dearer over the years.

Today it seems like a commemorative piece, in the manner of service medals. I look at it with good memories—never bad. Ghouls can't walk past my door when I wear it. How did Betty ever know it could become *this* important to me? Ah...yes. I remember—she was born with the caul. She knew.

CHILD POW

My Nonie explained many things while answering questions. Sometimes our relatives' responses were so innocent, that I felt eighty years old. When My Nonie told them she cut off and traded my long hair to a guard in Kobe for fishing line, Uncle David said, "But Nonie, you don't even eat fish. You've never liked it."

My Nonie and I looked at each other a minute. We remembered how proud we were when we caught a fish. They were tiny, but each little piece was nutrition for us. Lots of the questions were naïve. How could we make them understand? Maybe they shouldn't.

"Did you make any nice friends there?" someone asked.

"*Beg your pardon?*" Nonie responded, stupefied, as though struck dumb. I couldn't quite understand the question either. Our thoughts raced. Was it important we had friends? My mind sped ahead. I was nearly in an out of body experience. Reality disappeared suddenly but only for a moment. Frantically we scurried through our minds for the answer to our family's question. Such a simple question yet what mental complication it brought to both of us. For years we had survived by excluding all other people. It was paramount for the survival of each of us to focus only on the other's well-being.

Why were we being asked about friends? Friends? Were we supposed to make friends? Nobody told us to do that. If we had friends would we have come home sooner? My reasoning suddenly went all out of whack. We couldn't have friends. They might do something we'd be blamed for if guards knew we associated with them. We were just trying to survive.

How could we explain we didn't have *time* to make friends in Japan. At bayonet point, we either worked sixteen to twenty hours each day—or, exhausted from heavy work, malnourishment and sleep-deprivation, in a frenzy we scrounged for little bits of flammables to make a small fire to cook our fish and rice—or we tried to get warm enough to sleep, in preparation for the next day's labor. In addition, friends could be dangerous. We might become compromised by their activity if they displeased the captors.

Life was safer if we stayed by ourselves, but, most importantly, we had no friends because we had no time left for friendships. We didn't even learn the names of all of the people in our go-down. They didn't care and we didn't care. This wasn't like going to summer camp. Our lives depended on our ability to forage and to work very hard every single day. There were no days off. We couldn't afford the luxury of the distraction of a friend. It was work or die.

I could recount these events to my family only if I had loving arms around me to shelter my body and spirit. Those arms made anything bearable to discuss. I realized now, in the thinking about the absence of friends, just how lonely we had been those years. We didn't recognize it at the time. We were too busy shoveling, loading, searching, and trying to last one more day.

Over the years more memories return; then they subside, and I put them away from me once more. Many events are extremely difficult to think of—even now—but the horrors are over. At home we needed to pray for all those left behind and for those lost to the war. So many beautiful lives are gone. I think about this and many, many times I wonder if I have known a soldier who might have found the cure for a dread disease had he been spared. Did I know someone destined to write a beautiful anthem or create a sublime painting? I'm sure I must have.

So many lives of value were lost from this world due to that damn war. In the end, I feel it was all for greed, money, and macho power. What other reason is there?

The rest of our family, apart from My Nonie and me, had all fared well during the duration of WWII. Uncle Jim True, a civil engineer, finished his job as head of the construction of the local military airfield. He was commissioned an Army officer in 1940. He went to Alaska where he built airfields for the impending hostilities.

Although Alice and Jim were extremely close, she felt the need to establish her own profession, prior to commencement of hostilities. Jim strongly endorsed her idea.

The United States knew war was at hand. A large build-up of men and materials commenced in early 1940. Shipyards sprouted. Army hospitals opened in new places across the country. Aircraft construction was funded. America knew it was coming, not exactly when, and certainly not that Japan aspired to land the first blow. The general thought was that we'd fight the Germans in Europe as happened in WWI.

Independent as ever, Aunt Alice joined the Army Nurse Corps to accrue time in service and a few levels of rank. She and Uncle Jim both assumed his assignment would be to England, so she planned to seek assignment there as a nurse. They thought the separation might be only a few months. Yet, the army—which consults with no one—sent her to the Philippines instead, while Jim flew to England to build more airfields. He and his darling never saw each other again in this life.

He was a major, who eventually supervised the building of his self-designed Mulberrys, huge concrete pontoon structures.

These were patterned after his original design for present-day concrete floating bridges on Lake Washington and Hood Canal in Washington State. Mulberrys were wonderful floating harbors used on D-Day, on Normandy beaches.

Sadly, Uncle Jim died of a heart attack in September 1944. Aunt Alice was on a hospital ship in the Pacific. In 1945 while anchored in Manila Bay, Philippines, she helped retrieve POWs from Cabanatuan and other camps when Japan surrendered.

A violent typhoon hit the rescue fleet shortly after that, and our people learned most port facilities in Kobe, among other port cities, were destroyed. My Nonie and I realized, once again, we had been snatched from death in the nick of time. Pure luck.

Aunt Alice's mailed report of observing the surrender in Tokyo Bay was exciting, but her accounts of recovering prisoners from Japan were horrendous for us all to read. She lightened it as much as possible, for my grandmother's sake, but data "between the lines" was painful.

We had sent Aunt Alice lists of names we remembered, names of POWS who might be freed, yet she saw none. Released prisoners were immediately sent aboard hospital ships to be vetted concerning their health status and given medical treatment before a return "back to the world" on any type of ship headed that way. She actively looked for our friends, our fellow prisoners. With nurse friends, she distributed our lists on other anchored hospital ships, but those men we sought were never found.

It seems only a fraction of POWs incarcerated on mainland Japan, as we were, ever survived. One who did survive was our old friend Captain Tug. The announcement of his return from Japanese camps was front page news in local papers. Apparently most POWs were murdered in Jap coal mines immediately before or after the surrender so they could not bear witness to abominable treatment.

We learned later of POWs who spent part of WWII in terrible "research hospitals," where dreadful and inhumane experiments were performed on them. They were executed and buried in Tokyo, Kobe, Osaka, and other cities. I will not dwell on the types of torture, since many authors have written entire books about these "research hospitals." All I know of these awful places is what I have been told.

Since that time, we have always felt certain that execution would have been our fate if we survived the typhoon destruction. It appears, however, that POWs who worked on the docks did not survive. We were told later that the guards deserted their posts and left the prisoners to the mercy of the crashing seas that swept ashore in Kobe Bay.

I wonder who coaled the ships after that? Perhaps there was no dock to tie a ship to after the destruction passed, so they'd no longer need coalers like we had been. I wonder who did the job in peacetime? Were smaller freighters needed after the war or were they, too, all sunk in the typhoon? Maybe the luggers didn't survive the typhoon, either. We never knew. We were gone before the typhoon and cessation of hostilities. Lucky again.

Many prisoners were murdered—simply to keep them from exposing evil! The Japs killed them, yet our government still wouldn't allow a freed POW to tell about what he saw with his own eyes. We needed that friendly trading partner more. This cover-up continues to disgust me!

Oddly, Kobe and Seattle became Sister Cities years after the war. Each city acts quite proud of it. Good grief! Now a strange idea has been formulated by nitwits in both countries. They have decided to make Mount Rainier and Mt. Fujiyama "sister mountains." How ridiculous. This is nonsense. There is absolutely no comparison and furthermore it is insulting to even consider it.

It was a time of great joy for us now at home, except that my dear grandfather, my Bum Bum, who in heavy Scots brogue always called me his "Babby," had died eighteen months before our return.

My Nonie and I often tried to reconstruct time lines. One date we are sure we estimated accurately was a stormy and cold January night in Kobe and the night our Bum Bum died in Tacoma. According to our tiny, handwritten calendar, which she kept hidden while a prisoner, Bum Bum must have died that night while Nonie swam to the foreign ship and received our sweaters, socks and caviar.

My grandfather's spirit must have compelled that decent sailor to help Bum Bum's two darlings. We always felt there was more than coincidence to this strange happenstance. Now we knew why we had that feeling.

Our family always has agreed strongly with our conclusions about this.

Uncle David held me tight when he told me Bum Bum's death had been sudden—a cerebral hemorrhage. I was glad he hadn't suffered; we saw far too much suffering in Asia.

The day we arrived home was exactly six weeks before the first and second atomic bombs were dropped on Hiroshima and Nagasaki. Mercifully, those bombs ended years of our planet's worst devastation, which had touched almost every person on earth in some way. The cessation of war due to the atomic bombs dropped on Hiroshima and Nagasaki saved many hundreds of thousands of lives of people on both sides who would have died if the war had continued to the invasion of the Japanese home islands.

Another deep sorrow for us all was when My Nonie and I told our family, through tears, of the death of My Sweet Friend in the Philippines, along with all her family members. Our loved ones were each stricken to their core at this news. She was an integral part of our extended activities when she studied at my American boarding school. Our family was particularly angered and heart-broken when we told them about the last time we saw her. Little Lily, gone to the angels, her dead body lying limp in her mother's arms on the floor of the confiscated Bayview Hotel in Manila on the second Tuesday of January 1942.

As though he wrote it for our Lily, Poet Houseman said:

There now...she lays like a silent instrument at rest:
A silent instrument——whereon the wind
Hath long forgot to play.

Aunt Alice was transferred to Madigan Army Hospital in Puget Sound as a major until her discharge in 1947. She was a school nurse in Fife, did hospital nursing, worked for a dentist, and was a public health nurse. She bought her new Ford convertible with the Pan Am refund for the other half of the round trip tickets Nonie and I were not allowed to use. Apparently Pan Am *finally* assumed responsibility for refusing to board us when combat started, when they feared passenger contamination from my polio. All my grandmother's chicks had come home to roost.

Our old friend, Captain Tug, later gave an oral history interview, which I found most interesting. His experiences were comparable to ours. We were sorry he had to undergo this imprisonment, but we were glad to have corroboration of our own life stories. He explained how he mentally dwelt on food during his captivity. He also learned how to deal with unjust punishments in the same way we had done. He said that after the first few blows of a beating he would go limp and appear defeated because Japs soldiers would stop. He also discussed "hell ships," which took POWs to work-camps in Japan. The captain was fairly reticent to speak at great length, but I felt he corroborated all My Nonie and I had seen and endured.

I found his account interesting; in the many ways it validated my own experiences. At no time did he ever discuss meeting his father face to face in Asia, during the Swedish Red Cross inspection. I have often wondered if the two men decided to abide by America's forced demand for confidentiality, rather than breach it and have further contact with posturing government officials or pompous military staff.

American officials intimidated us and other freed civilian POWs to an extreme degree. After WWII, they were such nuisances and seemed constantly underfoot. One stereotypical behavior they exhibited was arrogance, sometimes even visibly but silently sneering, indicating, "You want me to believe that?"

Worse yet, it felt like they thought, *"You've survived POW camps, and you still want me to think you're my equal? You are tainted!"* We deeply felt each *hurtful* sneer and insult. Several actually flared their nostrils and curled their lips like we smelled bad. Not nice human beings, at all.

This silly secrecy business is the probable reason most real stories of POW survivors have been squelched for years. None of our military wanted accountability for their misfeasance, stupidity, and malfeasance concerning our freedom and return. It is as if the military believed officials who had dealt poorly with civilian POWS might eventually die, if everyone remained silent long enough—and you cannot sue or punish a dead man. They basically covered each other's mistakes and derrières. In my mind it was criminal conspiracy over and over again to deny us our Constitutional First Amendment right to speak out. Yet I do understand why they got away with it so easily—we were ex-POWs, and we were flotsam washed up by accident and, additionally in our case, we were women. Even Eleanor Roosevelt, the president's wife, wasn't safe from jeers and arrows of the under-educated, mentally unwashed electorate. Women were definitely second class in those times. It's not a wonder some of us continue to be so shrill.

After the war my stepfather, whom my mother and I loved tremendously, became a high school principal in a nearby city. He and Old Swede frequently met during civic meetings, but strangely, our families never had any contact after the war. It seems the experience might have drawn people together.

When a new high school was built, Papa was involved in the decision to name the school after Old Swede. The older gentleman was very grateful.

It may have been my mother who chose to distance herself from anyone who might know of her ordeal in the Far East. She was extremely ashamed of those experiences in her life. She shouldn't have been, but I think this was the reason the families had no contact.

My Papa remained grateful and maintained a friendship with Old Swede and Captain Tug, father and son, through their fellowship in Rotary. It was a red-letter day when I was inducted into Rotary in October, 1987, as one of the first women members. I was also the first woman president of my club. I am proud to be included with such wonderful citizens. My dear Papa had not lived to see it. I wish he had.

Captain Tug had been sent to Japan to work in the mines. After the war was over, he remained there voluntarily for several weeks to help nurse the sick in his group. He was eventually repatriated and sent to Hawaii for further processing. There, in his attempts to return to the mainland, he was flummoxed by our government, much as we had earlier experienced. (We returned to America five months earlier than Captain Tug.) No telephone calls were allowed. No helping hand gave this freed prisoner assistance to get home. Most noticeably, since he was not military personnel, there was no bureaucratic way to process him back to the United States. Repeatedly he told government officials he was a civilian contractor captured on Wake Island.

"Oh," they said. "Then you must be under Naval orders."

Our Navy, in turn, refused to do anything for him either.

As unbelievable as the following may sound, it is true! This tug captain, a former POW was temporarily penniless and unable to even pay for a long distance telephone call or cablegram to the United States, finally allowed himself to be declared "mentally ill" by a sympathetic doctor in order to get passage home to mainland America!

Fortunately, shortly before this bogus departure his father— by then a Captain in the Navy, crossed paths with his son and the red tape was immediately cut. They returned home together on an aircraft carrier—a small ship called a "Jeep carrier" because of its size. When they docked in Puget Sound, Captain Tug's mother, skippering her own tugboat from the family's fleet of

329

boats, met them carrying her son's overcoat over her arm. It was a chilly day—but a warm reunion!

CHAPTER 28

THE ARMY, THE NAVY, AND NEW YORK CITY

America! America!
God shed his grace on thee
And crown thy good with brotherhood
From sea to shining sea.
——*Katherine Bates*

I have castigated our government for what I still perceive as
their lack of response to help us. We were devastated citizens! However, I would be wrong and ungrateful to ignore
one thing that definitely did ease our way, or at least My Nonie's
way, back into civilized society.

Once we were met at Ft. Lewis by an intelligence officer, a
colonel, in company with another colonel who was a psychiatrist. Now more than sixty years later, I believe the psychiatrist,
naturally a medical doctor, was present to discern if we told

about things that truly happened to us or if we were not sane. These men were friendly, warm, encouraging, and also professional warriors who had often seen much death and destruction. Several times their eyes teared during our three or four meetings that often lasted hours, and that response was more than we had hoped.

"If we could make anything happen to make your future better, what might that be?" they asked Nonie at the end of our first of many sessions. It seemed she spoke so quickly she hadn't had time to even take a deep breath before she said, *"Give me a past."* She explained to them, *" I need to work. I need to support my child and help my family. My husband is a Navy veteran who was injured in battle three times in landings on Pacific islands. I need employment references to cover our past four years."* She spoke so quickly she was breathless for a moment. Her voice was animated as she went on to say, *"I'm so afraid employers won't hire me because of my personal wartime history, and I'm not sure I can undergo questions and comments from strangers. Maybe someday, but not now."*

Somewhere, someone with great resources pulled together union officials—later indicted for corruption in the aircraft industry—international construction companies and a few smaller businesses as references. Nonie's cousin, a long time upper management employee of Bechtel who lived most of his professional life in Saudi Arabia, seems to have assisted here Within two months she was assured all was in order. From that day on she had no problem with employment.

When I was asked if they could do anything special for me, I replied, *"Yes. We can stop these interviews. We have told our story probably fifty or sixty times. The story never changes because the facts won't change. The story continues to stay the same. You people need to realize that every time we are forced to detail those awful times that we have to relive them. We want to stop living in the past. We want you to leave us alone."*

It's only marginally possible my statement had some influence on them, but they began to remove themselves more and more from our lives.

I sometimes have such a strong need to find out how Nonie's professional history was created. Now that My Nonie is dead it might be all right to investigate, but I won't inquire since it was something she did not want revealed. No one could benefit, and the action might, in fact, cause harm to those who protected her.

Nonie in Balboa Park, San Diego
prior to leaving for New York City

Her "new" job references listed her life and jobs with aircraft companies in San Diego during the war. She had copies of personnel records and paycheck stubs. She was given references and commendations. She was even mentioned in an internal memo as one who could be counted on to give their all for the war effort. Her FICA tax was paid. Phony records also showed she had supported me at school. The school was identified as one I had indeed attended one year, so officials there were happy to cover upon request. They provided me with report cards for the time in question. Wonder of wonders, they even invited me to return to their school.

I was included in a list of children who purportedly were baptized by a Reverend Raymond Atteberry in the Fort Lewis chapel. I was included because I *could* have been there during that time. No one realized I had received the Baptismal sacrament in infancy.

These men were wonderful. They both extended their power, their imagination, and their compassion to the two of us when it might have caused them irreparable harm, if discovered. Once again, we were tremendously lucky to be in the right place at the right time with the right people. *The power of the caul.*

With all the positives in life there are also other times that show up more negatively. Government staffers in California did a purposefully rotten thing: they kept us apart from Papa while we were in California in "rehabilitation."

Papa was admitted three days prior to our exodus from the same naval facility. He was recovering from his last war injuries. We were all frustrated to realize we could have been together. Neither he nor we knew of the other's location, which would have been just a few yards apart.

Hospital personnel must have known we were related, considering the unusual last name. Additionally, Nonie had been interviewed about her financial condition and had provided both social security numbers as well as Papa's military serial number. The fact that no one told either party of the other's whereabouts indicates they knew all along, yet they decided to keep us separate, probably to hide our sorry physical state. No wonder "the Grey Ladies" sneered at us. We felt manipulated once again for no good reason. Weren't they a pitiful little bunch of bureaucrats? What was there that robbed them of the slightest compassion for others?

As soon as my grandmother told us of Papa's location, My Nonie called and bought train tickets on the chair car, and we headed south to meet up with Papa. We had arrived home on Thursday evening and by Saturday morning we were on our way again. We could finally spend joyous days together as a family!

One day Papa asked me if I had ever finally been confirmed in my home church. Since we were at home such a short time, confirmation was delayed. He knew how important it was to me. I told him how dear to my heart it would be when it finally happened.

He acted somewhat secretive, but said when he had flown to California from Hawaii for treatment of his broken back he was accompanied by three special sailors. One was a Navy chaplain; another was an admiral, receiving a check-up prior to big, anticipated fleet battles and the invasion of Japan; and the third good man was the admiral's aide.

The admiral had earlier been quite sick with shingles and had painful residual neuropathy. He, his aide, the chaplain, and Papa had dinner several times, played cards, and talked about their families. Papa told of his loved ones' misfortune to become POWs lost someplace in Asia. The other men, also husbands and fathers, were horrified at Papa's tale. They offered to provide any assistance he requested. Now, two days later, Papa knew we were on our way to join him and he quickly accepted their fine offer.

Papa asked if the chaplain, now a good friend, could do the honors and confirm me as an official Episcopalian. Since this is something correctly done by a bishop of the church, the chaplain attempted to arrange something for me. I was worried that I didn't have a male relative present to act as godfather. Papa told me not to worry, the issue was already handled. He said he had a friend who *asked if he could be honored by becoming my godfather*. I couldn't *imagine* who would volunteer for such a thing.

The chaplain assisted the nearest Bishop who came to the hospital chapel for my confirmation and, wonder of wonders, my godfather was none other than Fleet Admiral William Halsey. I had come from a prison camp where I was more worthless than something stuck on the bottom of a shoe and yet now was in the presence of this illustrious and famous hero dressed in formal uniform with medals and gold braid. I was agog, I was mute. I was nobody. He had volunteered to be my godfather. Unbelievable.

After the ceremony concluded, the Bishop accompanied the rest of us to the Officers' Club for a celebratory dinner. The Admiral and I had pork chops with applesauce. He talked to me at length about his own confirmation, about his family members and how he missed them. He told stories about his boyhood and some funny stories about when he was learning to fly an airplane. He preferred his battleships.

I remained silent, not knowing what to say and fearing to offend or be thought a ninny for making an inane comment. Finally, I asked him if he was also called "Bull Halsey." He frowned ferociously and told me he hated that nickname. I clammed up immediately, knowing I had innocently put my foot in it but the Admiral said, "Well, if you don't know what to call me, just call me Bill." He said this with such charm and a big grin that I relaxed immediately and finally began to chatter away.

All of the participants signed my Prayer Book. I was so proud. I carried my Prayer Book to church for the next thirty-five years and was regularly reminded of the day of my confirmation.

We had a wonderful two days longer with the Admiral and his aide. We were driven to Balboa Park and then to Coronado Island for a long leisurely lunch, where we *all* traded war stories. When they left they flew back to where the Admiral again assumed command of the fleet that would be in the vanguard of the invasion of Japan. I prayed so hard that nothing would happen to any of these fine men.

Once, many long years later, I left my Prayer Book in our pew and when I went back to get it, it was gone. Later that day it was returned to the parish office, but the "names" dedication page was removed. Apparently we had a fellow parishioner who was an autograph hound. Sometimes I get so thoroughly disgusted with my fellow man, but then I have to remember, churches are for sinners. Good grief!

I never saw him again, but "Just call me Bill" and I exchanged Christmas cards for years, until his death. I treasure the memory of that great man who wasn't too busy, or too impressed with himself to become part of a little girl's life. He gave big hugs He smelled of Old Spice cologne. Only in America.

THE ARMY, THE NAVY, AND NEW YORK CITY

One policy that still irritates me is the low remuneration that was given to separated or discharged service personnel. Papa and millions of fellow servicemen became members of the "52/20" club. After giving their lives, health, and in many cases their futures, our veterans merely received an insulting twenty dollars, for fifty-two weeks. America needed lots of government money to rebuild Japan, but that money should have stayed here and taken care of people who really earned it! Greed wears an ugly face.

After Papa was released from the hospital, we almost immediately left for New York City, where Papa finished his Naval career as an intelligence officer. In addition, Papa attended Columbia University, where he was awarded his Masters Degree in Secondary Education.

The G.I. Bill was a social and educational phenomenon. If a veteran chose school or formal job training, our government paid tuition, books and gave a $100 monthly stipend. For most vets this allowed for food, but the fellow lived in squalor while he was in school; or he lived decently but scrounged for food; or people doubled up and pooled their resources. Those dollars didn't go far.

We pulled it off in a small two-room sublet flat on the north end of Manhattan Island only because of Nonie's bank roll from the savings account our grandmother and Papa had set up. I thought we were in heaven because our flat had rose-colored walls and floral furniture. The three of us grew together as a family while both parents attended photography school. Later, they opened a photography studio but Papa was too lonesome for kids and soon went back to teaching in public schools. For many years he was an administrator and a high school principal.

We had a fine time living on the cheap as we did, always taking the A-line subway. We were eligible to use the Brooklyn Navy Yard for medical care, and we did lots and lots of walking. Our favorite outings included going to The Cloisters at Fort Tryon above the Hudson River—a wonderful museum laid out as a medieval castle, complete with The Unicorn Tapestries. We ate at Chili Charlie's under the Third Avenue El and felt like we were at The Stork Club or "21."

We climbed to the sky-high nosebleed section at the old Metropolitan Opera on Saturdays, hearing Tosca or Rigoletto. Once, to my delight during Christmas season, we heard a Saturday matinée of Humperdinck's "Hansel and Gretel." Shades of my pre-war California life. I barely restrained myself from singing along.

I was tested to see what grade level I should be in and was assigned to 8AR2. I was twelve years old. Top students were "A" level. An "R" allowed for rapid, more difficult curriculum.

I received an unusual, enriched education at Public School 52. Unusual because I had never had such difficult information come at me as quickly in past schools. I believe I had one of my best intellectual years. This school was incredibly organized, even which stairways we used. Boys on one and girls on another, separated by a chain-link fence.

Sadly, teachers, for no apparent reason, were attacked on a regular basis. My teacher in 8A2, Evangeline Gerard, was attacked one day for no reason. She was a wonderful teacher. When she was a child she had typhoid and lost all her hair as did My Nonie. In Miss Gerard's case, her hair never grew back and she wore a wig. Big, rough boys would poke at her head with the long window-opening pole. These ruffians heard she wore a wig and tried to knock it off. They were bigger and older because they had been held back so many times.

This was my first experience with American "juvenile delinquents." I'm sure they became part of New York City's underworld when they were adults. They were vicious and not unlike some of the guards I had known. They hurt others just for the sake of doing it and just because they could. Incidents like these caused me to fear most of the kids. Other than those few bumps in my road, I loved my New York school.

There were rigid requirements in scholarship, behavior, and dress code, but the strict structure was perfect for my needs. I was absolutely no problem, whatsoever. My only regret was having to leave to eventually return to the Northwest.

In the meantime, since both parents were out of the house all day, five days a week, I had the run of New York City from about 2:00 to 7:30 p. m. My Nonie and Papa would have been horrified at the time to know of places I went, but I had a lot of street smarts. I definitely knew how be cautious for my personal safety, and was quite resourceful. I still regard those times as some of my life's best! Perhaps I was foolish, but I sensed no danger and fearlessly made friends all over town while I carried my subway tokens in my shoes.

Once a few ladies noticed how I followed them, out of curiosity. They had been walking in single file, wearing head scarves and murmuring a prayer. I was curious and tagged onto the end of their line.

They invited me to accompany them to a special service at their synagogue, to celebrate a new mother's recovery after childbirth. They invited me to be part of their "kaffeeklatch" group. They asked me stories about being Episcopalian and I asked them about being Jewish. We traded life stories. Several had escaped from Nazi Germany before the war with their families. We had a bit of common ground. One was a piano teacher from whom I later took lessons. My parents thought I had met her at PS52. I loved her so much. I had my lesson at her house in the Bronx. She had French doors onto a small garden. I was so impressed.

The ladies thought it was funny when I teased them about how rich I felt associating with so much precious metal as in Goldfarb, Goldstein, and Goldberg.

With these kind ladies I learned to make halvah and knishes. In turn, I showed them how to substitute vegetable shortening, and we made my favorite Philippine dish—lumpia, the tiny spring rolls I had grown to love. I was pleased they liked them, a menu option that fit their religious cooking practices. We learned a lot together. They would call out "hello" and laugh when I'd visit with them. They'd say, "Here she comes. Our little gold digger."

I'd tease them back and say. *"No, no. The only metal I ever dug was in China in the tin mine,"* whereupon they'd roar with laughter and tell me not to make up such stories. They were good to me.

There was a Chinese family who, not knowing I understood what they said, commented on my silver charm bracelet and wondered among themselves why I was alone in Chinatown, down on Mott Street. They considered it a dangerous area for a young girl. I wonder if Mott Street is still dangerous for young girls. I hope not.

As usual, I didn't heed my elders. I answered them in fair Mandarin, to their delight, and explained the bracelet and charms were a gift from an auntie and uncle who had assembled it for each birthday and Christmas we were enslaved as Japanese POWs.

I told them I loved Chinese people and their kindness, like the men I had met at the China tin mine. They held me close to their family after that and treated me bossily, as though I too was Chinese; I loved them for it. I asked them to talk more slowly for me.

They checked my arithmetic homework, no language barrier there, although they used an large abacus in the store, and made me get smallpox vaccinations in the Oriental community, to ensure my health. They probably didn't trust I'd show up at school on immunization day. After all the hospitals we had been in recently, I was immunized against almost everything already. Somewhat too late now, as in Asia I had already either developed a personal immunity or had not been exposed to the illness. Most importantly for now, this family insisted I speak exclusively Mandarin with them. I was thrilled.

"Plactice, plactice, plactice," Soo Mei said, as she "placticed" her English.

The whole family, father Wu Han, his wife Soo Mei, and their three small children walked me to the subway each evening when I'd head home. Like adoptive parents, they came to my school spelling bees and other events.

We lived at 25 Cooper Street, a little tree-lined, two-block long area of small apartment houses. Blocks and blocks of apartments in our area had a main connector street, Dykeman, lined with stores, shops, businesses. It was a lot like living in a small town as one had no need to venture further than a few blocks to satisfy all life's needs. Parking was at a premium and everyone rode subways.

I found that most of the neighborhood residents were pretty small-townish. Lots of them had never been to the Metropolitan, for instance. No one knew exactly how to get to the Statue of Liberty. Some had never been to see the Rockefeller Center Christmas displays. I couldn't believe how backwoodsy they were. This wonderful city was being wasted by them. To this day I remain envious of them. I hope they have expanded their lives somewhat and taken advantage of the richness of their city.

Subway travel took the Wus about fifty minutes from their stop to our home; it was a straight shot from one end of the A-train line to the other. It was quite an adventure for them and a little scary, too, since generally they never left the Chinatown environs, ever. I was surprised they took the subway to the north end of Manhattan Island, just to hear me and my classmates show off—in a language the Wu parents could barely speak! The children, Pan, Fei-li, and Song, were all in elementary school and spoke very good English. They were completely bilingual. My contention, again, is that kids can learn languages so easily it's almost scary, if they're started young and immersed in them. What good friends the Wus were.

To the Wus, it was like they entered another foreign country. Americans did not speak Mandarin, and the Wus command of English was still limited, although the adult attended night-school and were learning rapidly. After I'd been living around Asians for so many years, sometimes I felt like the Wus were more my family than my English-speaking Caucasian loved ones were.

The Wus made their way up Manhattan to my school, followed directions exactly, and seemed a little braver each time. I was ashamed I couldn't enjoy their food though, especially since these good Chinese people ran a restaurant.

One Saturday at school, both the Wu family and My Nonie and Papa came to see me perform in a history play-off. I was always good at trivia. It was a proud day to introduce my two families to each other and bask in their attention. The Wus imagined Papa and Nonie spoke Mandarin since I did. They chattered away in Chinese for a long time before they realized no one answered. Nonie and Papa were dazzled to meet them and to find out about our fairly long-term friendship.

Their English was about as good as Nonie's Chinese. Papa had no language skills except for household German. For me, languages were as easy and refreshing as breathing a new scent, each different, but quickly mastered. As a consequence, I was proud to translate, thanks to the Wus' drilling.

After the event, where I handily won the grand prize, a book on European history before the First World War, we all went to a "Chock Full O' Nuts" coffee house restaurant chain for dessert and tea. My parents treated the Wus as honored guests. They were absolutely stunned and honored since Caucasians were most often quite rude to Chinese.

It was infuriating to the Wus, and to us, when they were called Chinks, slope heads, slant eyes and other derogatory names. They were amazed my parents treated them as guests, hosted them in the restaurant, and smiled like long time friends.

The Wus did not realize my family treated everyone this way, without bigotry; we were simply color-blind. Each person was judged as an individual.

Nonie and Papa were grateful for the Wus' assistance to me when I needed it and told me they were an excellent moral influence. We saw them often after that. They even came to our flat once for dinner. I had not told my parents about my Chinese family for fear they'd forbid me to go to Mott Street again and that is exactly what happened.

I was glad My Nonie and Papa were able to meet my oriental family. My parents later remarked how surprised they were that I had met such nice Chinese people, and that these busy business people would come to the north end of the island for me. Because their restaurant was a family enterprise, when they came to my school functions they had to close the restaurant and lose income.

Papa and Nonie were very impressed at the strength of support and friendship the Wus showed to me. What an honor to have them as part of our lives! Nothing should surprise us. Dozens of interesting people crossed my life in New York City, and I enjoyed them all. We were so sad to leave them. Papa and Nonie talked about sending them tickets to come to Puget Sound someday to visit. They had the encumbrance of finding someone to run the restaurant honestly while they were gone, but it was still a wonderful idea.

Shortly after we returned to the Pacific Northwest, a letter to the Wus was returned to us, marked "Undeliverable," with a handwritten notation on the envelope saying, "Burned Out." Papa immediately called a former colleague still in the Navy there. We learned, sadly, a fire in their building had destroyed the restaurant and the entire Wu family. They lived above the restaurant and all had perished upstairs. For a while I was struck mute with grief. I thought sad times were behind me after we came "back to the world." It was hard to lose my Chinese family.

Sorrow is universal, and even as a child I had to understand tragedies happen in America, as well as elsewhere, yet I still love the Big Apple. I highly recommend it as a destination to anyone, and regret I haven't been back since 1946, more than a half-century ago.

CHAPTER 29

THE EYEBROW

*...the whining school-boy, with his satchel and shining morning
face, creeping like a snail, unwillingly to school....*

——*Wm Shakespeare*

*School enrollment day
back in Puget Sound*

For years now, I've tried to break the habit of worrying about what people will think of me, after undergoing all this torment. I've felt spooked and assumed people were critical. I think it goes back to my high school years when my personal dragon lurked around corners.

CHILD POW

When we came back to Washington, Papa and Nonie went with me to enroll in the second half of the eighth grade. I was excited until we met the vice-principal of the school. Nonie explained she and I had been POWs, so my education had been interrupted, then resumed in New York and I had done well. We produced the requisite grade reports, showing straight As with a C-minus in mathematics, which I boldly told the vice-principal I despised. I always barely squeaked through math classes. (I've heard there's a condition called calculatis. I wonder if that's my problem? It really sounds more like something that happens to your teeth, doesn't it. Hmm.) Horror of horrors, I learned this man was also a math teacher. I paid for my comment about hating math for the rest of my school years.

This official immediately challenged the veracity of my records; he asked how anyone from a deprived setting like a prison camp could retain enough information to excel. In addition, how could I have been out of school four years, yet test into an A level group with students a few years my senior. I volunteered to take any entrance exam he might offer. Explanations from Nonie and Papa were met by him lifting a supercilious eyebrow, in this case a single black eyebrow, indicating disbelief. He acted like we all lied.

I stiffened in anger and could barely contain myself from yelling at him. This evident, I was duly excused from the room. I couldn't believe this person—obviously an incompetent buffoon—could dare judge the honesty of my decent, honorable Papa and Nonie!

When I entered the ninth grade as a twelve-year-old, about to be thirteen, it could have been a joy. Instead, that awful man spoiled my high school experience for the next four years. He was a reverse intellectual snob. If you succeeded, he implied you were showing off. If you could not accomplish a task, he said he *knew* you could not do it. If you answered a question he asked, he said you lied. If you didn't answer, you were defiant and obnoxious. There were no winners.

I was enfolded in a peer group in Puget Sound and was nurtured socially. I had nice friends, met decent people.

A few teachers did excel. The Lackeys, a marvelous husband and wife duo, taught math, economics and debate with humor and style and great elan. Our brilliant physics and chemistry teacher, John Corbally, went on to the presidency of Syracuse University. Who could possibly be surprised at that? He was so special. In the summertime, he sold sewing machines to make ends meet. I still have the one he sold to my parents for a Christmas gift for me.

Geometry and Latin were taught by Dorothy Mae Getty. Prim, very proper, gentle, shy, she was a gifted teacher who absolutely terrified us, but the students taught by Miss Getty were the lucky ones.

And then there was Margaret Mace who taught English Literature with a clear and resonant voice and the most perfect diction. What a joy to hear her read to us. She was dignity personified and I adored her. She was the daughter of Ambrose Russell who designed most of Tacoma's finest buildings in the early twentieth century. She, herself, had two daughters, Peggy and Nancy who grew to be loving, wonderful, brilliant adults with many talents.

Inadvertently Margaret Mace helped me recover from much of the heartache I felt over the death of my dear friend Ari. Ari was drowned in a barrel of water just a week after he turned fourteen years old. He was just a boy.

Margaret Mace announced to our Literature class that we would be studying "Evangeline" the great epic poem. My mind, still fragile, blocked out all normal and present activity and I ran from the schoolroom. I could only think of Ari and his terrible death. I grabbed my coat and ran cross-country for the three miles it took to our family homes. I was almost hysterical by the time I ran in our kitchen door and told my grandmother what had happened.

"You have to get me out of this class," I told her. She sat quietly holding my hands and then spoke.

"No, my dear, you must go back. The study of Evangeline will help you deal with Ari and your sadness about his death. If you do not take part in that class you will be insulting his memory. I know you don't want to do that. You need to remember all the good times with him and all the good and decent things he did with all the children. Don't dwell on the manner of his death. You will honor his memory by your participation in something that he felt was important enough to teach all the little ones about."

She was right, of course and when I returned to school my papa went with me and spoke to Mrs. Mace about the situation and my abrupt flight from school. She never spoke to me about it directly but once stopped me as I went from the room after class and said, "Alice, sometimes we can gain a great deal from the great poets. One of the things they can teach us is patience." It was an unusual statement and I wrote what she said in my diary. I still have it, dated January second week, 1947.

Other greats were a French teacher, Marie Helmer, and a wonderful English teacher, Mrs. Gibson, who made the *love of reading* any printed matter her goal. She didn't care what a student read. If one read comics, OK. If they read Scripture, fine. If they read novels, autobiographies, history, or geography, great. If all one read were advertisements, good. She wanted to impart the love of reading for its own sake, and I think she did.

The two teachers who were the very best in my opinion were Leroy Alsbury, who taught me history, and Louis Heytveldt, who taught almost anything asked of him. Both of them were super-special human beings and excellent teachers. Alsbury planted a great love of history still firmly rooted in my head and Heytveldt taught me sound social relationship skills that I still use today.

At our interview, The Eyebrow had announced I'd be on *permanent probation*. Politely, I questioned why was this so? He admonished me to be more respectful and then said my "flippant questioning was no more than expected." I didn't understand what I had done. Also puzzled, Nonie and Papa asked him to more fully explain.

He rather viciously told us that since this was a public school he was required to admit me, but he didn't want any student around who undoubtedly had been exposed to the treatment I must have received. He said I would be a figure of distraction to innocent boys and girls, and because he was a figure of some authority in the district, their parents would require him to assure their children were not spoiled by contact with me. I felt like I was back stuck on the bottom of someone's shoe again. So demeaning.

In addition, the first time I said anything about being a former POW, he made it clear the consequence was expulsion! We were stunned. He didn't understand the last thing I would have done would be to expose my past like that; I never told a single high school student about being a prisoner. I wanted to learn how to be a normal kid. I needed to graduate; it was my single motivation to stay in school!

This vice principal said he did not like me, because I was "too experienced." He did not like my parents, they were pushy. I kept my mouth shut but I immediately found fault with him for making up his own mind so quickly without any facts. My parents were many things, but "pushy?" Not very likely. Yes, since he was forced to admit me, he would seek any opportunity to reverse the fact.

Good grief! I had no "sexual interests." That was absolutely the furthest thing from my mind. Just because you've been to the ballet doesn't mean you want to dance. He was so foolish. Poor man so filled with hatred.

Papa and Nonie left it up to me. Would I go ahead and attend this nearby school or did I want to go back to boarding school? I chose the local public school for two reasons: I wanted to be part of a family and the boarding school was expensive. While we could afford it, that money should be kept aside for the building of our new family home—"Nonie's house."

I discovered later that my Papa had previously beaten out The Eyebrow for a big school administration job in a large nearby town. Papa flourished and loved his job, the staff, the parents, and most of all his hundreds of kids. When Papa died ten years after being retired, hundreds of his former students came to his memorial service. This other person could not have filled the bill.

He was a misanthrope from A to Z, and certainly no moral example. Admittedly, with some success, I tried to make his life miserable. I had the knack for it. It's a gift.

One of my best pranks was with my childhood pal, Heidi. One Saturday morning, we were sent to cheer on our newly proposed swim team at another school. It wasn't a regularly scheduled event, but a single trial. She and I took one look at that humidity-filled space which was the other school's underground pool, and since we both had "important dates" that night we decided we would not stay and take all the curl out of our hair.

After some discussion we devised a means to cancel the swim meet. We decorated the pool with large chunks of Tootsie Rolls from the corner drugstore. The pool was closed until it could be drained and cleaned because people who saw those big floating brown lumps assumed it had obviously been vandalized. For an unknown reason, the swim team idea was disbanded right after our visit to the pool, so there were no more needed repeats of what we had thought was a good idea—and our hair looked great that night!

We got caught—we always did. As a result, I spent the next two weeks sitting on a bench outside The Eyebrow's office. Heidi was regarded as simply having fallen in with a bad companion. The principal was humiliated by the complaint from the other school. I was overjoyed at his discomfort, as were My Nonie and Papa—quietly. However they refused to help me plan future events to upset him. Deviously, I was able to pull several other capers worthy of the Scarlet Pimpernel, but alas, I was repeatedly caught and punished.

For a while I felt I had a flare for crime, but I was too lazy to invest time in the lifestyle. I spent most detentions on the seat outside his office immersed in novels tucked inside my zippered notebook. People probably thought I was diligently completing school work. I didn't care if the work was done or not. Getting by was good enough. The Eyebrow was bound to find some way to demean or detract from any curricular achievement I might develop. I didn't care. I just wanted out.

The foolish man had been one who stayed home from the war with his feet up on his desk. Worse yet, for someone in his position, supposedly as a churchman and a moral leader, he had a relationship with his secretary after he became the high school principal. It was common knowledge. If you were made to sit on the bench outside his office, as I was—far too many times—you couldn't avoid hearing the activity. I was not a voyeur. I was repelled. I would never tell anyone about what I heard, though I thoroughly disliked him. I simply did not entertain the thought of spreading the tale. Wretches seem to appear in all countries, not only in Asia; I certainly wouldn't be one here.

Other students asked why he hated me, but I couldn't tell them. I honestly did not know, but it was obvious. His hatred of me was irrational and embarrassing.

Admittedly, there were times I wanted to burn down the school building, though I never did. Scouts honor. Once I got an "A" on a Latin final and The Eyebrow, ever vigilant over my shoulder, made me take it again to rule out cheating. Latin was a graduation requirement; without it, I'd have lost a foreign language credit I needed for college matriculation. He landed that one on me over Memorial Day weekend, immediately before graduation. Needless to say, a re-test was taken under the visual supervision of our well-loved chief librarian of exemplary reputation, and again I did fine.

Nonie wanted me to continue to study languages, and New York schools had built on what I already had learned, although they didn't offer Mandarin nor Japanese. My Chinese friends on Mott Street had really pushed Mandarin language practice. Because I became proficient, I fancied to one day work for our government as a translator.

It's too bad I'm no longer fluent in Kanji—the Japanese language of ideograms, nor in Mandarin, but I can hold a sprightly conversation in both languages. Other languages came and went during my education, but my favorites remained Mandarin and French. Mostly though, I tried to stay out of the way of The Eyebrow.

I went from a child who had no trouble getting "A" grades to one who didn't care if the work got done at all. I believe The Eyebrow made me dread and hate school in general. Left up to me, I'd have taken only sewing, composition, history, debate, and languages—the right choices for me. They are the ones I have used as an adult.

Throughout my school years, arithmetic remained a throbbing black hole to me. I don't balance checkbooks. Someone else appears to be happy to do that for me. I don't figure the size of flower beds by measurements or great formulas. If it looks about right, it must be right. I don't figure gas mileage. What difference might it make? I'm not changing cars. We need to get real about curriculum; to make it functional for today's world. I think that's happening, and I applaud it.

I didn't graduate with a lot of happy memories, as I was constantly skidding around corners, trying to keep ahead of

CHILD POW

The Eyebrow, now promoted. It seemed as I advanced a grade level, his job also stepped up. His schizophrenic egotism seems to have been his stepping-stone to higher jobs. That, and the fact he had been around long enough to know where all the skeletons of other administrators were buried.

A previous principal, the one whom he directly replaced I believe, was dismissed from the district because of his extra-curricular interest in one of the teachers. Now The Eyebrow was doing the same and, somehow, it was swept under the rug. I won't believe he got his job on merit, but then I wasn't the hiring authority, was I?

Years after we graduated, The Eyebrow became superinten-dent of schools in that district and, in spite of my opinions, I've been told he was a near genius regarding school district fiscal matters. The poor sad man just should never have been around children.

At our fifty-year class reunion, when this man was intro-duced, everyone stood to clap, everyone but me. The crowd separated—I sat, stared into his face, and smiling gave him the finger. I'm infrequently accused of being ladylike. I admit he had some grief from me as a student, but he started the problems.

Sounds like a kid's excuse, doesn't it? It is, and I'll never think of him with anything but a child's memories, due to his constant cruelty. He died within weeks after our fiftieth class reunion.

I felt he had no reason to treat any student as he did me; I was a good child. I may have been hyper-excitable, but I was never disrespectful to a teacher; I did not create disturbances that needed quelling by administrators. He *made me* his problem and assisted in broadcasting scurrilous, twisted lies about me among the staff, which also may or may not have reached students. I don't believe I could have been the only one he treated this way, but if there were others, they remain anonymous to me.

During his retirement years this former principal owned a business. There was a time My Nonie and Papa asked me to pick up something for them. Not knowing it was The Eyebrow's business, I jauntily walked in the door. He sat front and center at a desk. I was immobilized in anxiety just as I had been some thirty years before. He glared at me a moment, then said, with thick sarcasm, "So, you did survive to adulthood, after all."

I immediately turned, walked out, and had Nonie call to have the material sent by mail. He just never let up. Such a sad human being.

After years of good jobs, college, one expulsion from a college, a degree from another and a further degree from yet a third school, I experienced a rotten marriage, the birth of two adored children, and a divorce. Then I met and married a man who also had two children, and he became the light of my life. He was an exemplary father to my children and a loving and indulgent husband our entire married life.

He was probably a far better husband than I was a wife. He constantly thought of us first, whereas I had many irons in the fire and nearly drove him to distraction with my multi-tasking. If I wasn't taking twenty-two Girl Scouts camping overnight, I was handling my two apartment buildings with tenants who required him to keep order on more than one occasion. At one time, I measured all men against my very first love, but after I married my second husband, I could tell he was the person the good Lord had put on earth for me.

CHAPTER 30
HONORING AMERICANS

S ome truths need to be considered:

- *Work as hard as you can at whatever your job. It may save your life.*

- *Be willing to take a chance. It may save your life.*

- *Remember what Jack Kennedy said: Always forgive your enemies, but never forget their names.*

- *Learn the words to our Pledge of Allegiance and say it every day. It may save your life—and make your life worth saving.*

- *Say an "Amen" after the Pledge of Allegiance in remembrance of all who have loved our flag and all those who perished to protect it.*

- *And, most important: Love and honor your parents. They may give you life more than once; my mother did.*

*Alice and Nonie at
Nonie's retirement party-1982*

362

It is helpful to consider that history books are most often written by committees of learned people who weren't even there when the events occurred. On the other hand, here I am, a real, live eye-witness. I was in a place, at a time in history, where few people had a chance to record the events. These accounts occurred in front of my eyes. My sometimes cynical comments about our past and present government during this era of WWII are based totally on my own impressions, vivid memories, and educated opinions. I can defend them to anyone. Bring it on.

When I was in high school after the war, my mother and I took a day train to Portland, Oregon to shop at the big Meyer and Frank shopping mall. As we walked up a concourse, an unseen man nearby yelled a demeaning form of address and an order at My Nonie in Japanese. It required a filthy, humiliating response. He had called her "white legs" and demanded she "bend over and get ready for big Ito."

Out of reflex, we both stopped immediately, faced the rude man who had shouted and properly bowed our heads in an ingrained, *hard learned*, ritualistic sign of respect. This practice was to avoid looking at the face of the person who had addressed my mother in the same way she was spoken to in POW camps. In another instant, we realized our surroundings and straightened, embarrassed.

Passersby gaped at us, as though we were performers in a skit. One man in the bustling crowd yelled, "Where's the cameras?" He must have thought we were making a commercial.

CHILD POW

The Japanese man stood in the mall and laughed with uproarious glee. Then we recognized him—by his derisive laughter! I remembered his laugh, amidst the screams and torture of innocents. This monstrous freak was one of our former guards. As in the past, he brayed like a jackass and jumped from one foot to another. The differences this time were: he wore no uniform and no one had been set aflame.

We gave him vile glares, then attempted to walk on, my precious mother in tears. In Japanese, I shouted out that *his* mother was a *Korean,* an enormous insult to traditional, older Japanese men like him. After everything she had been through, how dare he speak to her like this? I felt such a surge of rage, I wanted kill him! I was homicidal! I had nothing to use for a weapon. People who had stopped a moment to watch us had different reactions.

Sensing our pain, several stepped forward to shield us from this evil man. Though they did not understand the exact problem, they heard his threatening tone and chose to intervene, like real Americans! They stepped toward us and held their arms out, to act as a barrier to the monster. Several placed their bodies between us and the man. One person stood directly in front of him and made the sign of the cross to ward off evil.

Dear reader, if you were there that day and intervened, please know how many times we have blessed your presence. We felt we were in grave danger and you helped us. I don't know how the danger would have been expressed to us, but we felt it as strong as a drum-roll banging on our chests.

Suddenly from the back of the crowd a man in a tan trench coat called out to us.

"I was a POW in Sumatra, and later in the Philippines. I know what he said to you. Were you prisoners, too? Are you all right?"

Since we now had assistance, our other rescuers walked away. The guard had disappeared by this time. My Nonie told our new acquaintance that this former Japanese soldier's sudden appearance had thoroughly frightened us both. She also said we were under the impression we would never see those horrible soldiers again. Where had he suddenly come from? Were we his target?

With such gentleness, he shepherded us to a small, quiet café, where he bought us coffee and conversed for almost an hour. He was a fine gentleman. We learned he had been an army surgeon, but his hands were crushed by the Japs to the extent he could never operate again. He was now obtaining credentials in psychiatry at an Oregon college. He briefly recalled the grotesque treatment of prisoners in his camps. The hour this man gave from his busy life was the single time anyone who truly understood what we had been through had offered us any help. I'm not sure we ever learned his name.

"I strongly believe you both need emotional support, to put the war behind you," this gentleman suggested. He said we should try to find psychiatric services in our home area.

When we demurred, he told us today's unfortunate event should show both of us our minds and emotions could not heal without help. In retrospect, he was right. In the future we made many appointments, individually and together. Our problem was that we never found a professional who had the specific knowledge needed to help former prisoners, let alone civilian POWs.

If a person was never there, how could they comprehend what it was like? They did try. They honestly wanted to help. Yet in frustration, we always concluded professionals were unable to understand, because they *had never* experienced or dealt with such atrocities. It was excruciating for us to explain and relive incidents with each new therapist, while at this same time in our lives, we were trying to block out all those memories.

One psychologist said we caused each other additional grief, through a form of crowd psychology. This "professional" erroneously supposed most or even all of our experiences did not actually happen, but instead were a conglomerate of stories, gossip, and rumors we had heard. My Nonie returned his invoice unpaid, marked "Refuse to pay. No service rendered." Of course, we didn't return to the foolish man again. He was a nitwit, personified.

Good people spent a lot of professional time trying to help us. Every tool of their educated profession was called upon to help us. Between them and us, we just couldn't seem to draw a therapeutic package together.

Most *psychologists* we met wanted to develop a treatment regimen; to focus on each of us as an abused woman. Time after time they addressed only the sexual assault portion of our incarceration. That was a fair assessment, but was only a very small part of our mistreatment. At least they recognized that part of it had been real. The far larger part had to do with the loss of self-determination and constant raging fear and terror. To live with terror twenty-four hours a day for years is not able to be adequately described to a therapist. The scope is too large.

Psychiatrists, on the other hand, wanted to give us a new form of medication at the time called tranquilizers. They felt the severity of our emotional upset could be dampened by medication and therefore enable us to deal better with our mental ghosts. That, too, was a good idea, but didn't address our fundamental problem of acceptance and release of painful memories.

In addition, the pharmaceutical recommendation was not a viable long-term option, since it made us "zombies." Perhaps we were given an improper dosage or perhaps we were just extra sensitive to the medication, whatever; we each emphatically declined further drug treatment after a couple of doses. When we did *not* take drugs, at least we felt capable of fleeing or defending ourselves if we were ever accosted again by a former captor, like the monster in the Portland mall.

These treatment practitioners were good people; they simply had no handle on Post Traumatic Stress Disorder. After four more decades, this syndrome was finally acknowledged. We needed another way to recover, so once again we were on our own. Even in American, our mantra remained: "We just have to get through today."

The mall event obsessed our thoughts; we both had nightmares. Day after day, we didn't feel safe unless the other was present. We were prisoners again—at home! If I missed the bus home from school, my mother thought a terrible event must have happened to me. If she did not meet me on time at a destination, I panicked and thought someone had harmed her. One fact was clear—the encounter with the former guard re-traumatized us both.

Over time, we grew *enraged* and absolutely *astounded*: Enraged with ourselves that we hadn't freed ourselves from the camps' hold on our minds and emotions, even after all this time; and we were *astounded* by our own naïvety in wondering why this monster in the mall was allowed into the U.S.A.

For years we blamed ourselves for our anger. We refused to play the role of a "victim," but we still needed to blame someone. In the absence of anyone else, we blamed ourselves. We blamed ourselves for feeling humiliated in front of this criminal. This is a stereotypical victim response. Thankfully, through the years the monster in the mall was the only guard we ever saw in America. Previously we had imagined he was probably tried after the war, pronounced guilty, and hanged. How could he have escaped a trial? Who cold have sent him here? Why? He was so evil. He enjoyed pain and death. He was a monster. Whoever sent him was a monster, too.

This same Japanese devil flayed a helpless American prisoner—skinned him alive! I was there. His blood remains vivid in my memory; it splashed on my feet. It smelled like rusty metal. As a child, I was commanded to watch an American patriot, The Basket Man, vomit, being forced to eat his own skin. His screams still reverberate in my ears.

To this day, I can't bear to have anyone scream. Even a child's tantrum almost destroys me, and I have to get away from it. I wouldn't allow my babies to scream when they were tiny. People said I was spoiling them. That turned out to be completely untrue. It made them very contented and happy children and wonderfully secure adults.

Shame, shame, shame on whomever allowed that maniac an entrance into our free but innocently naïve country. If he wasn't involved in a criminal enterprise, how had he obtained enough money to come to the states? He had no skills other than killing or torturing others. By American standards, he was unemployable.

Who paid his way to America and what was he doing in Portland? Was he Yakuza, Japanese mafia? Was he here as a assassin? Surely he couldn't be after us, yet we remained terrified for months and sleep came infrequently at best. We reverted to keeping watch for each other. Nonie and Papa would retire early while I professed I had schoolwork to keep me up. Nonie would rise and spell me off so I could have a few hours before leaving again for my school day. We did this for many months. We about drove ourselves around the bend worrying and obsessing about that freak.

We later told an intelligence officer at Fort Lewis about the incident, but we heard nothing further. We were "debriefed" on the fort by intelligence personnel many times. The intelligence people were extremely kind—the only military department that ever was. Yet we concluded from their responses that our experiences were so horrible, so impossible, that they did not believe us.

For example, when they asked for corroborating witnesses, we said they were undoubtedly dead. The army was in a much better place than we were to trace these individuals. We could sometimes give them names and hometowns. We could only offer our two broken bodies, with x-rays and scars for evidence. Yet it didn't seem to convince them even though they would continue to call to seek out information.

We had told them everything. They had it all. We didn't have anything new to offer to them. They smiled. They thanked us. And each time that seemed the end of it. Until they called again to have another "talk." We tried so hard to cooperate with them. We wanted to help. What they couldn't seem to understand was that each interview with them required that we relive terrible memories. We were unable to heal our minds because of the continual need to recall: who did what and when did it happen?

CHAPTER 31
OUR AMERICAN SOCIETY

Only because of the gifts and talents of the many, from whom all mankind have benefited, and from those who have sought the free shores of this America, have we earned the right to be called The Lighthouse of the World.
— *Wendell Wilkie*

B y way of explanation, some former civilian POWs were meanly compensated through a token stipend each month in post-war years, but *they* could prove where *they* had been. They had passports and in some cases, they even had ship manifests, showing where they had been taken and by whom and on what ship.

My Nonie and I were stateless persons with no identification, thanks to the infernal confusion in Manila in the first days of the war. I remember the day my mother was told to hand over her passport at the transport desk outside the Bayview Hotel. The passport mentioned me only as an after-thought; "accompanied by female child."

In retrospect over the years, I believe the document may have accompanied us until we were sent to Baguio. I'm sure we didn't have it after that, and that may be the reason we were transported with such confusion to China. I'm positive we didn't have it on the hell ship to Japan because I recall with clarity that we had only a small paper packet of food, given to us as we boarded. We carried no other items in our hands, and of course, we had no pockets in which to secrete anything. The absence of identification affected us in many ways, for the balance of our time in the Orient. Another thought is that Japanese officials were in charge of all the documents and may have simply mislaid ours, or even, after we were misdirected on the dock and were mistakenly sent to China, when they couldn't find us, they threw our information away.

Attempting to reach Prisoner of War support groups has been a futile exercise. It was necessary to produce identification documents, copies of camp rosters, shipping orders, anything, to prove we were legitimate. We had nothing that would suffice.

Anything my mother had from the government that got us from Australia to America was destroyed by her years ago in an effort to block out her personal tragedy. I retained nine pictures from that time. They were on a roll of film I took with a Bon Voyage gift Brownie box camera. I threw the camera away when we left the Philippines the second time. My Nonie kept the roll of film tucked under her breast for four years. When we came home we traded with other former POWs for the Fuji, Kobe, and Foochow snapshots. Strangely enough, although they show no military secrets or information, the military was very interested in these snapshots and made copies of them many times.

One day I discovered someone in my own Rotary Club had been in camp with us. That day, after I had given a program of abbreviated memoirs of our experiences, more like a synopsis, leaving out Baguio, of course, he called to me outside when we were going to our cars. He asked me if I remembered him from another place. I really didn't. He said, "Do you call your mother, Nonie?" I told him that I did. My curiosity was high. He asked me if I had ever been to Cabanatuan Camp #3. I told him I couldn't remember the designations of any of those camps. I was still too sick at the time and it was such a long time ago.

"I was there with you and your mother. I remember the pretty lady, Nonie, who had the little girl. I remember how wonderful your mother was to all the wounded and the dying men she cared for. She should have been given a medal for all of that. She was the one good thing that ever happened to any of those men, or to any of us around there, at that time." He hugged me real tight and told me he had wanted to ask me about it for a long time. He recalled, "When you were inducted as club president, I wanted to say something to her that night at the banquet but I just wasn't sure how she'd respond. I didn't want to open any old wounds, if she had them. How is she now?"

I told him that she had taken her brightness with her into death. She was very ill for a long time and sought the release from this life just as she had helped others go so many years before. I told him how we, my daughter Jeannie and I, had tried to comfort her and tell her that it was okay to let go of this world now. I remember telling him how she smiled at me one time and said I was using the same words she had used so many years before. It pleased her that I did. I wasn't aware of it, but then I began to remember how she would talk to the dying men about God's great love for them and how they were so lucky to be able to soon be in His Presence and how they seemed so comforted by that. She always had a way of taking away the fear from the bad things. She had the magic.

He actually was the one who "outed" me and revealed my past history, not understanding this information was kept just within our family. It's okay though, I don't need to prove any-thing to anyone. *I've been to see the elephant.*

Many horrific, monstrous acts were done to us and in front of us. This memoir, this recitation of those four unbelievable years, is as hard to tell as it may be to read. Yet you need to know this information. The wonderful stories of our great heroes such as Nimitz, Halsey, Clay, Patton, Marshall, Rickenbacker, Doolittle, and Pershing, on and on, so many others, should be part of required history courses.

Our children need to know who the heroes of this country are. Children need to look up to heroes to establish pride in themselves as being fellow members of our great nation. It pro-vides each child with national identity. It's a healthy thing. The horror of POW life is a part of American history not taught in schools and may never be. It is not politically correct to expose or tattle on a former enemy, a country who is now supposedly a close ally of our economy. Greed, for gain, ignores the past. I think the road to hell is paved with stolen gold.

There were people we met as prisoners, though, who should be remembered in kinder ways, like the Japanese officer who for reasons known only to himself, added us onto the trans-port list for repatriation; the sailor from an unknown country's merchant marine who gave us food and his own woolen socks and shirts; the Japanese guard who arranged to exchange my hair for fishing line and hooks, thus providing us a means to supplement our food.

Many times we depended on the kindness of strangers. None of these men had any connection with us. We could give them nothing in return. Each was in major jeopardy, if caught. Why do you suppose they gave us their little bit of protection? I think they acted with the basic decency and goodness that knows no racial heritage or color of skin.

Another concern of mine is how we still have not fully honored and adequately recognized a highly decorated unit in our United States Army, *all of Japanese ancestry.* These men are true Americans, the 442nd Regimental Combat Team. They are aging veterans now. Time's wasting. They have earned much more tremendous respect. We particularly owe them honor because their own home country, America, imprisoned many of them and their families in relocation camps. All were from the West Coast, not the East Coast, nor the Deep South. What sense do you make of this? Why the Americans of *Japanese ethnicity*? Because they looked different? I think so.

May I ask you to consider some other "different looking" Americans? Tiny, bandy-legged John Adams, our second president? Smart as a tack and a brilliant leader. What about homely, gangly Abraham Lincoln, our 16th president? The soul of kind compromise and cool-headedness at a bad time in our history. What about Teddy Roosevelt, the original land steward who devised our first national parks? Deaf as a post, bellowing everything he said, brave as any man ever was, and with a gap between his front teeth wide enough for a butterfly to go through. What about William Howard Taft, who had a terrible time getting out of his enormous bathtub due to his incredible corpulence? One of the most brilliant legal minds of the 20th century.

Different looking? Yes. Grand Americans, every one of them. Just as are the veterans of the 442nd who looked so different to the Caucasian Americans of 1941 that they were demeaned, stolen from and then put in camps. Can't we do something a little bit extra for them? It's a true national guilt we bear about this.

These loyal citizens and families were stripped of property, which was never returned. They had owned homes, businesses and broad farmlands. Unfortunately, all were sold to white American scavengers who sometimes paid as little as ten cents on the dollar. As further insult, around 1990 our government authorized each imprisoned Japanese-American to receive $20,000. This was a demeaning pittance, compared to what was taken from them by the government. Pardon me. Not by *the* government, by *their own* government. We are told politicians are honorable, but if you believe that you might believe anything. Good grief!

A Japanese friend was born at Manzanar Camp in the California desert during the relocations. Her mother went into labor. Several people helped her to the camp dispensary. Tough hours later she gave birth. She was hustled to her feet and told to leave. She felt quite weak and shaky and asked if she could stay a while.

"There aren't any rice paddies available here to stretch out in," the Caucasian doctor said.

This lady, an American citizen and a university professor, was treated with grave disrespect for no provable reason! Her husband, also a citizen, was an active American serviceman at the time, fighting in Italy with U.S. forces. At the time his little daughter was born, he was part of the 442nd who was rescuing the Lost Battalion of Texans who had become cut off. The 442nd sustained tremendous casualties. Who remembers?

What sense does this make? My friend's mother was never reinstated at the university after the war, either. Yet, as proud Americans on their living room wall they display with pride her husband's multiple medals and citations for bravery under fire.

Shame on us. Shame on us! Why didn't our government stop its noisy, cranky bureaucracy long enough to say: "Wait a minute. What's wrong with this picture?"

Why were *our own citizens* imprisoned, in disregard of the guarantees stated in our Bill of Rights, in the first place? Why were naturalized American citizens of German and Italian ancestry put in camps, as were our West Coast Japanese Americans?

If you seek villains, there's a complacent bushel-load with large salaries in Washington D.C. Included in this bunch of nitwits are the late Henry M. Jackson and Warren Magnuson, Washington's long-revered senators. Lawmakers are all referred to by the title: "The Honorable Senator from Washington State" and "The Honorable Chairman" of a specific committee, which makes me furious! The aforementioned heroes of the Potomac were *not honorable* when they pushed our Japanese *citizens* into camps, allowed their property and businesses to be stolen, then made them exist under horrendous and demeaning conditions in the camps.

These people were their constituents, for crying out loud! Follow this line of reason: Constituency requires a voter's registration card, which must be obtained by proof of citizenship. Yet both these former senators voted to segregate our American citizens simply because of their race. This makes them honorable? Revered? By whom? Not me! On the contrary, it smacks of dictatorship.

Is it any wonder I became a civil rights advocate? It would only be amazing if I had *not* done so. Do I sound angry? I am, and I have been for the past sixty-five years. And good grief, now we have the "Patriot Act!" I hope someone in Washington, D.C. has a memory long enough to keep abuses like these from happening again to Americans, though I'm merely too old and too tired to jump in the middle of it again. I miss the old days in one way though; it was always such fun to win. And win, we did.

CHAPTER 32
DAILY FORGIVENESS

It is impossible to make people understand their own ignorance, for it requires their knowledge to perceive it; and, therefore, he that can perceive it, hath it not.

——Jeremy Taylor

My life has been checkered with great success and miserable tragedy. Coming from such a loving and devoted family, I was injected into the chaos of WWII. After the war, after my high school graduation, I entered college at my parents' demand. I won scholarships; I failed required PE courses. I became fluent in two more languages; I began to forget how to read and write in two others. I had the ultimate grand love affair; he was sent away and he killed himself. I celebrated too much for being hired for "the dream job"; I fell and broke both legs. At the hospital I was told that I had been carrying a child; the child of my lost love had not survived my fall. I had lived my life too much, too fast, and in such turmoil that it all caught up with me at once.

I spent the summer months in total seclusion with Aunt Betty and Uncle Carl. I retreated into somnolence, anorexia, and silent contemplation until one morning I woke and the past was gone.

I was no longer a victim. I was a survivor. My mother gave me this gift years before. As I woke from my self-imposed stupor, I was finally ready to open her gift and use it for the betterment of my life. Life is good.

It is interesting to me that in attempts to forgive my enemies, I have experienced a rebirth as a person. For many years, my constant, raging hatred of Japan and Japanese nationals blinded me to an important fact. In carrying this emotional burden around every single day, I denied the biblical teaching I believed and had learned as a child: Compassion and forgiveness should be offered to any of God's children.

Over time, my hatred had consumed me and kept me from seeing worthiness in others. Until I saw myself as a survivor, rather than still as a victim, I could never forgive or heal. I am no longer a victim. I am a survivor. I will never be a victim again.

My mother gave me the gift of survivorship. She showed me how to really live, sometimes with passive resistance—of necessity—rather than merely to exist as air-breathing detritus washed up on a beach. As I age, however, I find my ability to forgive others becomes more passive and is floppy, lethargic I'd much rather go to the barricades and fight once again. Both needs remain: forgiveness and fight, but I'm simply too tired to become embroiled in it again. It takes great bolts of energy to sustain the fight for rights. Perhaps now it's someone else's turn. Perhaps now someone can do it better than I did, but oh how I loved it and the fight for it and the winning of it.

Each election year we *must* exercise our right to vote, especially when an astonishing number of fools pop out of knotholes to run for office or endorse other nitwits who do.

In this country, we must not let the voices of charlatans, soothsayers, or ignoramuses dictate our national policy. A major area in which we Americans often get bamboozled is in our incorrectly cited history. Watch out for this.

For example, an ultra-conservative commentator on Fox Network television has described an incident during WWII where "terrible American forces in Europe perpetrated a massacre of German officers at Malmedy." If it were true, it would indeed have been awful. However, the reality and truth of it is, *it did not happen. It's the other way around.* The fact is *Germans* killed many hundreds of American soldiers in the Malmedy Massacre. The correct account is taught at West Point, as a matter of U.S. Army history. It is also a matter of Belgian, French, German, and Polish history. Where did this poor man learn *his* history? And from whom? And how does he retain his network job when he's such a fool? Good grief!

Other examples of ignorance are those people who claim the Holocaust never happened. What idiots. Did all of the "survivors" form a gigantic conspiracy to invent a fable of some sort? Of course not.

A most recent idiocy is that of movie makers who have jumped up to change more of our history just to sell their movie tickets. There is a film about a fictitious few Japanese on an island battlefield. The writers and producer have actually proposed, "The Japanese are just the same as us." They suppose the recorded rampant villainy was done by Japanese who didn't really understand us, so now we can all kiss and make up. Did this movie star/producer/director ever have a prisoner's blood splashed on his feet and ankles? I did. He wasn't even there. Who are you going to believe? Let me tell you something. They *were not* "the same as us."

It's true that *after* American forces found caves on captured islands in the Pacific with bodies of their fellow soldiers and Marines tortured, emasculated, and burned to death, they took hard action against the Japanese. Excuse me please, once again, where I come from what our troops did is called "street justice." Just don't let anyone tell you that they are the "same as us." Here's how to assess the statement and decide for yourself:

Our troops didn't *drown innocent children in barrels* or *behead ill soldiers for the fun of a gambling game.* Our soldiers didn't kill a prisoner by *crushing him slowly* to death. Our soldiers didn't *flay an ill and starving soldier and make him eat his own skin.* I was there. Don't you dare let them tell you that the Japs were "the same as us." They were *never* "the same as us." The lie is stomach turning.

Don't let these foolish storytellers get away with such absurdities. I am so angry. Don't let them say, " Get a life. Don't worry about it." There have been *a lot of American lives* spent on foreign shores to assure the First Amendment rights allowing these nitwits to publish this garbage; what about the value of *those* lives? Get a life, indeed. Don't let them tell you, "It's just a movie." If so, then they shouldn't be selling it as fact-based history. Good grief! They're trying to change our nation's history to be something it never was. No. No.

It's angering to know the perpetrators of this fraud will be fêted, probably given Academy Awards and be lionized for showing our enemies' "humanity." We must call them on it and make them either shut up or show the truth. At the very least, these media-adored frauds should apologize.

We must confront these lies at every opportunity; our children have a right to know the truth. We know what did happen.

Think of a way to castigate them or at least join in boycotts against their foolish prattle.

When we hear an unusual fact or claim from any national figure, in politics or the media, we *must* check the sources carefully. When we don't call nitwits to account, we allow recidivists to change our history. We can't let that happen. I know these people are liars! They were never "the same as us." I was there!

It is not easy to be either a survivor or a forgiver. Each day, I thank God for the freedom and the blessings of this country. Each day I also mentally take my country to task for perpetrating idiocies on the electorate. Each day I thank God that only by chance I was born an American.

I can dissent, and yes, I am even expected to dissent.

Government will never be perfect. I think the nature of the imperfection of we mortals comes in here someplace. Consider this: if the United States is such a bad place, why do people die trying to flee their former countries to come here? Believe me, this country, with all its imperfections, is as good as it gets, *anywhere*. Quit knocking it.

Count your blessings every day that you are an American. Then thank God on your knees and count your blessings one more time. You may never understand what you have until someday when you might lose it. America may not be paradise on earth but it's as close as we'll come in this mortal lifetime.

Each day, I have to specifically remind myself that on this day I will forgive the Japanese: they caused us such physical pain; they tried to erase my mother's spirit; they ripped out her merry heart and adventuresome core; they murdered My Sweet Friend and her wonderful family; they cruelly executed young Ari for his silly exuberance; they stole my childhood, despoiled my young girlhood, made me an angry woman, and caused me to strongly distrust men who aren't Anglo-Saxons.

Each day I say aloud I will forgive them, but the effort is definitely daily, not a one-time event. Some days I forget to forgive them. Other days I don't care if I forget. It's far too personal. I still try. Forgiveness is a hard process. But then, no one ever said life is easy; and neither is it fair.

My mother is dead now. None of these experiences could be discussed while she still lived. Her personal sense of decency toward others was inexhaustible. She was a lady who loved unconditionally and she never understood why the Japanese treated her so indecently. My Nonie's only true failing was to believe our incarceration was her fault.

She always felt she was unable to protect her only child from gross villainy, and she never reconciled that self-criticism. She was wrong. My Nonie protected me where and when she could, and she taught me that special things in life are often hard won. Be assured, she did not fail me, in spite of what she may have thought. If she *had not* taken the actions she did, we'd have died. Instead, she brought us both home alive. She was a hero.

My late husband who told me he loved me with the last breath he took, asked me when we were first married to abide by one wish. During his lifetime, he wanted none of my POW experiences mentioned to our children, his friends, his family, or ones who did not already have this knowledge—ever. I did abide by his request, although it was difficult.

Sometimes when he told a story about WWII, it sounded as if he had won the war in the Pacific single-handed, although he spent his entire Navy career in San Diego. He was a man from an older generation who didn't know how to deal with abuses to the person he most dearly loved.

He was a man raised in a geographic area and at a time when men took violent umbrage at any aspersions cast upon a lady's character. Such insults were settled in a physical manner, usually with a gun.

Forced into it by chance, he would have had to strike out in my defense and we agreed that wasn't anything we wanted in our lives. I had too much killing in my lifetime and didn't ever want to see another death from violence. He, in turn, didn't want to be forced into "settling things up" because a town drunk let his foolish tongue wag. My past was secured with silence until after Robert died.

As an example of the violence of that time, we moved to a small mining town that had bloomed overnight from 2000 inhabitants to over 10,000. There were several murders a week for the many months we were there. It wasn't right, but that's the way it happened. It's a matter of public record in the newspapers of the time.

One day, our five-year-old, Jeannie, was sitting in a corral on horseback talking to a ranch wrangler. A cowboy came up to the corral fence, leaned in, and shot the wrangler dead, accusing him of being the paramour of the cowboy's wife. The cowboy was never tried. It was considered to be a 'defense of the sanctity of his marriage.' These were different times and places than I was used to after growing up in Northwest civility and lawful order. At first I was appalled but eventually recognized it as another time, another place, and I accepted I was the outsider and unable to criticize the manner in which they implemented their own laws and societal norms.

My husband was kind, gentle, and much older than I and did not want to defend my past. He also did not want me to feel shamed in other people's eyes. I never have. What happened to me was not by choice. It was done through slavery.

Because I was "damaged" in my mother's eyes, it was difficult over the years for her to love me as I hope she had wanted to do. I was no longer her perfect child. In my adulthood, she sought a "daughter figure" from among her brother's granddaughters, and from young women who worked for her. Yet she always continued to demand more of me than from others. I couldn't always meet her standard of excellence or often even understand why she imposed it.

If whatever activity or action she wanted from me was forthcoming, she said nothing, seeming to believe she had encouraged me in natural self-expression. If I somehow failed to meet her standard, she withdrew from me in aloof silence. Soon a recurring phrase was heard: "You could have done it, if you had wanted to."

I frequently worked myself into a depressive state; it seemed I couldn't earn her approval. I deliberately did what I knew would infuriate her. I smoked cigarillos. She hated the filthy habit. As do I. I dyed my hair. It came out a strange color of salmon pink. I drank too much whiskey. I drove like a mad woman gone to hell—with an excuse for every negative action! I was outrageous simply to get her attention, and the more she ignored me, the worse my behavior became. Pretty self defeating.

I think My Nonie viewed my inability to meet her dreams and demands as personal affronts, perhaps because she felt I blamed her for our wartime experiences. Actually, it was because of my illness that we were captured and in our terrible situation.

"Stop blaming yourself. Just once, blame me and put it all to rest if you need to blame someone," I used to say. Yet she could not.

"You were never to blame. You gave me life, a second time. You taught me what is really important: Love, decency, truth, steadfastness and faith," I told her. In how many ways did I have to express it?

Sadly, over the ensuing years we angered and disappointed each other in many little ways. It rankled me how each year on my birthday, she and Papa deliberately went to dinner with a friend, avoiding any acknowledgment of the special day.

In a similar vein, holidays were a curse to me. I would plan, decorate and cook for the big day, only to be hoisted on the see-saw of her rejection at the last hour. After pre-planning, my husband and children would eat our Thanksgiving or Christmas dinner for five days rather than one or two because our loved ones chose to go elsewhere at the last minute. I finally quit asking them to come for the holiday dinners.

I continue to carry the hurt that she would not fully recognize my precious son, Tom. He was a gentle, loving, dependable boy. He was so kind. He loved animals, his family, his school, his church where he was allowed to serve as an acolyte. He loved his 4-H cow and cats. He didn't have a mean or awkward bone in his body, yet Nonie continued to seek perfection. Most of the people who knew Nonie professionally never heard of Tom. The night after Tom's funeral when my heart was breaking and I needed to be with them they went to a dinner party with people she worked with. Tom was a wonderful person, yet she hid his existence from most of the world because he was mildly retarded. Others have told me they felt she wasn't ignoring Tom as much as she was punishing me for bringing forth a mildly retarded child. I'm not sure about that because I think Tom, even in his disability, was as perfect a person as God could make.

This is the only life criticism I have about My Nonie, yet she herself was so perfect. Wasn't she entitled to one little flaw? It tears at my heart sometimes how much I long to hear her voice. There are days when I wake and yearn for her wisdom and courage and quickness of sparkling wit so strongly that for a moment I don't think I can go through the day.

To Nonie's almighty and often verbalized displeasure, she remained most furious with me because I did not become an opera singer. My voice actually dropped an octave in early teen years and developed a raspy quality. I have always thought it was due to the inhalation of great quantities of the coal dust in Japan and the racking, untreated bronchitis we both suffered in captivity and the reality is that I never *wanted* to be an opera singer in the first place.

Thankfully, hours before My Nonie drew her last breath, we reassured each other of our steadfast love for each other. I miss her immensely. Everything I have and everything I am, she gave to me. She was my mother. I loved her so. I still do.

It is wise to gather and store memories while they are sweetest. It's wonderful to have a library of them in your mind's eye, to pull out and enjoy all over again.

I remember many times in camps we passed people softly humming the "Star Spangled Banner" or whispering our Pledge of Allegiance, complete with an Amen. How dangerous it was for us to do this yet we did it as it was the one tie to our homeland. I remember the panic in one man's voice one day when he whispered frantically, "I've lost it! I've lost it!! I can't remember what comes after…the rockets red glare, the bomb bursting in air…For God's sake tell me…what comes next?"

One evening as we sailed toward Australia and freedom, the galley crew of the Drottningholm fixed us a special chocolate cake for dessert. It was exciting to think about because chocolate cake was always high on our lists of "comfort food" when we dreamed about someday going home. As the blond young mess stewards carried in our dessert we saw that each piece of cake had been speared with a tiny American flag on a toothpick. It was the first time since 1941 that we had seen our beautiful flag with her forty-eight stars and thirteen stripes. In spite of our many years of yearning for the chocolate cake, none of us could eat it. We could only sit and weep at the sight of our beloved flag—the emblem of all we had yearned for over the last tragic years. Our tears were of joy, relief, and sorrow; all in one.

You may be sure that whenever an American prisoner has been held in a foreign country, after being freed, at the first sight of an American flag, there will be tear-filled eyes. It really does mean that much. Our flag is the gorgeous reminder of all we hold dear. It is the significance of home. It is the symbol of America.

God Bless America

AN EPILOGUE

I wrote the following poem for My Nonie's birthday, January, 1995. Her family always called her Brownie as a child, because she was tiny, sweet and kind and had those huge brown eyes. Years later, loved ones called her a short version: "Nonie." Papa called her Nonie or "Poko," for " little one."

The poem follows major events through Nonie's life. It begins when she was kept away from school because she lost her hair during a typhoid epidemic in 1916. Her brothers teased her. Her dad sent the boys to the mines so she could go back to school. My biological father betrayed her and left her with a child. War came. She aided others during the war at great expense to herself. Then as a POW she put her mind far away in a safe place and endured. She was loved by soldiers for her kindnesses. aps tested her strength. God protected her and brought her to reedom. We learn from her about the unconditional love that sks for nothing in return.

"THE BROWNIE"

Spirit of gentle courage steps forward in grace,

Love lightens another's burden. Small girl with huge brown

eyes. Shy smile.

Small girl so easily hurt by another's darts.

Small girl searching for hierarchal place, but it won't be.

Strong Ones deride the Brownie's dreams.

Help! Help! Strong One demands a moment's satisfaction at

Expense of Brownie dreams. Is Brownie always the lesser

brown-eyed sister?

Flee from this love disguised tyranny.

Tall, dark stranger. Commit yourself forever.

Can you protect this soft kind heart?

Dark eyes flawed with inconstancy, hurt the Brownie's heart

But leave the gift of new life. Go far.

Your love ripple fades with time to memory of fine days past

Illusions torn apart by war-thunder, but Brownie waits.

Dreams can come true. Future can come again.

No more do Strong Ones override the gentle heart.

In early silver streaks of sun the Brownie watches

As her heart love helps to heal her battle dreams.

New crust of life creates and gives the Brownie forest

patterns.

All air is clear as Brownie streaks across the sky,

Her mind with those who are not earth-bound.

Courage and joy are offerings

to those who need the Brownie's gifts.

Freely given in softest steadfast love.

Special sweetheart, revered. Dark-mind nights grow long.

The Brownie heart despairs, yet waits for light.

Good God who brings relief from mind pain

help the Brownie now.

CHILD POW

Strong Ones will question Brownie's strength.

Can she withstand the love-grief as it scourges her

tenderness?

Good God takes back the suffocating sorrow.

His window opens and He takes the Brownie home.

The Brownie is free. For the first time, the Brownie is free.

As forests and wide sun-hot earth of deserts

Draw us to the quiet in our minds, we seek the Brownie

places.

The goodness. The sustaining hope of Earth Ones.

The encompassing love that asks for no self-return.

The brave un-vanquished sweetness

that seeks to teach the life secret of freedom

to be unique and not an imitation. The goodness of the heart.

The secret of the Brownie

AN EPIGRAPH

LIFE'S PATTERN

Not until the loom is silent, and the shuttles cease to fly,

Will God unroll the canvas and explain the reason why

Dark threads are as needed, in the weaver's skillful hand,

As the threads of gold and silver,

In the pattern he has planned.

—by Eleanor Jopling Gilderoy, 1950

Maternal grandmother, 1878-1980, 102-years

ABOUT THE AUTHOR

A.L. Finch was born on the plains of Montana between the Greasy Grass and the Little Big Horn. She was raised in Puget Sound. At the age of eight, her ill-fated vacation trip to the Philippines with her mother resulted in a subsequent four years as a prisoner of war in three countries.

At almost twelve years old, she returned to America, eventually graduated early from high school, went to a private college, minored in Languages and majored in Political Science. Two weeks before graduation, celebrating excessively after final exams, she fell off a fire escape, broke both legs and was expelled.

She transferred to a state university and received her Bachelor of Fine Arts, then earned a Master of Political Science. To repay her college debt to an uncle, she worked as an investigator of voting rights abuses.

After five years of marriage, two children and a divorce, she met her true love and moved to the American Southwest, where he was involved in the uranium and copper mining industry.

They relocated in the Pacific Northwest in the 1960s. She again worked for the government, monitoring and investigating abuses in civil rights. Eventually, she was hired by a federally mandated state agency to spearhead advocacy, investigation, and protection at a large facility.

She established and developed a training program to support the rights of disabled adults under guardianships. She devised and maintained a nationally acclaimed, sophisticated Human Rights Committee within a major facility for persons with developmental disabilities. Her only son died in 1982 while living there.

In addition to speaking multiple languages herself, she coordinated and established a formalized system of response for non-English speaking travelers to this area. In the early days of this venture, the local Port Authority was the major user of what developed into the present "Language Bank." At one time over sixteen languages were available through translators and assistants on a twenty-four hour basis.

In 1969, she established the original sexual assault center in her local area and developed a program to provide advocacy and intervention for women and men who had been assaulted or sexually abused.

Ms. Finch has lectured around the country and continues to provide training to college and university students regarding civil rights and ethics, particularly regarding the rights of children, disabled citizens, and the elderly.

Ms. Finch lives in the house her Nonie designed, amidst the rambling gardens on the same property where she grew up. To her delight, her adored daughter, a classical musician, lives next door in the house inherited from Aunt Alice. She identifies herself as "the mother of pugs," her constant, funny, brave and noisy companions. She describes herself as undoubtedly the most contented woman on Puget Sound and she daily, and gleefully, counts her blessings.

To order additional copies of this title call:
1-877-421-READ (7323)
or please visit our web site at
www.annotationbooks.com

If you enjoyed this quality custom published book,

drop by our web site for more books and information.

www.winepressgroup.com

"Your partner in custom publishing."

Printed in the United States
131563LV00001B/168/P